Praise for *His Sword a Scalpel*

"Beautifully written and fact filled. A great job of historical writing."
—**Dr. John L. Cameron**, Alfred Blalock Distinguished Service Professor of Surgery and former Chief of Surgery at The Johns Hopkins Hospital

"General Charles Stuart Tripler was the first Medical Director of the Army of the Potomac. It was he who envisioned and built the medical infrastructure for the Union army near the beginning of the Civil War—a model that has served as a template for all subsequent iterations of the medical departments of the United States Army. Unlike so many other Civil War generals, Tripler did not have the opportunity to burnish his own reputation through post-bellum memoirs. He died in 1866, just months after the end of the conflict. In an unfair twist of history, Tripler's legacy was almost completely eclipsed by that of his successor, Major Jonathan Letterman—but no longer. Jack Dempsey's thoroughly researched and well-documented *His Sword a Scalpel* does a masterful job of restoring the reputation of this humble, compassionate and extremely capable servant of the medical profession. Health care workers may be especially drawn to items in the Appendix, including the Mexico Report and features on the Tripler ambulance wagon and his Crimean oven. It would be well for every modern-day physician and surgeon to emulate the life and service of this noble American doctor."
—**Dennis A. Rasbach** graduated from Johns Hopkins University Medical School, has more than three decades of experience in general surgery, and is an author of Civil War titles *Joshua Lawrence Chamberlain and the Petersburg Campaign* and *I Am Perhaps Dying*

"This work is a very thorough and cogently argued treatment. It offers a very persuasive defense of Tripler's reputation, which has been unjustly maligned. Tripler had to adapt to an entirely new structure and scale of warfare."
—**Dr. Martin J. Hershock**, historical author; Dean and Professor of History at University of Michigan-Dearborn

"Author Jack Dempsey has done history, Michigan, and all of us an enormous favor by telling for the first time the story of Dr. Charles Stuart Tripler, a career military officer and physician who did more than anyone to advance battlefield medicine at the beginning of the Civil War. His insights and reforms undoubtedly saved countless lives, then and later, before politics ousted him from his post. *His Sword a Scalpel* is compelling, and is best read in combination with *Heart In Tatters: Eunice Hunt Tripler and the Civil War*, the story of the heroic physician's wife, who survived her husband by nearly half a century."
—**Jack Lessenberry**, award-winning journalist, editor, columnist, author, and former president of the Historical Society of Michigan

"A fabulous work with extensive and thorough survey of the relevant primary and secondary sources. A really wonderful read presenting a lot of new insights."
—**John Lustrea**, author, editor, M.A. in Public History, former director of education at the National Museum of Civil War Medicine

HIS SWORD A SCALPEL

Publications of the
Michigan Civil War Association

Heart in Tatters: Eunice Hunt Tripler and the Civil War
His Sword a Scalpel: General Charles Stuart Tripler, MD, USA

HIS SWORD A SCALPEL

General Charles Stuart Tripler
MD, USA

MICHIGAN CIVIL WAR ASSOCIATION

Copyright © 2023 by the Michigan Civil War Association

All world rights reserved

No part of this book may be reproduced, stored in a retrieval system, or transmitted in any form or by any means electronic, mechanical, photocopying, recording or otherwise, without the prior consent of the publisher.

Readers are encouraged to go to www.MissionPointPress.com to contact the author or to find information on how to buy this book in bulk at a discounted rate.

Published by Mission Point Press
2554 Chandler Rd.
Traverse City, MI 49696
(231) 421-9513
www.MissionPointPress.com

ISBN: 978-1-961302-25-9
Library of Congress Control Number: 2023918741

Printed in the United States of America

Second in a series

❋ ❋ ❋

Proceeds from this volume benefit the Michigan Civil War Association in preserving and sharing Michigan's role during the American Civil War.

At the time of this publication, the MCWA is raising funds to erect a monument honoring Michigan's contributions to victory and to Emancipation at the Battle of Antietam,

Sept. 17, 1862.

❋ ❋ ❋

The Michigan Civil War Association is a Michigan 501(c)(3) non-profit corporation.

Its corporate purpose is to pursue cultural, historical, and economic development opportunities to preserve and promote the history of Michigan's role in the American Civil War.

Founded in 2013, the MCWA has acted as a careful steward of all donations received.

More information is available at https://www.facebook.com/michigancivilwarassociation.

Board of Directors
Bradley M. Egen
Kalamazoo
Brian James Egen
Monroe
Will Eichler
Washington Township
David D. Finney Jr.
Carmel, Indiana
Margaret O'Brien
Portage
Jacqueline Tinney
Livonia
Matt VanAcker
Lansing
Jack Dempsey
Plymouth Township

Publications Committee
Margaret O'Brien
Matt VanAcker
Jack Dempsey

Editorial Consultant
Dr. Martin J. Hershock
Dean of College of Arts,
Sciences, and Letters
Professor of History
University of
Michigan-Dearborn

Contents

Illustrations   ix
Preface   xi
Introduction & Editorial Note   xv

❋ ❋ ❋

Part One: 1806—1860: Building a Reputation   *1*
Part Two: 1861—July 1862: Leading on the Front Line   *29*
Part Three: August 1862—1866: Continuing Care   *143*
Epitaph   *173*

❋ ❋ ❋

Appendix   *201*
Bibliography   *255*
Index   *283*
Acknowledgments   *291*

Illustrations follow page 142

1. Charles S. Tripler
2. Columbia College Medical School
3. Sandy Hook, Md., Aug. 9, 1861
4. Seven Buildings HQ
5. Camp Winfield Scott
6. Corps General Hospital near Yorktown
7. White House Base
8. Cumberland Landing
9. Field Hospital, James Peninsula
10. Pre-war view of Savage's Station
11. Savage's Station Rolling Stock
12. Field Hospital at Savage's Station
13. Harper Hospital, 1865
14. Tripler Hospital, Columbus, Oh.
15. Tripler Ambulance
16. Gravestone
17. Monument

The first duty of a physician is, plainly, to devote himself to the recovery of such sick persons as may confide themselves to his care. No one is disposed to evade this duty, we fully believe .... I may ask, however, whether we are as industrious as we might be in the pursuit of more and more attainment in the science we profess; whether we consume the midnight oil in storing our minds with the daily accumulating facts resulting from the labors of our fellows in all parts of the civilized world; whether we permit nothing to escape us that may qualify us the better to discharge our duties to our patients, but so make all true knowledge our own, that we can avail ourselves of it promptly and in season whenever the occasion for its application may be presented. ...

The importance of a life can not be measured ....[1]

---

1. Charles Stuart Tripler, *The Duties of Physicians in Relation to Popular Medical Delusions: An Address Delivered Before the Covington and Newport Medical Society, June 14, 1859* (Covington: S.G. Cobb, 1859), 3-4.

Preface

No other time of US history has captured the imagination and fascination of people than the American Civil War. It is said that there have been more books, articles, blogs, and materials written about this pivotal period than there are individual days since 1865. The history of this monumental conflict interests not only those in this country, but around the world.

I am not sure if any historian has completely determined the exact reason for such interest in this era, but most agree that its impact was severe and the single most monumental test to the great experiment of a constitutional democracy. Although expressed in different forms, its impact has direct and relevant connective tissue to our lives today. Even a casual comparison of today's events to the past can illuminate this precisely. As a country, we are still defining what it means to be a more perfect union.

Metaphorically, the fire of our country's steam boiler was lit on June 21, 1788, with the ratification of the Constitution of the United States. The pressure built over the waning decades until it burst with the opening salvos at Fort Sumter on April 12, 1861. After four years of devastating conflict, the precarious precipice of a democratic government maintained. As President Lincoln stated, the nation would "have a new birth of freedom and that government of the people, by the people, for the people, shall not perish from the earth."

The tidal wave of grief that washed over the country from 1861 to 1865 was unprecedented and for years its people and landscape bore scars, often as mute testimony, to the tremendous suffering and sacrifice. Approximately one out of four combatants were killed, equating to about 2.5% of the population. New research suggests that the actual deaths from the Civil War are more accurately around 750,000 compared to the previously noted 620,000. At 2.5% of today's population, this would equate to 8,275,000 American deaths in four years. A staggering and unfathomable number.

The result of the American Civil War did finally answer the question of states' rights versus a strong federal government. Prior to 1865, the United States was referred to as "are" and afterward, "is." Though much was determined and settled by constitutional amendments and laws, there was a considerable amount of work yet to be done in order to deliver on the promises of the Declaration of Independence.

Challenges to those determinations, as acutely seen throughout the years since 1865, are still with us today. Current events have highlighted there is still healing and work to do. Our history and the lessons of history are so preciously relevant and the common sense understanding of the past should command ascent to the learning curve of today. Though needing curation to meet our current circumstances, history provides lesson plan tools in our navigational journey.

Innovations and common positive outcomes have been born from colossal conflicts, disasters, and challenges. The Civil War is no exception with hundreds of innovations and progresses. Advancements in medicine, processes, and treatment flourished. Triage as a form of medical attention during a mass casualty event was created. Coordination of transportation, care, and organizational support of the wounded and logistics sustaining armies were developed. Patents for improved industrial and agriculture machinery and equipment flourished to match the demand for a strained country. It was during this time that Martha Coston invented signal flares as a form of distress signaling.

During extreme circumstances, great social innovation emerges. Union victory at Antietam on September 17, 1862, provided President Lincoln with the military success needed to issue the preliminary Emancipation Proclamation. Ultimate war victory ensured the enforcement of the 13th, 14th, and 15th Amendments. Though national and grass roots organizations worked toward abolition for decades prior to the Civil War, I have always felt that January 1, 1863, with the formal issuance of the Emancipation Proclamation, was the start of the Civil Rights movement as this was the first time the Federal government put into action momentum that has led to the achievements made since.

History is rife with unsung heroes whose contributions, for both known and mysterious reasons, have been overlooked or lost. Michigan, especially during the Civil War, has many. General Alpheus Williams, with a sterling military record, was instrumental in many engagements and campaigns. He often had temporary Corps command because of his abilities on the field and in military science, yet he was never given permanent command status. Colonel Norman J. Hall, the "Forrest Gump" of the Civil War, was a participant to several major events that no other individual can claim. Graduating from West Point in 1859, he was sent to Harpers Ferry during John Brown's attack, came back for his execution, was present at Fort Sumter, took over Brigade command at Antietam after it was decimated, led the amphibious Union assault across the Rappahannock River at Fredericksburg, and was one of two Brigade commanders that repulsed Pickett's Charge at Gettysburg. His actions in all of these were superb and exemplary at the highest levels but no substantial book or piece has been created about this soldier.

General Charles Stuart Tripler is one of those unsung heroes from Michigan that deserve substantially more recognition and veneration. Tripler served in the regular army, being sent to various posts and locations. He participated in the Second Seminole War and the Mexican–American War where he served as Medical Director during the Mexico City Campaign. Through experience and astute observations, Tripler began to correct the previously adhered to medical procedures of the Army. Soon after the outbreak of the Civil War he was appointed Medical Director of the Army of the Potomac. Due to political pressures and lobbyists, he subsequently was replaced and went on to serve as Chief Surgeon of the Department of Great Lakes. His replacement,

Jonathan Letterman, having been the Medical Director at Gettysburg, gathers all the attention and notoriety with the medical aspects of the Civil War. It was Tripler's advancements, innovations, and foundation that his successor enjoyed and built upon.

I implore you to let history percolate as an influence in your life. Not that you have to be actively engaged in the field or public history, although that would be most welcome, but that you have an appreciation and respect for the past. Allow the stories to educate and inspire you in your life today. What we all share in common is that we have descended from ancestors of the past. They all had hopes, dreams, concerns, challenges, and achievements, large and small, that should fortify us in the continuation of our story.

The Michigan Civil War Association is pleased to offer another work in the series of publications that we hope tell these untold stories. We want to provide a voice for those who can no longer speak and a platform for voices that have been marginalized, forgotten, or censured. Please know that your support in this mission is critical to not only the efforts of the MCWA but to secure from the clutches of obscurity the stories of those everyday contributors to the tapestry of our national story.

Tuebor!

—Brian James Egen
President, Michigan Civil War Association

Introduction

Sickness and death. Personal courage. Hygiene. Pestilence. Endemic disease. Self-care. Vaccination. Triage. Exhaustion. Public health policy and politics. Bureaucracy. Supply chain issues. Shortages, controversies, mismanagement. A bitterly contested presidential election in which racial issues take center stage.

Although such terms and phrases represent the year 2020 when a virus took dogged grip on the lives of Americans, they apply equally to the nation's greatest crisis, the Civil War, 1861-1865. During those four years, some seven hundred fifty-thousand soldier deaths resulted from a cataclysmic breakdown of the national political process resulting in armed conflict between Americans. The war also caused an untold number of civilian deaths and inflicted pain, suffering, and grief on families and communities all across the continental United States. It was a gruesome era, "fought at the 'end of the medical middle ages.'"[1]

Perhaps because of this incomprehensible butcher's bill, students of the Civil War era have tended to focus on causes, strategies, and tactics. Many visitors attend to the great and familiar sites of the battlegrounds such as Little Round Top, Dunker Church, Henry Hill, and the Hornet's Nest. Fewer have sought out locations where combat wreckage had its reckoning: the Pry House near Antietam Creek; the XII Corps field station on Gettysburg's Hospital Road; Mt. Zion Church on Battlefield Memorial Highway near Richmond in

---

1. Drew G. Faust, *This Republic of Suffering: Death and the American Civil War* (New York: Vintage Books, 2008), 4, quoting William A. Hammond (see *infra*).

Kentucky; the Carnton House outside of Franklin, Tennessee. Perhaps a glimpse comes from the safety of a couch or other viewing platform: the pan-back scene of wounded in the Atlanta square in *Gone With The Wind*, or an episode of *Mercy Street*, or William Holden ministering to John Wayne in *The Horse Soldiers*.[2]

The long-standing, classic understanding of Civil War medical treatment is of an ill-informed, almost barbaric practice. An example is in the one-volume history that inspired so many post-World War II readers to become fascinated by the epic struggle:

> For the unfortunate Civil War soldier, … he enlisted in the closing years of an era when the science of medicine was woefully, incredibly imperfect …. [H]e had almost no chance to get the kind of medical treatment which a generation or so later would be routine.
>
> Both the Federal and Confederate governments did their best to provide proper medical care for their soldiers, but even the best was not very good. This was nobody's fault. There simply was no such thing as good medical care in that age—not as the modern era understands the expression. … [T]he treatment of wounds and disease, consequently, ranged from the inadequate through the useless to the downright harmful.[3]

If Bruce Catton wrote it, surely it must be unvarnished and poetic truth.[4] Many historians have since agreed, as in how "the state of

---

2. See Appendix.
3. *The American Heritage Picture History of the Civil War*, narrative by Bruce Catton (New York: American Heritage Pub. Co., 1960), 359-360. See also James McPherson, *Battle Cry of Freedom* (New York: Oxford University Press, 1988), 486. But see Justine S. Murison, "Quacks, Nostrums, and Miraculous Cures: Narratives of Medical Modernity in the Nineteenth-Century United States" in *Literature and Medicine*, Vol. 32, No. 2, Fall 2014, Johns Hopkins University Press, 419.
4. In his seminal study of the main Union Army in the East, Catton hardly discussed medical matters and never mentioned C.S. Tripler. Bruce Catton, *The*

medical science had little to offer" in aid of the sick or wounded. It seemingly took as much fortitude and moral strength to endure medical treatment as to go into battle.⁵

What credit Catton did assign for decent care went to the United States Sanitary Commission, a volunteer private organization that "set themselves the task of raising hygienic standards in camps and hospitals" run by an apparently callous Union military.⁶ Catton was no outlier. The common understanding surrounding the bulk of the 20th century was that "other than the efficacious work of civilian medical organizations, especially the US Sanitary Commission, the war was generally a medical disaster."⁷

Only the physicians knew the genuine story. One renowned battlefield surgeon could lament, a half-century after the war, the state of respect for their labors:

> We had served faithfully as great a cause as earth has known; we had built novel hospitals, organized such an ambulance service as had never before been seen, contributed numberless essays on disease and wounds.... What has been our reward? The great leaders in war have been promoted and universally honored. Countless statues commemorate in Washington and elsewhere the popular heroes. Statues of generals are in every town, some of them memorials of men it were wiser

---

Army of the Potomac Trilogy, Gary W. Gallagher ed. (New York: Library of America, 2022).

5. Gerald E. Linderman, *Embattled Courage: The Experience of Combat in the American Civil War* (New York: The Free Press, 1987), 28. See also Earl J. Hess, *The Union Soldier in Battle: Enduring the Ordeal of Combat* (Lawrence: University Press of Kansas, 1997).

6. Catton, *American Heritage Picture History*, 371.

7. Shauna Devine, "'To Make Something Out of the Dying in This War': The Civil War and the Rise of American Medical Science" in *Journal of the Civil War Era*, Vol. 6, No. 2 (June 2016), 151. Ironically, it is a Centennial era motion picture (see Appendix) that more accurately portrays the state of period medical care than the later (1990) *Dances with Wolves* where a wounded officer saves his foot by evading surgery.

to forget, some of whom history will judge severely. Every village has its statue to the private soldier. There is not a state or national monument to a surgeon.[8]

Scholarship in recent decades has begun to paint a different picture.[9] Rather than a "medical disaster" marked by a commonplace reality of "inexperienced physicians and surgeons hacking off limbs with unsanitized medical equipment" with no anesthetic or post-operative care, those practitioners are increasingly being seen as unsung heroes of a conflict overwhelming in its scope and effect on health and welfare.[10] True, "the existence and importance of the pathogenic microbes" was unknown during this period—on the other hand, ether and chloroform were in regular use.[11] "Historians once characterized Civil War medicine as medieval," says a current Civil War encyclopedia, but "recent scholarship" is helping change that misperception.[12] The National Museum of Civil War Medicine, founded in 1990, provides educational resources revealing "brilliant innovations" that

---

8. S. Weir Mitchell, "The Medical Department in the Civil War" in *Journal of the American Medical Association*, Vol. LXII, No. 19 (May 9, 1914), 1445, 1449-1450. Mitchell lobbied for marking of the Gettysburg hospital sites by its battlefield commission, the tablets to include the names of surgeons. Id. 1450. They remain standing there today.
9. A Centennial book purports to be "the first to present the overall medical picture of the period." Stewart Brooks, *Civil War Medicine* (Springfield: Charles C Thomas, 1966), inside front flap. See Margaret E. Wagner, Gary W. Gallagher & Paul Finkelman eds., *The Library of Congress Civil War Desk Reference* (New York: Simon & Schuster, 2002), 623-664.
10. Shauna Devine, *Learning from the Wounded: The Civil War and the Rise of American Medical Science* (Chapel Hill: University of North Carolina Press, 2014), 1-2, 6.
11. Paul E. Steiner, *Disease in the Civil War: Natural Biological Warfare in 1861-1865* (Springfield: Charles C Thomas, 1968), 4; William W. Keen, *Surgical Reminiscences of the Civil War* (Philadelphia: Transactions of the College of Physicians of Philadelphia, 1905), 104. Keen became president of the American Medical Association.
12. Lorien Foote & Earl J. Hess eds., *The Oxford Handbook of the American Civil War* (New York: Oxford University Press, 2021), 21.

marked the care received by soldiers during the conflict. It annually bestows the "Major Jonathan Letterman Medical Excellence Award" to honor the legacy of innovation and service to wounded warriors begun by Letterman, the second Medical Director of the Union Army of the Potomac. Recognition has gone to Surgeon-General William A. Hammond for founding the Army Medical Museum (now the National Museum of Health and Medicine), the first military attempt at scientific study, and for laying the groundwork of a medical history on the conflict.[13] A recent study notes that hospitalization during the American Revolutionary War caused death in "about a quarter of all patriot soldiers." By contrast, the rate during the Civil War "dropped to around 14 percent."[14] A 2022 book argues that the war elevated the practice of medicine, ushered in the debuts of female and African-American physicians, and produced "a huge field of heroes"—doctors who have never received their due.[15]

Why chroniclers have corrected the record by elevating some participants into near-heroic status but on the back of one particular physician deserves inquiry. Why is not this practitioner lauded? Does revisionism require reviling of Letterman's predecessor? Encountering the bulk of this otherwise refreshing literature, one would think so.

The story of career officer and doctor Charles Stuart Tripler has either faded from view or been despoiled. He had built a sterling reputation in the antebellum Army. Holder of a medical degree when few did, he attended classes at West Point related to his field

---

13. Id. 150. For the history of Hammond's brainchild, see Michael G. Rhode, "The Rise and Fall of the Army Medical Museum and Library" in *Washington History*, Vol. 18, No. 1/2 (2006).
14. Michael Stephenson, *The Last Full Measure: How Soldiers Die in Battle* (New York: Crown Publishers, 2012), 392. This work criticizes care during the 1862 Peninsula Campaign and uncritically praises Letterman and Hammond. Id. 396.
15. Carole Adrienne, *Healing a Divided Nation: How the American Civil War Revolutionized Western Medicine* (New York: Pegasus Books, 2022), ix-x, 1. Containing a bibliography but no footnoted sourcing, regrettably, this book omits the doctor who is the subject of the present work.

before receiving a commission in 1830. Veteran of the Seminole and Mexican-American armed struggles, chief medical officer on a typhoid-ravaged New York-California voyage, Tripler studied, wrote, and lectured on advances in military medicine. His 1858 *Manual of the Medical Officer* became the standard US Army guidebook. An inventor, he devised improvements in battlefield ambulance transportation. Appointed inaugural Medical Director of the massive Army of the Potomac after the ignominious Union defeat at First Bull Run, Tripler confronted the daunting and unprecedented task to build a medical infrastructure for America's largest armed force ever. At over 100,000 strong, it amounted to the ninth or tenth largest city in the country.[16] His leadership put that force on a footing to nearly capture the Confederate capital and deliver a perhaps fatal blow to the Rebel cause in the second year of the war.

He was 55 years of age when the Civil War erupted. Too old to contribute to the success of Union arms, says the conventional line. Perhaps so, looking at how historians have treated his age class. Charles F. Smith was 53, Robert Anderson 55, George Sears Greene 59, and Edwin V. "Bull" Sumner was 64. Of these four, none has been accorded the kind of adulation paid to peers on the Rebel side. Albert Sidney Johnston was 58, Robert E. Lee 54 at commencement. Their character counted more than chronology—but only for them.

Tripler served as Medical Director of the Union's largest army from August 12, 1861, to July 4, 1862. He served at the front. He led its medical care during the lengthy Peninsula Campaign in Spring 1862 in which the Army of the Potomac fought in numerous hostile encounters, including the Seven Days Battles. This concluding weeklong series of actions produced casualties on a scale never before experienced by the American people. A major factor lay in technological change. The Minié ball had been invented in 1846[17] and first used in

---

16. A modern comparison would include the ticketed capacity of certain college football stadiums, the Daytona International Speedway, or the Pimlico Race Course.
17. By French Army officer Claude-Etienne Minié (1804-1879).

the Crimean War of the mid-1850s. Rifles were replacing muskets. Rifled cast iron artillery weapons supplanted smoothbore brass guns. Artillery became larger in its capacity to deliver ordnance. Shrapnel via exploding case-shot made its appearance. The "unwelcome messenger"—canister shot, a cylinder filled with iron balls—turned heavy weapons into giant shotguns.[18] Wounds were more horrible, and good military doctors, surgeons, and nurses were critically needed.

As night fell on June 25, 1862, the Army of the Potomac outnumbered its opponent, the Army of Northern Virginia, and had advanced within several miles of Richmond. It perched on the brink of triumph. It was not debilitated from disease, and its wounded from the three-month onslaught were being cared for in newly created hospitals constructed so as to nurture them back to health. But the Union commander, Major-General George B. McClellan, did not press his advantage. He waited; he surrendered the initiative to Lee, the recent replacement as head of the Rebel force when General Joseph E. Johnston, age 55, had been incapacitated by a battle wound. The outcome: a hurried, unplanned, bloody Union retreat that turned the tables in the shocking space of seven days.

The outcome for Tripler was to be replaced. His appointment by President Abraham Lincoln to a promotion within the Army Medical Department had been voted down by the US Senate. Therein lies its own ugly story, and he had cause to resign his commission. Given a choice of postings, he decided to return home to his family in Detroit, Michigan, and to continue to serve his country for the next four years. He helped launch a medical installation for soldiers that continues today as a university research and learning facility. Within his limited orbit, he labored untiringly. Only his untimely death in 1866 at age 60 put an end to his Army career.

Cancer took Tripler's life, but politics had torpedoed what likely

---

18. *The War of the Rebellion: A Compilation of the Official Records of the Union and Confederate Armies* (Washington: Government Printing Office, 1880-1901), series I, XXVII, pt. I, 901 [hereinafter *OR*, and with reference to series I unless otherwise stated].

would have become greater contributions. The principal culprit was the Sanitary Commission, which offered much help to Union soldiers and deserved credit for it—but undermined that legacy with self-aggrandizement, back-stabbing, and racist research. Its unsanitary side has been largely overlooked by historians. Its chief personage achieved fame in another field, insulating him from critical examination of his Civil War work. This work attempts a fresh and balanced review of these and other relevant facts.

Tripler did history a favor, one that it has long ignored. He penned a massive retrospective detailing his intensive efforts to help ameliorate disease, dress wounds, amputate with care, and save lives during his tenure as Medical Director. He chronicled his efforts as the first medical leader of the largest military force that the United States had ever fielded, offering up a specific account for others to study and build upon in their work. He confronted war on an unprecedented scale and left instructive guides.[19] No soldier was more qualified by training or experience to lead medical care for the Union's foremost army during its formation and first major campaign. No battlefield surgeon more deserved his nation's gratitude. Few have received less.

A companion volume to this work published in 2022 brought to light the story of Eunice Hunt Tripler, wife of the Army surgeon from 1841 until his death. She never remarried before her death forty-four years later. From her memoir, much can be understood about their lives, their devotion, and her efforts to ensure his legacy would not be forgotten.

Perhaps this current work will contribute to the record as it should stand, one where students and historians grasp how Union Civil War

---

19. Union doctors in the Western Theater simultaneously were investigating improvements. See, e.g., Middleton Goldsmith, *A Report on Hospital Gangrene, Erysipelas and Pyaemia, as Observed in the Departments of the Ohio and the Cumberland* (Louisville: Bradley & Gilbert, 1863). For the experience of a nurse in the Theater, see Annie Wittenmyer, *Under the Guns: A Woman's Reminiscences of the Civil War* (Boston: E.B. Stillings & Co., 1895). For the organization, see *The Western Sanitary Commission: A Sketch* (St. Louis: R.P. Studley & Co., 1864). Soldiers' aid societies also made major contributions on the health front.

medical care did care, and brought to bear the best knowledge of the era, to benefit each soldier patient.

Editorial Note

This is a work of historical inquiry.

The reader may wish to consult the companion volume to this study, *Heart in Tatters: Eunice Hunt Tripler and the Civil War*, published by the Michigan Civil War Association in 2022. As a memoir fashioned from oral reminiscences first published under the title *Eunice Tripler: Some Notes of her Personal Recollections*,[20] it lacked references or citations to undergird its first-person accuracy. *Heart in Tatters* supplied that element and demonstrated the remarkable verity of Eunice Tripler's memory, a characteristic she retained well into her eighth decade. It told, more fully, a story of fortitude in a remarkable woman who loved a physician-soldier during and long after their marriage ended in his premature death. Its publication carried much advance praise.

The present work relies on *Heart in Tatters*, on original research, and on a multitude of original and secondary sources. Aid was provided by Tripler family and history colleagues, all of whom sought to furnish the storehouse of a historical record on Dr. Tripler that had never been assembled. At first, the work proceeded from a simple notion: publish in one volume the voluminous and informative report that Tripler submitted in early 1863, from Detroit, on his tenure as the Medical Director of the Army of the Potomac. Those 40,000 words had been included in the *Official Records* but divided into two disparate volumes, with omissions (and in a post-war history). Close reading raised many questions. Conventional histories claimed that Tripler had brought his demise upon himself; why, then, did his report claim many successes? Might it have laid the groundwork for subsequent improvements? Aside from being Eunice's husband, what was the doctor's life story—who, really, was he? Why was his grave

---

20. New York: The Grafton Press, 1910.

at Historic Elmwood Cemetery in Detroit marked by an impressive memorial funded by military colleagues? Why did a Civil War general military hospital carry his name? Was naming an Army medical facility after him in 1920 just another mistake in how military installations have been branded? Why had this Michigander fallen into obscurity during the last century?

For a lifelong student of the Civil War whose understanding of its medical matters could only be regarded as rudimentary—and, in retrospect, highly flawed—such questions required investigation. The result of that inquiry—this present volume—proves again the necessity of returning to primary materials, thereby gaining an accurate understanding of the work of this remarkable physician-soldier.

It also led to a re-examination of the service record of another Army doctor, one better known to the editor. Duncan Alexander Cameron, born in Calumet (the "Copper Country") in 1905, obtained his medical degree from Wayne State University in 1928 and practiced in Livingston County before America entered World War II. He joined the US Army and served in the North African and European Campaigns. In the latter, he landed at D-Day+14, virtually on the heels of the first assaults. Attaining during his service the rank of Major, he also received a Bronze Star. Pieces of his story are found in a book with a title expressive of the risk he faced: *Front Line Surgeons*.[21] He was younger brother of my mother's father, and we knew, respected, and revered "Uncle Dunc" before he passed away in 1979. But at family holiday gatherings around the Cameron dining table, no one spoke a word about his military experience. He, like Dr. Tripler, had worked to save lives of soldiers who had volunteered, like him, to serve the people of our nation in the cause of human freedom. How is it possible that such heroes are overlooked?

When the PBS series *Mercy Street* aired during 2016-2017, it portrayed medical care at a Union hospital in Alexandria, Virginia, not

---

21. Clifford L. Graves, *Front Line Surgeons: A History of the Third Auxiliary Surgical Group* (San Diego: Frye & Smith Ltd., 1950).

on the battlefield. Perhaps, for that reason, it lasted but two seasons. Not many attempts have been made to film a drama in which medical experience under fire in the War of the Rebellion is seriously treated (see Appendix). For students of the bloodiest war in American history, the recounting of its medical aspects deserves much greater attention than most of us have devoted to it.

As ever, any errors herein are the sole responsibility of the undersigned.

—Jack Dempsey, Editor

HIS SWORD A SCALPEL

Part One
1806—1860

Building a Reputation

Youth and Family:
1806-1846

Charles Stuart Tripler was born January 19, 1806, "on the 'Bowery'" in New York City.[1] Formerly dominated by farms on the outskirts of the city, the street and its surroundings had been part of a main route to the north out of the 75,000-person municipality. In the first decade of the 19th century, it underwent a mercantile transformation.[2] His father was a merchant, and his mother was a daughter of a British national.[3] When a little boy in New York, he heard songs in the street calling on citizens to defend against the British during the War of 1812. His future wife recounted her husband's youth thus:

> The home of his parents was on the "Bowerie." Orchard St. marks the place of his father's apple orchard. The half-brothers of Dr. Tripler built "Tripler Hall," which was opened by Jennie Lind. Dr. Tripler's father was a very stern man. He died a year after our marriage, and I never saw him. Madame

---

1. This section is based on *The Army Medical Bulletin*, No. 61 (April 1942), 176-181, and Tripler's *Recollections* as recently annotated (see n.21, n.26), as well as Howard A. Kelly & Walter L. Barrage, *American Medical Biographies* (Baltimore: Norman, Remington Co., 1920). For information on another notable New York-born physician, see Appendix.
2. Kenneth T. Jackson ed., *The Encyclopedia of New York City* (New Haven: Yale University Press, 2010), 148.
3. Although some sources report her father as Hugh Stuart, governor of Bermuda, that name is not among the roster of officials who have held the position. There is documentation regarding a Lieutenant Hugh Stuart, Royal Garrison Battalion and acting engineer for His Majesty's government on Bermuda in the 1780s.

Tripler lived with us at Fort Gratiot two years just before Dr. Tripler went to California. She died at the home of relatives in Toronto. A brother of Dr. Tripler was Grandfather of the inventor of liquid air.

Dr. Tripler's father had been a successful merchant in New York. As he prospered, he invested in land, then comparatively cheap. He sold his estate on Orchard St. and went farther North. At last Dr. Tripler's two half-brothers became involved in business entanglements and got their Father to become their security. They failed and he lost his whole fortune, the creditors taking even the family silver with the crest. This I learned from Madame Tripler, for Dr. Tripler never referred to the matter from mortification at his Father's and Brothers' conduct. These Brothers went to South America.[4]

Because of reverses in his father's business affairs, the young boy was apprenticed to an apothecary who had studied medicine. Tripler received "a good practical education in his off hours," leading to a decision to become a student in the College of Physicians and Surgeons, affiliated with Columbia University, in lower Manhattan. It laid claim to lineage as the oldest medical education institution in America.

The school was in a small building at 3 Barclay Street, just west of Broadway near the City Hall Park. Lecture halls occupied the first two floors, with the top floor housing an anatomical amphitheater. Tripler's attendance required no relocation in a city now populated by over 100,000 residents. The faculty consisted of distinguished members of the Medical Society of the County of New York to which

---

4. Michigan Civil War Association, *Heart in Tatters: Eunice Hunt Tripler and the Civil War* (Traverse City: Mission Point Press, 2022), 29; Tripler, *Recollections*, 83-84. Tripler Hall, on "the west side of Broadway, nearly opposite Bond Street," was "one of the largest music halls in the world." It became Metropolitan Hall before burning down in 1854. Rebuilt, the theater was leased in 1855 by Laura Keene of *Our American Cousin* fame. T. Allston Brown, *A History of the New York Stage: From the First Performance in 1732 to 1901*, Vol. I (New York: Dodd, Mead & Co., 1903), 424-426, 431.

were added instructors formerly in the Columbia medical program. In 1820, the governing board reported that the institution was rapidly improving, and in 1822 it boasted of drawing students from distant parts of the nation. It possessed a library containing the most significant works on medicine. A split occurred while Tripler was a student, with the faculty resigning to form a rival school. The Regents promptly appointed successors consisting of accomplished practitioners. Some ninety students were in attendance in 1826.[5]

Tripler graduated in 1827 along with eleven fellow classmates.[6] He had become a resident assistant physician at Bellevue Hospital in New York City the year before, as a function of his studies, where his experience included contracting smallpox and typhoid fever. During his short stint, he published a set of remarks on delirium tremens. The facility was located on the East River between 25th and 28th Streets (where it remains), originally designed to house the poor and subsequently housing the sick, the indigent, and criminal defendants.[7]

The young doctor was offered a position with the East India Company, perhaps through his mother's connections, likely a lucrative career choice. But he had set his mind not on riches but—for some unknown reason, though perhaps based on those street songs—on medical service in the uniform of his country. He moved up the Hudson River to the military academy at West Point, accepting an invitation from Surgeon Walter V. Wheaton, under whom he studied and worked.[8] On October 30, 1830, age 24, he was commissioned

---

5. John Shrady ed., *The College of Physicians and Surgeons, New York, and Its Founders, Officers, Instructors, Benefactors and Alumni: A History* [Vol. I] (New York: Lewis Pub. Co., 1903), 51-56, 58, 66, 80, 85.

6. John Shrady ed., *The College of Physicians and Surgeons, New York, and Its Founders, Officers, Instructors, Benefactors and Alumni: A History*, Vol. II (New York: Lewis Pub. Co., 1903), 425.

7. Robert J. Carlisle ed., *An Account of Bellevue Hospital, with a Catalogue of the Medical and Surgical Staff from 1736 to 1894* (New York: Society of the Alumni of Bellevue Hospital, 1893), 22, 30, 35, 147, 322 (his name is misspelled as "Trippler").

8. *Official Register of the Officers and Cadets of the U.S. Military Academy, West Point, New-York, June 1841* (New York: J.P. Wright, 1841), 6. Wheaton served

as Assistant Surgeon, US Army, his papers bearing the signature of President Andrew Jackson.[9] It was the beginning of a thirty-six year career devoted to the Army and the nation it protected. To receive his commission, the doctor needed to take this oath:

> "I, _____, appointed a _____ in the Army of the United States, do solemnly swear, or affirm, that I will bear true allegiance to the United States of America, and that I will serve them honestly and faithfully against all their enemies or opposers whatsoever, and observe and obey the orders of the President of the United States, and the orders of the officers appointed over me, according to the rules and articles for the government of the Armies of the United States."[10]

Since university-educated medical practitioners were "an almost insignificant proportion" of the whole field,[11] the Army could count itself fortunate to have someone of such background become part of its six-thousand man force. He was versed in Latin, Italian, French, and Spanish. The top official of his department was Joseph Lovell, the 8th Surgeon-General of the Army, a post assumed in 1818 during a four-year period when Congress replaced the position of Physician-General and allowed one Assistant Surgeon-General as an aide.[12]

Tripler's first duty station was with the 3rd US Infantry at Natchitoches, Louisiana, from December 1830 to March 1831. He next became post surgeon at Fort Towson in present-day Oklahoma, serving until January 1834. After four months' leave, he became post surgeon at Hancock Barracks near Houlton, then at Fort Sullivan, both near the border of Maine with Canada. Between July 1836 and August 1837, he served in Florida with troops engaged in the

---

as an instructor on the faculty of the Academy.
9. Shrady, Vol. II, 425.
10. https://history.army.mil/html/faq/oaths.html
11. Devine, "To Make Something," 152.
12. See, e.g., Act of April 14, 1818, 3 Stat. 426.

"Second Seminole War." He would return to that duty twice more, from November 1837-September 1838 and October 1838-December 1839. In between, he was "on duty in office of Surgeon General at Washington, D. C." and, briefly, at Fort Sullivan. He was promoted to Major and Surgeon on July 7, 1838,[13] his commission signed by President Martin Van Buren. Although subject to a court of inquiry "in relation to furnishing wood to steam-boats at Picolata, Florida" in 1839, it appears no fault was found or discipline taken.[14]

After a brief stint at Buffalo Barracks, N.Y., in January 1840 he was assigned to the Detroit Barracks in Michigan. It proved to be the most significant posting of his life, for there he met the woman he would marry. Their relationship became a love story lasting a quarter-century. She would give birth to nine children. After her husband's death, she would not remarry and for the rest of her life held fast to the memory of the man to whom she bestowed her heart.[15]

Eunice Hunt was a descendant of American patriots. On her father's side, Thomas V. Hunt fought at the Battles of Lexington and Concord on April 19, 1775, when he was but twenty. He was wounded in the Battle of Stony Point on July 16, 1779, and again at the climactic Battle of Yorktown. After the war, he married Eunice Wellington of Waltham, Massachusetts, continued to serve in the US Army, and attained the rank of Colonel. The Hunts were blessed with twelve children, the fifth being named Thomas (likely after his father), who served in the War of 1812 and fought at the Battle of Brownstown near Monroe, Michigan. He died on August 16, 1808, at fifty-three. His grave, and his wife's, are in the Jefferson Barracks National Cemetery

---

13. Shrady, Vol. II, 425.
14. Adjutant General's Department, *Subject Index of the General Orders of the War Department, from January 1, 1809, to December 31, 1860* (Washington: Government Printing Office, 1886), 57, 129.
15. Service record is primarily based on C.B. Burr ed., *Medical History of Michigan*, Vol. II (Minneapolis: Bruce Pub. Co., 1930), 782-783, which indicates reliance on "War Department records, Brigadier General Wahl's letter, Adjutant General's office."

in St. Louis County, Missouri.[16] Eunice Hunt was also grand-daughter of Robert Allen Forsyth, a veteran of the War of 1812. He married Margaret Lytle in 1797, and they had three children, the last being named Alice Mariane Sophia. Thomas Hunt (1791-1838) and Alice Forsyth (1803-1888) were married in Detroit on September 29, 1821. They had six children, the oldest born on October 11, 1822, in Washington, D.C., and named Eunice. According to one chronicler of early Detroit, Colonel Hunt "had two very pretty daughters, Eunice and Ellen. The former married Dr. Tripler, surgeon, U.S.A."[17]

When Tripler arrived from Buffalo in January 1840, a journey of at least a week, he brought a servant, a beautiful sleigh, a small trunk, a few books, a gun case, and a flute, to be supplemented by a piano that arrived via a lake vessel in the Spring. After their first introduction, Eunice "saw him every day in spite of his duties all over the city in attending officers." Tripler would feign interest in her uncle's livestock and would use it as a pretext to pay her a call. She was not an easy catch; with a "spirit of mischief," she recalled, "I would not go to receive him, but get my Mother to appear in my place. This would bring a note from him on return to the city, so that he either saw me or had word directly from me each day." Their courtship was not overlong. On the announcement of their engagement, the commanding officer in Detroit threw them a celebratory dinner.

On March 2, 1841, Eunice Hunt and Charles Tripler were married in an evening ceremony at St. Paul's Church on Woodward Avenue in Detroit by Samuel A. McCoskry, first Episcopal Bishop of Michigan. The garrison commander's wife took care of readying the groom's outfit. It was a favor returned in gratitude for the doctor's care and curing of their child. The new couple began to establish themselves as part of

---

16. Edward G. Longacre, *The Man Behind the Guns: A Military Biography of General Henry J. Hunt, Commander Of Artillery, Army Of The Potomac* (Cambridge: Da Capo Press, 2003), 20-21.
17. Friend Palmer, *Early Days in Detroit* (Detroit: Hunt & June, 1906), 891, 942; Ellen married "Chas. Bissell, dry goods merchant (his second wife)," id. 891, and their son Charles T. served as a Union officer in the Civil War. A cousin of Eunice's was Henry Jackson Hunt of Civil War artillery fame. See n.356.

a growing community in the river city, now just over nine thousand in population. They first resided in a boarding house on Fort Street and then moved to "The Parsonage" on Woodbridge Street and Rivard. Their first child, named after his father, was born on May 8, 1842. An officer who had served with Dr. Tripler at Tallahassee came from New York for the baptism and served as godfather.[18] Such an act demonstrated the kind of comradeship that Tripler had fostered in the Army.

The difference in age between wife and husband was not insignificant. He was 35; she was 19. It caused Eunice anxiety from a "constant fear of appearing too young for Dr. Tripler." For his part, he likely had little or no concern about marrying a "very pretty" young woman who would survive her child-bearing years and live into her eighties. She was from a well-known family line, both in D.C. and Detroit; his family background was not the subject of bragging.

In 1841, an issue roiling the Army's physicians was their status within the military. A congressional enactment of 1834 had established more defined ranks and pay, and ostensibly it made doctors eligible for the same trappings and benefits of the rest of the officer corps. The Secretary of War, however, had proposed to limit such related aspects of service. The Surgeon-General's office issued a circular to all members of the Medical corps inviting views. Over the next three years, a number of "able papers" were sent in. Some were by "the more distinguished members," and Tripler's name was within that group.[19] In July 1843, Tripler served as one of the three surgeons staffing the annual session of the Medical Examining Board. They interviewed fourteen candidates, of which only four passed the exam.[20] It was not merely a task but vital to screening out less than capable physicians before they could begin to treat soldiers.

In March of that year, the Triplers moved to a house on Congress

---

18. Thomas Childs (1796–1853), West Point Class of 1814.
19. Harvey E. Brown, *The Medical Department of the United States Army from 1775 to 1873* (Washington: Surgeon General's Office, 1873), 170 [hereinafter "Brown, *Medical Department*"].
20. Id. 172.

Street two doors west of Shelby Street. When a renowned figure from the War of 1812 came to Detroit, Winfield Scott made sure to pay the happy couple a visit. Eunice was pregnant again. Their unfettered joy was short-lived. Their infant boy died on September 7, 1843. Alice Hunt Tripler's birth on December 19 assuaged the couple's grief. She was named for her grandmother and nicknamed "Allie." Another boy was delivered on February 19, 1846, and given his father's full name in hopes his life would be prolonged (it was).[21] That year brought another move to a house on Jefferson Avenue opposite the Biddle House, one of the city's hotels. Two months later, the Mexican-American War summoned Tripler from Detroit to duty in full-fledged combat.

---

21. Progeny information is taken from the family Bible, courtesy of Dr. Charles D. Cullen of Wichita, Kansas.

Duty Calls:
1846-1860

The Triplers' domestic life was interrupted when Congress approved a declaration of war against the Republic of Mexico on May 13, 1846. The troops of the Detroit Barracks, Tripler among them, were sent to Newport Barracks, Kentucky, and then down the Mississippi River to New Orleans. They became part of the army of Major-General Scott, which landed near Vera Cruz in March 1847 and laid a successful siege to that city. Tripler was assigned as medical director of Major-General David E. Twiggs's 2nd Division of regular Army troops.[1] He served as chief surgeon in the series of actions during the advance upon Mexico City, including the battles of Cerro Gordo, Contreras, Churubusco, Molino del Rey, and Chapultepec. Twiggs incorporated praise of the services provided by Tripler and assistants in official reports on these conflicts. So, too, did patients. One officer wrote home about how "Dr. Tripler attends me, and says my wounds improve every day."[2] General Twiggs commended him (and others) after hostile action, reporting that they "spent the entire night exposed to the pitiful storm in dressing the wounded and alleviating their sufferings." Another officer praised Tripler for "prompt and able attention to the wounded."[3] It appears from his wife's memoir that this conflict was where he first performed a battlefield amputation.

Upon the capture of Mexico City on September 14, 1847, each

---

1. Brown, *Medical Department*, 185.
2. *Democratic Free Press*, Detroit, Mich., Oct. 14, 1847, 2.
3. Brown, *Medical Department*, 190.

Division established its own hospital arrangements. A Thanksgiving service was held, and Eunice Tripler would relate that a "little band of officers communicated, at their head Gen. Scott. Major Duncan Stewart, a Paymaster, once told me Dr. Tripler saved more souls than any other man in Mexico — by doing, rather than saying, the right thing." Tripler's moral life, he told her, "was a perpetual sermon." Despite religious differences, Tripler befriended and provided medical care to several Mexican priests.

In December, Tripler was assigned by Medical Director Richard S. Satterlee[4] to organize and operate a general hospital for the Army.[5] This evidently meant putting to use a number of buildings: the Bishop's palace, the Governor's palace, the Iturbide palace, the Inquisition, the College of Mines, and the convent of Santa Isabella. But difficulties arose because of the wide dispersion of the locations, the shortage of medical officers, and the abilities of the personnel. On the whole, however, "its administration by Tripler was decidedly creditable."[6] When it came time to withdraw the troops and return North, Tripler was co-director of the effort to remove the wounded and ill.[7]

Tripler continued his practice of observing religious services while a part of the expedition, being a faithful church-goer. He became an original member of the Aztec Club, organized in 1847 along the lines of the Society of the Cincinnati for the officer veterans of this war.[8] The cadre included a number of officers he would serve with during the Civil War. When gaming and drinking were proposed

---

4. In 1862, when the Surgeon-General was retired, Satterlee was a candidate to take the position as the senior officer in the medical fraternity.
5. Brown, *Medical Department*, 195.
6. *The Army Medical Bulletin, supra.*
7. Brown, *Medical Department*, 197.
8. Cadmus M. Wilcox, *History of the Mexican War* (Washington: Church News Pub. Co., 1892), 711; William H. Robarts, *Mexican War Veterans: A Complete Roster of the Regular and Volunteer Regiments in the War Between the United States and Mexico, from 1846 to 1848* (Washington: Brentano's, 1887), 7.

for the club's activities, General Scott enlisted Tripler—"his fellow Episcopalian and moralist"—to help shut it down.⁹

The US Army losses in the Mexican-American War would be dwarfed by the carnage wrought during the next great conflict in the 1860s. Nonetheless, each wounded or ill soldier carried his own importance, and comparisons of war casualty totals overlook the individual human cost involved. It can also diminish the impact on the caregivers who strive to aid those who have suffered. Dr. Tripler's experiences in trying to save lives south of the Rio Grande formed part of the expertise he would bring to the War of the Rebellion, but it also shaped part of his own emotional makeup. He related the story to his wife of the battlefield amputation where the patient was killed by hostile fire in the midst of the procedure. Such vignettes provide insight into the psychological cost of combat to those who manned a weapon as well those who tried to ameliorate the effects on the human frame of those devices.¹⁰

Although the campaign proved successful, a significant number of soldiers fell ill. Among them were several medical officers, one of whom died of disease. Yellow fever attacked without regard for line of duty. Tripler apparently escaped becoming ill.¹¹ The Surgeon-General of the Army called for reports from the medical directors of each Division on their analysis of the situation. Tripler complied on July 6, 1847. His report sought out and included the input of his subordinates, and it identified a number of contributing factors. The

---

9. Lloyd Lewis, *Captain Sam Grant* (Boston: Little, Brown & Co., 1950), 268.
10. The psycho-traumatic effects of the War have received detailed attention in recent works, e.g., Eric T. Dean Jr., *Shook over Hell: Post-Traumatic Stress, Vietnam, and the Civil War* (Cambridge: Harvard University Press, 1997), and recently in Dillon Carroll, *Invisible Wounds: Mental Illness and Civil War Soldiers* (Baton Rouge: Louisiana State University Press, 2021). Louisa May Alcott wrote of one case in 1863; see n.351. A recent anthology looks at this and other aspects of trauma. David Seed, Stephen C. Kenny & Chris Williams eds., *Life and Limb: Perspectives on the American Civil War* (Liverpool: Liverpool University Press, 2015).
11. Brown, *Medical Department*, 189.

document shows that Tripler was then stationed east of Mexico City, in Puebla.[12] When the US Senate ratified the war-ending treaty, it was Tripler who brought the good news to other officers.[13]

The doctor was on duty again in Detroit in May 1848. Reunion was short-lived, since he spent June-November at Jefferson Barracks near St. Louis, Missouri. On November 22, he resumed his role as post surgeon at Detroit Barracks.[14]

The 1850 Census recorded the "Trippler" family in Detroit, Charles in the profession of "U.S. Surgeon" with his wife "Uniz" and three children: 6-year old Alice H., 4-year old Charles, and 3-year old Ellen M. (for Mackintosh), who was actually quite still a baby. She, their fourth, was born in Detroit on September 8, 1849, and died on October 8, 1850, not long after the census taker's visit. In only the first decade of their marriage, the Triplers had suffered the deaths of two of four children.

Tripler's reputation led Surgeon-General Thomas Lawson to appoint him as representative of the Medical Department of the Army at the annual meeting of the American Medical Association in Cincinnati in May 1850. The veteran of the late war "was very cordially received," and he brought "to the notice of the Association the claims" of the Army medical staff. He had also joined the Michigan State Medical Society. Not long after, the Army post at Detroit "was broken up." In July 1851, the Tripler family transferred to Fort Gratiot, a Federal military installation in Saint Clair County, Michigan, along the St. Clair River just south of Lake Huron.[15]

Tripler's participation within both organizations reflects recognition by the profession of the need to advance its qualifications and general public reputation. The Society had been organized in 1819

---

12. See Appendix for the text.
13. W.A. Croffut ed., *Fifty Years in Camp and Field: Diary of Major-General Ethan Allen Hitchcock* (New York: G.P. Putnam's Sons, 1909), 323-324. Signed on February 2, the treaty received US Senate ratification on March 10, 1848.
14. Burr, 783.
15. Brown, *Medical Department*, 203. Lawson's term of office was from 1836 until death on May 15, 1861.

and had among its goals to prescribe requirements for studying to become a physician, qualifications to obtain a license, conditions for its revocation, and providing means to partner with an established practitioner. It engaged in approving local medical societies along similar lines. Reciprocity with licensing regimes in other States was approved. With Michigan still being sparsely populated during the early 19th century, the effort to ensure "a clean, well educated, honest profession" was an ambitious and visionary one.[16] The AMA was founded in 1847 as a national professional organization comprised of delegates from State and local medical societies, institutions of learning, hospitals, and other medical facilities. The Association enacted the world's first national code of medical ethics.[17] Its goal to "improve the healing art" was to be achieved:

> by securing more complete and thorough courses of instruction to students; and by raising the standard of requirements of those admitted into the ranks of the profession;—by investigating the causes of the diseases which prevail in certain localities, and by seeking the way by which these causes may be removed, or their effects counteracted;—by collecting reliable histories of the different epidemics which, from time to time, spread over our country, and by endeavoring to discover the means of arresting their progress;—by offering prizes for the most useful discoveries and improvements in medicine; and by promoting every measure tending to enlarge the boundaries of our science or increase the efficiency, and augment the usefulness of our art.[18]

---

16. Leartus Connor, *The Michigan Medical Society; Its First Eighty-three Years; Present Wants and Suggestions for Their Supply* (Detroit: John Bornman & Son, 1902), 2-8.
17. *Code of Ethics of the American Medical Association, Adopted May, 1847* (Philadelphia: Turner Hamilton, 1871).
18. *Reception of the American Medical Association at Independence Hall, Philadelphia, May 2, 1855* (Philadelphia: T.K. & P.G. Collins, 1855), 3-4. The Association had been organized in that city.

Although the AMA would not commence publishing its journal until after the Civil War, practitioners like Tripler did have the benefit of other American resources. One was *The Medical Repository*, first published in 1797 and continuing for a score of years.[19] The *American Journal of the Medical Sciences* first appeared in 1827.[20] Tripler himself would complain of the "country doctors, accustomed to a village nostrum practice," who would prefer their known remedies to "the rigid system of the army."[21] Not all of the surgeons who sought Army service kept up to date.

Eunice and Charles were able to spend three years together before the next assignment came. On August 21, 1851, their fifth child, Ellen Cass, was born at Fort Gratiot. Named after Eunice's sister, Ellen would outlive her father and older sister Alice, becoming the fifth child to die.

The gains from the war with Mexico included the territory along the Pacific Coast south of the Canadian border. Tripler received orders to report at New York for a sea voyage to the Isthmus of Panama and thence up the Pacific coast. He expressed strong concerns to the War Department that a summer crossing of the jungle would be extremely hazardous from a medical standpoint. The Washington bureaucracy waved off the warning. As Tripler feared, "the ill-fated trip was an irremediable fiasco." The ship was overcrowded, the weather was oppressively hot, and passengers were always on edge. And that was just on the Atlantic side.[22] Eunice would relate her husband's experience of the journey across to the Pacific:

---

19. Samuel L. Mitchill, Edward Miller & Elihu H. Smith (New York: T & J. Swords).
20. Philadelphia: Lea & Blanchard. A survey of early medical literature is found in H.R.M. Landis, *The History of the Development of Medical Science in America as Recorded in The American Journal of the Medical Sciences* (Philadelphia: Lea Brothers & Co., 1901).
21. *OR*, V, 79. Tripler might have meant the use of patent medicines, or the informal customs of such a practice.
22. Ron Chernow, *Grant* (New York: Penguin Press, 2017), 71–72.

It was June, 1852. The crossing of the Isthmus was fearful. Shiploads of laborers for the railway died as fast as they came—or, as the saying was, "An Irishman for every tie." Miasma and pestilence were everywhere. The troops went by boat up the Chagres River which was covered with a heavy, green slime. Then they marched through mud so deep it was soberly said certain soldiers were actually lost in the mud and never found. Of course this meant that sometimes, while on the march, soldiers were attacked with cholera, and, being unable to keep their place in column, would lie down in the mud. Death at times came swiftly after the commands had passed on. Dr. Tripler said, when some such cases of sudden seizure were reported to him, he rode back to give relief but could find no patient at the point indicated. Out of 700 men, women and children, 70 died on the Isthmus and Dr. Tripler was their only surgeon. But a ship's surgeon at Aspinwall, for very pity's sake, crossed with Dr. Tripler to give him aid. The officer who so volunteered was Dr. Elisha Kent Kane, afterward of Arctic fame.[23] It was a heroic deed and appreciated by Dr. Tripler who had unbounded admiration for Kane. Years after, some time following Kane's return from the far North, the two met in Cincinnati and renewed their friendship.[24]

Tripler renewed an acquaintance on the trip. After reaching Panama Bay, the burgeoning number of sick were put aboard a vessel to be cared for by Tripler, with enlisted men converted into hospital stewards under his direction. They proved inattentive. Oppressed by the lack of cooperation, Tripler called for an officer to remain on watch to compel the stewards to do their duty and attend to patients. The officer assigned to be with him in this regard was Lieutenant Ulysses S. Grant, who had been stationed in Detroit in 1848-1850.[25] Somehow,

---

23. Kane (1820–1857) was a US Navy officer.
24. *Heart in Tatters*, 40–41.
25. Id. 42.

the two officers survived—in fact, another passenger wrote of how the medical team "did everything in their power" to prevent disease and to alleviate suffering, exhibiting "tireless energy and great presence of mind."[26] The team was led by the two who had first met alongside a fresh waterway: "Grant and Dr. Tripler fixed up an old hulk a mile offshore to act as a hospital ship where they could bring the sick;" "Grant and Tripler ministered to the sick."[27]

When Grant sat down to draft his memoirs in 1884, three decades had passed since that difficult voyage. He remembered it pretty vividly and included a story about a sea-sick lieutenant. He wrote about the cholera outbreak and how about one-third of the entourage died from it. He did not mention Tripler, however, and only referred to "the doctors" who had accompanied the regiment. Grant also glossed over any difficulties he experienced while stationed on the West Coast. He blamed his resignation from the Army on inability to support his family out of his military pay. He never mentioned the medical officer who proved helpful to his health on this and other occasions.[28] According to a recent Grant biography, his difficulties with alcohol became chronic, a result of his susceptibility to quick inebriation. From that cause, exacerbated by the separation from family, arose his decision to resign in April 1854. Eunice Tripler revealed her version of that situation:

> Grant was in my husband's care and Dr. Tripler was entirely frank and open in dealing with his case. He, at last, resigned from the Army and came East. From the difference in rank, first in Dr. Tripler's favour and later in Grant's, there was hardly intimacy between the two.[29]

---

26. Chernow, 74.
27. Ronald C. White, *American Ulysses: A Life of Ulysses S. Grant* (New York: Random House, 2016), 110.
28. *Personal Memoirs of U.S. Grant*, Vol. I (New York: Charles L. Webster & Co., 1885), 194-199, 210.
29. *Heart in Tatters*, 52.

The "case" might also have encompassed behavior that was related to gambling in San Francisco, involvement in "get rich quick" schemes, failed investments and projects, shifting duty posts up and down the coast, and loneliness. The ready availability of intemperate beverages contributed to Grant's misbehavior, and "overwhelming evidence" attributes his quitting the Army to "an alcohol problem."[30] It would explain not mentioning one of his treating physicians in 1884.

Tripler was appointed to the post of Medical Director, Department of the Pacific, and served in this position until January 1856.[31] He also managed, better than Grant, to endure the separation from family.

The time together in Detroit had been a blessing to Lieutenant Grant and his wife. Married in August 1848, they came to Detroit as newlyweds, a state that culminated in Julia Dent Grant's first pregnancy. Tripler acted as her physician. When he found her "not very well" at a key stage, Tripler advised a return to her family homestead for the birth. She followed his advice and, in May 1850, had her first baby without complication at White Haven in Missouri.[32]

While in California, the cost of living became so high due to the Gold Rush that Tripler went into private practice. He lived off this income and sent all his Army pay home to support the family, a salary that included a location premium of two dollars per day. While in San Francisco in 1853, he went into practice with a physician from New York City. After a year, when Dr. Hewitt had to return East, he borrowed $550 from his partner, a significant sum that would not be repaid until after Tripler's demise. The doctor's generosity extended to his family; at one point, he had supported three unmarried female relatives at the rate of $700 per year. Part of Tripler's fortitude continued to derive from his spiritual beliefs; he regularly participated in church activities while stationed on the West Coast. It was here that he met future Civil War comrades Joseph Hooker and Edward

---

30. Chernow, 85; see *Heart in Tatters*, 52.
31. Shrady, Vol. II, 425.
32. John Y. Simon ed., *The Personal Memoirs of Julia Dent Grant* (New York: G.G. Putnam's Sons, 1975), 66.

D. Townsend.[33] Tripler treated William T. Sherman's son and, in the estimation of both parents, saved his life.[34]

Was Tripler without humor? Eunice told this story about a conversation he had with a superior officer while stationed together out West:

> Gen. Wool[35] was a man of most egregious vanity and very unpopular with his brother officers and in the Army generally — but was quite obtuse to the fact. He, one day, dilated to Dr. Tripler on the subject of his own possible illness and death and the consequent trouble and care which would result to the command in the necessary arrangements for the funeral of an officer of his rank. Dr. Tripler long afterward used to chuckle over the reply he made. For he said, "Don't give the subject another thought, General. The officers will be simply delighted to attend to the matter." Gen. Wool looked rather wild at this.[36]

Upon his return and their 1856 reunion in New York—they had been apart some four years—the couple traveled to Washington so that Tripler could make the obligatory report. They hastened on to Detroit, "for Dr. Tripler wanted to see the children so much." They were not there long, but Tripler had time enough to appear in print for the first time in *The Peninsular Journal of Medicine and the Collateral*

---

33. *Heart in Tatters*, 52. Townsend (1817-1893), West Point 1837, served as Chief of Staff to General Winfield Scott and as Assistant Adjutant-General, 1861-1863. The Triplers named a child after him.
34. Id. 126-127. This according to Eunice, but Sherman made no mention of the story in his memoirs. William Tecumseh Sherman Jr., nicknamed Willie, born June 8, 1854, in San Francisco, died of typhoid fever in October 1863. Abraham Lincoln's son William Wallace ("Willie") died of the disease in February 1862.
35. John E. Wool (1784-1869), veteran of the War of 1812 and the Mexican-American War, Union Major-General in the Civil War.
36. *Heart in Tatters*, 54.

Sciences, a medically oriented publication originating from Detroit begun by a University of Michigan anatomy professor. His lead article was entitled "Case of Gun Shot Wound to the Stomach."[37] Very few physicians in the Army, or in the civilian population, had experience with such a trauma situation.[38] The family moved in April 1856 when he was ordered to Newport Barracks in Kentucky, where the Licking River meets the Ohio across from Cincinnati. Here was born their sixth, Edgar Macklin, and seventh, Edward Townsend.

Newport Barracks served as the recruit depot for all the western assignments within the Army. Given his role as post surgeon, Tripler capitalized on the opportunity to write a *Manual of the Medical Officer of the Army of the United States*, published in Cincinnati in 1858. Apparently the first of a projected series, this volume concentrated on the medical issues associated with recruitment. It soon became the recognized authority in the field.[39] He never finished any others, perhaps because spare time was taken up in the study of astronomy. Besides continuing his learning, he was afforded the opportunity to lecture at the Cincinnati Medical College. His presentations were compiled into a *Hand-Book of the Military Surgeon*.[40] While at Newport, Tripler

---

37. Vol. IV, No. 1, July 1856 (Detroit: John A. Kerr & Co.), 1-7.
38. J. Julian Chisolm, *A Manual of Military Surgery, for the Use of Surgeons in the Confederate States Army* (Richmond: West & Johnston, 1862), iii.
39. The precise title is: *Manual of the Medical Officer of the Army of the United States, Part I, Recruiting and the Inspection of Recruits, by Charles S. Tripler, M.D., Surgeon U.S.A.; Fellow of the College of Physicians and Surgeons of the University of the State of New York* (Cincinnati: Wrightson & Co., 1858). In 1866, a second edition was issued by the Government Printing Office. Later, Tripler's aide Charles R. Greenleaf authored *An Epitome of Tripler's Manual and Other Publications on the Examination of Recruits* (Washington: William Ballantyne & Sons, 1890).
40. There are two editions of this work, with Tripler identified as "A.M., M.D., Surgeon U.S. Army" (Cincinnati: Robert Clarke & Co., 1861). The Preface indicates that Tripler's contributions were based on lectures he gave "for the last three years" at the Medical College of Ohio and that his contributions were truncated because he "was summoned to report himself to [US Army] headquarters before his revision of his labors was completed." Co-author was George Curtis Blackman (1819–1871), professor of surgery at the College. One physician-historian

"became impressed with the magnitude of the impending civil conflict and tried to prepare for it. He had studied the Crimean War and other modern conflicts."[41]

This volume of less than two hundred pages is said not to have achieved the same kind of sales as the *Manual*. Perhaps its date of publication caused lower sales volume, but it still bears an examination given content suggested in its extensive subtitle: "being a compendium of the duties of the medical officer in the field, the sanitary management of the camp, the preparation of food, etc.; with forms for the requisitions for supplies, returns, etc.; the diagnosis and treatment of camp dysentery; and all the important points in war surgery: including gunshot wounds, amputation, wounds of the chest, abdomen, arteries and head, and the use of chloroform." Chapter 1—on the officer's duties—began with the admonition "not to suppose that he is to sit in his tent" and await a call to attend to a sick soldier; instead, he was to be "zealous" and provide "the greatest possible security against the invasion of disease."[42] What followed was a primer on providing medical care in order that even the inexperienced officer could do his job. Tripler referred to the "General Regulations for the Army," which controlled many of the aspects of medical provisioning. One example was:

> Before the action, the quartermaster of the division makes all the necessary arrangements for the transportation of the wounded. He establishes the ambulance depots in the rear, and gives his assistants the necessary instruction for the service of the ambulance wagons, and other means of removing the wounded.[43]

---

describes the work as "a premier military medical text." Mark J. Schaadt, *Civil War Medicine: An Illustrated History* (Quincy: Cedarwood Publishing, 1998), 81.
41. *Heart in Tatters*, 61.
42. *Hand-Book*, 1.
43. Id. 8.

As important as the medical matter was, in other words, it was necessary to understand that procedures had been established that were to be followed for regular order and good discipline. The Army was organized along departmental lines: the Quartermaster exercised responsibility for issuance and supplies and for transportation; the Commissary bureau had responsibility for provisions; the Ordnance bureau had overall control of ammunition, armaments, and weaponry. The Navy was a separate department with its own management, independent of the Army.

The book referenced European authorities, relayed real life experiences in Mexico and the Crimean War, and included practical items such as recipes for healthy eating. The chapter on wounds suffered from weapons referred to a number of authorities, demonstrating Tripler's wide reading. In the chapter on amputations, he related:

> Injuries of the patella do not require amputation, as was proved by two of my own cases in the Mexican war.[44]

He later referred to "a case of mine" in "the city of Mexico" versus "another in San Francisco" on a question that had not been settled.[45] He did draw a conclusion in favor of the practice since "[i]t does save life, and essentially diminish suffering."[46]

Interesting, given the predominant issue dividing North from South at the time, the term "negro" appears but once in the *Hand-Book*. It is merely a reference to a case, the patient being a person of African heritage in India who had an arm wound.[47] "Inferior" appears on three occasions, only in reference to an angle or organ.[48] There is an underlying assumption that Army patients will be Caucasian, given the state of the law, regulations, and society.

---

44. Id. 53.
45. Id. 54.
46. Id. 55-56.
47. Id. 43.
48. Id. 68, 99, 109.

Near to the time of this publication, a book was printed setting forth the regulations for Army medical operations. Roughly comprising eighty substantive pages, the volume contained a preface demanding "that they be strictly observed. Nothing contrary to the tenor of these present regulations will be enjoined or allowed in any part of the forces of the United States by any commander whatsoever."[49]

In October 1859, with this experience and scholarship providing qualifications for Tripler's membership, he was appointed to a five-member Army Medical Board to give recommendations on the number and type of tents the Army should obtain "for the sick and wounded and their attendants."[50] The Board also revised the Standard Supply Table "to include most of the modern improvements in medicines and hospital stores, instruments and dressings."[51] It examined ambulance models and, "by adopting the four-wheeled Tripler" and two two-wheeled models, provided the foundation of "the first organized American ambulance system."[52]

That year, Tripler became an individual member of the American Medical Association. On May 3, 1859, at its annual meeting in Louisville, he was elected as a vice-president of the organization.[53] On September 20, Tripler again was serving on an Army board to review applicants for vacant medical positions; the other two members were

---

49. *Regulations for the Medical Department of the Army* (Washington: George W. Bowman, 1860), 3. The language dates from March 6, 1860.
50. *The Medical and Surgical History of the War of the Rebellion*, Part III, Vol. II (Washington: Government Printing Office, 1883), 920 n.1 [hereinafter *Medical and Surgical History*]; Brown, *Medical Department*, 212. The *Medical and Surgical History* was published in three parts, each part having two volumes, making six volumes in total.
51. Brown, *Medical Department*, 212.
52. John S. Haller Jr., *Farmcarts to Fords: A History of the Military Ambulance, 1790-1925* (Carbondale: Southern Illinois University Press, 1992), 28. The report appeared as an Appendix in an 1861 publication that, it can be assumed, was part of Tripler's library, having mentioned him and his work by name. John Ordronaux, *Hints on the Preservation of Health in Armies: For the Use of Volunteer Officers and Soldiers* (New York: D. Appleton & Co., 1861). A different appendix appears in the 1863 edition.
53. *Detroit Free Press*, May 12, 1859, 2.

Finley and Satterlee, demonstrating Tripler's renown within the medical corps.[54] In 1860, Tripler received an honorary degree from his alma mater in New York.[55] His credentials at age 54 were extensive and well-recognized.

In domestic affairs, the Triplers welcomed their eighth child on December 21, 1860, a girl, and named her Eunice Montgomery.[56] She was born at Newport, becoming another representation of the sectionalism that was splitting the country. Kentucky was a slave State; a sister slave State, South Carolina, had on the day prior to her birth adopted an Ordinance of Secession, declaring its withdrawal from the Union and purporting to assume its own independent status. Five more Southern States would take the same step in January 1861. In February, a seventh joined and helped form the so-called Confederate States of America, based on a provisional constitution adopted on February 4 and a permanent instrument on February 22. Its cornerstone was prohibition on the power of government to deny or impair "the right of property in negro slaves."[57] Kentucky would remain officially in the Union.

As of December 1860, the Army's authorized strength equaled approximately 18,000 officers and men. A total of 16,367 soldiers were listed on the rolls. Of this number, commissioned officers totaled 1,108. Four were Generals; the remainder were either regimental officers or served in staff positions of the War Department. A total of 361 staff officers were assigned to the nine bureaus in the Department. Tripler was among a select group of approximately one hundred physicians in Army and Navy service. He stood out among those peers because of his experience under fire during the 1830s and

---

54. Brown, *Medical Department*, 212.
55. Shrady, Vol. II, 425.
56. After her mother and her parents' Army friend, Montgomery C. Meigs, whose father was a physician.
57. Article I, Sec. 9, Clause 4. Confederate Vice-President Alexander H. Stephens used this very term, declaring: "Our new government is founded upon ... its foundations are laid, its cornerstone rests, upon the great truth that the negro is not equal to the white man."

1840s and his yeoman work on the voyage to the Pacific. The Army had constructed but a single general hospital, at Fort Leavenworth in Kansas Territory. The Medical Bureau was a diffuse organization without complete control over the well-being of the soldiers. The Quartermaster-General and his Department held responsibility for the provision and supply of the Army, including medical items. At the head of the Medical Department was a Surgeon-General, with a rank below his peers. Despite a looming war, no effort was made to refit a peacetime structure for the needs of a revolutionary conflict.

Thomas Lawson had served as the top Army medical officer since 1836. He was seventy-one years old when secessionists fired upon and forced the surrender of Fort Sumter in Charleston Harbor, South Carolina, on April 13, 1861, precipitating the Civil War. Two days later, newly elected President Abraham Lincoln, whose only martial experience was an uneventful short period during the so-called Black Hawk War thirty years prior, invoked existing law to call up the militia in support of securing Federal property and maintaining the Union. He also convened Congress so that additional measures to ready the national government for conflict could be enacted. The ramping up of the US military would require time.

Lawson might have been up to the task of ensuring the Army's medical infrastructure could meet the demands of the nation's most engulfing war. It will never be known. He soon became ill and traveled to Norfolk, Virginia, in hopes of recuperating. He was stricken with a stroke on May 15 and died within a few hours.[58] His successor, Clement Alexander Finley, was nearly as old at 64. He was a career military doctor, having been commissioned as a surgeon's mate in August 1818. Finley had been in Florida, as had Tripler, and he had seen initial service in Mexico as Medical Director for the army commanded by Major-General Zachary Taylor. Taken ill, he was relieved and came back to the States. He returned in accompaniment of Scott's

---

58. James E. Pilcher, *The Surgeon Generals of the Army of the United States of America* (Carlisle: Association of Military Surgeons, 1905), 39.

expedition, but illness disabled him again. His actual battlefield experience, then, amounted to far less than Tripler's.[59] His tenure would be short, lasting until April 1862. He "did not fully grasp the magnitude of the problems facing the army after the South had fired on Fort Sumter."[60]

The Civil War would make careers, and it would undo them. It would also abbreviate many lives.

---

59. Id. 41.
60. Frank R. Freemon, *Gangrene and Glory: Medical Care during the American Civil War* (Madison: Fairleigh Dickinson University Press, 1998), 35. Finley died in 1879.

Part Two
1861—July 1862

Leading on the Front Line

Early War Months: April-August 1861

By the time war commenced by the attack on Fort Sumter, Tripler had built a strong record and won a high reputation both inside and outside the military. He had made "intellectual discoveries" that "contributed meaningful, informative ideas to military medicine."[1] He had authored a book that would become standard in Army readiness. He had lectured at a prestigious Midwest medical college. He had written knowledgeably on subjects that a minority of physicians had confronted. He was not a young man, but nothing suggested his life would be cut short unless it would be in battle.

As the Union mustered itself to confront the "Slaveholders' Rebellion," Tripler was a valuable resource. Lincoln was an unprepared Commander-in-Chief; his War Secretary had minimal military credentials. Heading up the Army was 75-year old Winfield Scott, suffering from age, service, and poor health. A significant number of West Point graduates from the South resigned their commissions and accepted officer positions in the Confederate military. Some ex-Army officers sought to leverage the situation to accept the choicest post; George B. McClellan was an example of that jockeying for position.

Tripler was an officer in the US Army on April 15, 1861. He had no choice of assignments and was stationed far from Washington and the Rebel capital at Richmond, Virginia. As Scott sought to

---

1. Dan Stouffer, "Officer Autopsy: Dissecting the Legacy of Jonathan Letterman" in *Surgeon's Call: Journal of the Museum of Civil War Medicine* (Special Edition 2015), 7-8. This publication contains commentaries on Stouffer's article, plus a rebuttal from the author.

muster up the Army, he turned to familiar names in whom he had great confidence. In charge of the Department of Pennsylvania was Major-General Robert Patterson, a Mexican-American War veteran. His command extended just to the west of that governing the nation's capital and northeastern Virginia. On April 25, 1861, Scott notified Patterson that "Surgeon Tripler, from Newport, Ky., has been ordered to join you."[2] The appointment answered the need for the services "of an experienced surgeon" from the regular Army to promptly organize and lead the volunteer medical staff.[3] It was an important department, encompassing the three States immediately north of the Potomac around Washington.[4] Patterson advanced his force across the River and into the Shenandoah Valley in order to draw the attention of Confederate forces under command of Generals Thomas J. Jackson and Joseph E. Johnston. On July 6, Patterson sent the War Department a report of his movement from Hagerstown, Maryland, to Martinsburg in Virginia. Hostile action had produced Union casualties of eight men killed and fifteen wounded. "As fast as the facilities of ambulance transportation offered, these men were removed to the general hospital at Hagerstown, Maryland, arrangements for their reception having been carefully provided by Surgeon C.S. Tripler, U.S.A., medical director of the army."[5] Patterson's report bore "testimony to efficient service" by members of his staff, including "Surgeon Tripler in attention to the wounded."[6] In this first action, Tripler had performed well.

An odd coincidence appears within official records this early in the War. It was a circumstance under which Tripler might have been superseded:

---

2. *OR*, II, 157, 600-601; Shrady, Vol. II, 425.
3. *OR*, II, 595.
4. Id. 607.
5. Extract from a Report of Services from April, 1861, to June, 1863, by Surgeon C.F.H. Campbell, US Volunteers, in *Medical and Surgical History*, Appendix to Part I, Vol. I (Washington: Government Printing Office, 1870), 10. Jackson gained his "Stonewall" nickname later that month.
6. *OR*, II, 160-161.

At the time of the attack on Fort Sumpter [sic], the command with which I was doing duty was stationed at Fort Mackinac, Michigan. The condition of the lakes, closed with ice, kept the command at that post until April 28, 1861, when navigation having opened, the troops left, and [I] reported with all possible dispatch at Washington, D.C. Having reported to the Surgeon General, I was detailed to organize and take charge of the Union Hotel hospital in Georgetown. Having organized this establishment, and having remained in charge of it until it was filled with patients, I was ordered to report to Major General Robert Patterson, as medical director. ** At the request of General Patterson, Surgeon Tripler was retained, and I was ordered to report again to the Surgeon General.[7]

Tripler's reputation and familiar service in Mexico likely made Patterson demand his retention.

As a surgeon in the US Army, Tripler proudly wore the uniform of the Medical Staff. Its distinctiveness arose from the letters "MS" in Old English script on their shoulder straps, a sash of "medium or emerald green silk," and one-eighth inch gold cord down the outside of each pant leg. His hat featured "US" prominent above the brim. Green trim marked the medical arm.[8] If they carried a sword, many favored the Model 1840 Medical Staff version.

On July 15, Patterson advanced his force on the Valley Pike to Bunker Hill, halfway to Winchester where Johnston's army stood. From the 17th to 20th, Patterson had his headquarters in Charlestown. He telegraphed Scott on the 21st from Harpers Ferry. Patterson had ordered the hospital depot at Hagerstown to be moved there.[9] In

---

7. *Medical and Surgical History*, Appendix to Part I, Vol. I, 230 (by US Army Surgeon George E. Cooper).
8. Philip Katcher, *American Civil War Armies (3): Staff, Specialist and Maritime Services* (London: Osprey Publishing, 1986), 5, B.
9. *OR*, II, 166-167.

his view, he had offered battle but found the invitation declined—thus, his troops had "done all that was possible" before moving back northward. He expressed thanks to his staff "for their efficient aid and devotion to duty."[10]

At Washington, the predominant view was that Patterson had utterly failed. He had not occupied Johnston sufficiently; instead, the Valley forces had entrained for Manassas Junction, where they arrived in time to turn the tide late on the day of Patterson's telegram, July 21st. The Battle of First Bull Run was the first major Union defeat (putting aside Fort Sumter), culminating in a retreat that degenerated into a rout. Casualties on the US side totaled around 1,500 out of a force approximating 35,000 under Major-General Irvin McDowell, but defeat became more bitter by inadequate preparedness in the Army's handling of its wounded. The official accounts by Surgeon William S. King, Medical Director for McDowell,[11] and others relayed that, since officers of the medical staff were attached to individual regiments with no other layer of care, it became the responsibility of a decentralized staff to figure out how to deliver aid in that moment. King reported that "after the action had fairly commenced and the wounded and the dead were seen lying on the field in every direction, I dispatched Assist. Surg. D.L. Magruder to the rear, with directions to prepare a church" to serve as a hospital.[12] Two nearby houses were

---

10. Id. 174.
11. William Shakespeare King was born on December 28, 1810. He was appointed from Pennsylvania as Assistant Surgeon in July 1837, promoted to Major and Surgeon in August 1856. He was 50 years old at First Bull Run. He retired from the Army in 1882 after receiving brevet promotions for faithful and meritorious service during the War. He arrived only seventy-two hours before the army had begun its march toward the enemy. Scott McGaugh, *Surgeon in Blue: Jonathan Letterman, the Civil War Doctor Who Pioneered Battlefield Care* (New York: Arcade Publishing, 2013), 49.
12. David Lynn Magruder, born in Pennsylvania on April 23, 1825, had joined the US Army in 1850 and became Captain and Assistant Surgeon in February 1855. He was 36 years old at First Bull Run. Promoted to Major and Surgeon in April 1862, he served in 1863-1864 in Louisville, Kentucky, as a medical purveyor and became a Brigadier-General after the war. He received a brevet promotion in 1865.

pressed into service once the church was filled with patients. Nothing had been prearranged to handle casualties. "Ambulances made their appearance," he went on to note, revealing a lack of organization and control and *ad hoc* action. One regiment had only a single ambulance in service, the rest having broken down, and there were too few ambulances at the hospitals to evacuate all of the wounded. In addition to a number of the wounded, several surgeons became prisoners of war. The aid stations had been set up too close to the battlefield to handle the precipitous withdrawal.[13]

McDowell had contributed to the medical misery. He wanted the advance to travel light; as a result, a twenty-wagon complement of medical supplies was left in Alexandria. The wagons accompanying his force had multiple purposes: for "ammunition, the medical department, and for intrenching tools." As a result, King had anticipated only skirmishing, and casualties were very light on the first two days of the expedition when the Medical Director "seemed most intent on keeping a list" of the killed and wounded. Altogether, July 21 was "a day of medical improvisation and chaos."[14] One surgeon described it as "utter disorganization, or rather want of organization."[15]

Newspaper reports in the North excoriated the Lincoln Administration and the Army. They extended this criticism to the delivery of medical care. One of the leading Eastern papers, the *New York Times*, railed against those in charge:

> We are inexpressibly pained to learn from Washington, that very inadequate provision has been made by the regular authorities, for the proper care of the wounded in the late battle. It seems incredible in a Christian, civilized community, but we are credibly informed, that some of our gallant soldiers, for sheer want of hospital garments, even yet lie

---
13. *OR*, II, 344-345, 371, 403.
14. Id. 305, 307; John J. Hennessy, *The First Battle of Manassas: An End to Innocence, July 18-21, 1861* (Mechanicsburg: Stackpole Books, 2015), 148-149.
15. Keen, 97.

sweltering in their bloody uniforms, festering with fever and maddened with thirst.

The ancient and fossilized arrangements of the Medical Department, planned only for a petty military force of less than fifteen thousand men—and few of them ever assembled, in a body a thousand strong—prove, as every dictate of common sense should have shown, utterly inadequate to the immense Army suddenly assembled.[16]

Two days after the battle, Scott inquired of McDowell whether he could not "send out for our wounded and stragglers?"[17] If still possible, it was a damning indictment of poor planning and lousy execution of medical care.[18]

King's embarrassing after-action report was published in a medical journal in early August.[19] The battle opened the eyes of the Northern public: this war would not be over quickly, and it would not be easily won. The medical profession experienced a similar epiphany. An editorial in the same periodical entitled "The Profession and the Crisis" began with a summons:

> We are for the first time as a nation engaged in a war of great magnitude, and one which will necessarily inflict a vast amount of individual suffering and national loss in health, limb, and life. ... The medical profession must rise to the emergency with singleness of purpose, purity of motive, and unanimity of action.[20]

---

16. July 27, 1861, p. 4.
17. *OR*, II, 758.
18. See Kevin Bair, "First Battle of Manassas: Unwarranted Deaths of Savable Men" in *Surgeon's Call*, Vol. 25, No. 1, a publication of the National Museum of Civil War Medicine (NMCWM).
19. Stephen Smith ed., *The American Medical Times: Being a Weekly Series of the New York Journal of Medicine*, Volume III, July to December, 1861 (New York: Bailliere Brothers, 1861), 94-95.
20. *American Medical Times*, 71-72 (Aug. 3, 1861).

The individual doctors in service had done their best, often at great personal risk, was its view. The Army central organization, however, had let everyone down:

> The recent battle of Bull Run adds its testimony to the heroism and devotion of the Medical Staff, and the inadequateness of the means at their disposal. The profession, as the conservator of life, asks in the name of the Republic the wounded were not brought off the field, and why the hospital was not guarded? It asks why the surgeons were not sustained and protected in the discharge of their duty, and why none but those able to walk made their way back to Arlington, and the hospitals? It does not appear that stimulants or nutrition were prepared in any quantity before the battle at the church at Centreville, or that any orders for the general guidance of the regimental staff were issued. ....[21]

A number of careers suffered. McDowell would not hold an important independent command again. Scott would retire within several months. Patterson was immediately relieved of command, and his discharge effectuated on July 27. An otherwise admirable service record now besmirched, he would attempt to remediate his reputation with a defense that placed the blame on Scott for not making matters clear or issuing appropriate orders.[22]

Other changes proceeded. Of the offers for command, Major-General McClellan had chosen to lead troops in western Virginia, where his success countered the embarrassing result at Bull Run in the view of the Administration. He was brought to the capital to replace McDowell. Congress acted to pass a comprehensive piece of legislation to modernize and implement "the better Organization of the Military

---

21. Id. 73.
22. Robert Patterson, *A Narrative of the Campaign in the Valley of the Shenandoah, in 1861* (Philadelphia: John Campbell, 1865), 49. This work added no more detail regarding his staff's conduct.

Establishment." The new law reshaped the Medical Bureau. It added numbers to the ranks of surgeons and assistant-surgeons, created a corps of medical cadets to serve as "dressers in the general hospitals and as ambulance attendants in the field," allowed for employment of female nurses to "be substituted for soldiers," approved an improved diet as the Surgeon-General of the Army would institute, and in all things sought to place the Army and Navy on something dramatically different from peacetime status.[23] Much more was needed than 90-day volunteers and aged commanders who would not communicate well with each other. New vigor and expertise were needed for the main theater of war in the East.

Tripler had not been stained by his association with Patterson. When former Massachusetts Governor and now Major-General Nathaniel P. Banks took over, he retained Tripler as Medical Director.[24] The surgeon's burden had not been heavy, with few casualties to handle and a small army to service. He remained an excellent candidate for a more important and taxing post.

In the month of July appeared a highly complimentary review of the *Hand-Book* in a prominent medical journal. In addition to extolling the practical aspects of the work, and calling it "admirable," "interesting and important," the review termed it "indispensable" for the physicians in, and entering, the service of the United States. It also highlighted the vital importance of proper medical care during the ongoing conflict:

> If there be any time when the value of true science and skill in medicine and surgery is properly acknowledged, it is in time of war. There can be no more uncompromising leveler of incompetence and charlatanism of every kind than the

---

23. George P. Sanger ed., *The Statutes at Large*, Vol. XII (Boston: Little, Brown & Co., 1863), 287-291 (37th Congress, 1st Session, Act of July 22, 1861).
24. *OR*, LI, pt. I, 428. Ironically, during the several days he reported to Banks, Tripler was the superior of W.A. Hammond.

necessity of military service, where every step becomes a question of honour and dishonour, of life and death.

Tripler's "clear and complete" writing, so the journal asserted, established "the high claims" of the volume, along with its citation in others.[25]

On such a basis did Charles S. Tripler receive a coveted but burdensome elevation four months into America's greatest and bloodiest war.

---

25. Isaac Hays ed., *The American Journal of the Medical Sciences*, New Series, Vol. XLI (Philadelphia: Blanchard & Lea, 1861), 213-215, 217.

First Medical Director, Army of the Potomac: August 1861-March 1862

The very next day after Bull Run, McClellan was summoned to Washington where "circumstances" made his presence "necessary."[1] On July 25, the War Department announced that McClellan would command the Departments of Washington and of Northeastern Virginia, with headquarters in the national capital.[2] By July 27, McClellan had reached Washington and issued his first order as commander of the Division of the Potomac from headquarters there.[3] The designation would change to that of the Army of the Potomac, but, whatever the nomenclature, the Administration and the Northern people had expectations of a vastly better organization and execution of the means to achieve military victory. The young General began assembling his staff and implementing a program of training and fitting out of the largest and most impressive army in the nation's history. On August 5, 1861—within ten days of McClellan establishing his headquarters—Tripler was ordered to Washington.[4] On the 13th, he was appointed Medical Director of the Division of the Potomac; on the 20th, he was announced in the same role for the Army of the Potomac.[5]

In his correspondence, McClellan did not need to explain Tripler's identity. The surgeon's renown was on a par with other notables in the

---

1. *OR*, II, 753.
2. Id. 763.
3. Id. 766.
4. *OR*, LI, pt. I, 446.
5. Id.; *OR*, V, 575.

Army who would join the staff: John G. Barnard as Chief Engineer; Stewart Van Vliet as Chief Quartermaster; George G. Meade as senior topographical engineer.[6] It was sufficient to indicate to the General's wife that "Dr. Tripler" would be his chief medical officer.[7] Looking back years later, McClellan would count himself fortunate to have had such "excellent officers" in charge of enforcing organization upon their respective departments "on a footing commensurate with the actual and future condition of affairs."[8] McClellan surely appreciated the importance of having a highly capable Medical Director—the career of his father, Dr. George McClellan, noted surgeon and a founder of Jefferson Medical College in Philadelphia, would have impressed the necessity upon the thirty-four-year-old General. As "a highly regarded surgeon" with combat experience, Tripler was a natural choice.[9] He was "a most able and accomplished officer,"[10] "one of the most observant and devoted officers of the branch of service of which he was an illustrious member."[11]

The extent of knowledge and experience that Tripler brought to the role likely cannot be precisely recounted. His scope can be imagined, however, in the types of associations he made. An example is John Shaw Billings (1838-1913), who passed the examination and

---

6. A Mexican-American War veteran, Meade served on staff for Taylor and Patterson. He was engaged in surveying the Great Lakes when the war arrived and would take command of the Army of the Potomac for the Battle of Gettysburg.
7. Stephen W. Sears, *The Civil War Papers of George B. McClellan: Selected Correspondence, 1860-1865* (New York: Ticknor & Fields, 1989), 76; George B. McClellan, *McClellan's Own Story: The War for the Union, the Soldiers Who Fought It, the Civilians Who Directed It and His Relations to It and to Them* (New York: Charles L. Webster & Co., 1887), 83.
8. *McClellan's Own Story*, 70.
9. McGaugh, 56.
10. William W. Potter, "Reminiscences of Field-Hospital Service with the Army of the Potomac" in *Buffalo Medical and Surgical Journal* (Oct.-Nov., 1889), 8.
11. Bernard J.D. Irwin, "Notes on the Introduction of Tent Field Hospitals in War" from *Proceedings of the Association of Military Surgeons of the United States* (n.p., ca. 1894), 12.

became an Army doctor in Fall 1861, managed Union hospitals, served as medical director of a Corps beginning in 1863, directed the library of the Army Surgeon-General after the war, and became a leading light at Johns Hopkins. He graduated from the Medical College of Ohio at Cincinnati in 1860, and it was here that Tripler witnessed him perform a delicate operation ("stricture of the urethra"). Once they both were on duty near Washington, Tripler would send cases to Billings for successful performance of this procedure in order to keep the soldier in service rather than be given a medical discharge.[12]

McClellan's expectations of Tripler do not appear in any contemporary writing. The General's attitude toward medical matters, however, may have been revealed in his report on the Crimean War. McClellan extolled how the best hospital was one where command and responsibility "is always vested in an officer of the line" and the surgeons "have not the slightest military authority or responsibility." This system, he recommended, had merit in the event of "any concentration of a large number of troops."[13] Rather than afford control over all medical matters to medical people, McClellan preferred that non-physicians be in charge.

The condition of affairs, and the acclaim that the General had received for his conduct of operations in western Virginia, placed McClellan in a position where he had the full backing of the Administration for practically whatever he wanted. He could have chosen anyone for Medical Director. A subsequent choice, Assistant Surgeon Jonathan Letterman, was stationed in California and did not come East until November 1861.[14] Another, William A. Hammond, had left Army service before the War and rejoined it on May 28, 1861. He was on duty as inspector of camps and hospitals for General William

---

12. John S. Billings, *Medical Reminiscences of the Civil War* (n.p., n.d.), 115, 116.
13. *Report of the Secretary of War, Communicating the Report of Captain George B. McClellan*, Senate Ex. Doc. No. 1 (Washington: A.O.P. Nicholson, 1857), 80. The work was republished in late 1861 by J.B. Lippincott & Co.
14. James M. Phalen, "The Life of Jonathan Letterman" in *Records of the American Catholic Historical Society of Philadelphia*, Vol. 58, No. 2 (June 1947), 127.

Rosecrans in western Virginia and, therefore, part of McClellan's overall command. Letterman and Hammond had both undergone exams in New York City, passed, and been commissioned on the same day, June 29, 1849. They would "form a far-reaching alliance."[15] When they both ended up serving together in early 1862, their close collaboration presaged developments later in the summer.[16] Joseph Barnes, future Surgeon-General of the Army, had been on the West Coast at Fort Vancouver until June 1861.

Perhaps the best choice would have been Major John M. Cuyler, stationed at Fort Monroe on the James Peninsula in Virginia, who had joined the Army as Assistant Surgeon in 1834. He had served in the Seminole conflict and the Mexican-American War and been stationed at West Point from 1848 to 1855. He was Tripler's age. Another would have met McClellan's penchant for favoring officers with US Military Academy backgrounds and regular Army records. John T. Metcalfe had graduated from West Point seventh in the class of 1838. After leaving the Army in 1840, he received a degree in medicine from the University of Pennsylvania and practiced in various capacities in New York City. His affiliations with numerous hospitals there, and authorship of "various papers on Medical Science, 1845-1887,"[17] suggested his credentials might have satisfied many constituencies.

Instead, of all candidates, McClellan selected Tripler. A full portrait of the new Medical Director was sketched before his arrival in D.C. It is informal, not an austere, posed drawing. It shows a certain flair by the subject, sitting cross-legged and drawing on a long pipe, with a rather dapper look.[18] It was not a classic physician's image.

The appointment of McClellan to command met with widespread approval. One of the first supporters to go on record was the US

---

15. McGaugh, 22.
16. Id. 64-67.
17. George W. Cullum, *Biographical Register of the Officers and Graduates of the U.S. Military Academy*, Vol. I (Boston: Houghton, Mifflin & Co., 1891), 699-700.
18. It may also hint at an activity leading to the disease that would claim his life.

Sanitary Commission, a relief organization authorized by the Federal Government to act as a private partner to the War Department. On July 29, its governing board adopted a formal resolution:

> That the Sanitary Commission assure Major General McClellan in advance, of all the moral support and sympathy of their numerous constituents, and beg him to believe that the humane, the intelligent, the religious, the patriotic, will uphold his hands in every endeavor to communicate a spirit of subordination, fidelity, and obedience to the troops, even by resort, if found necessary, to the utmost rigor of military law, believing that the health, comfort, and efficiency of the army are all united in their dependence on a strict, uniform, and all-pervading military discipline.[19]

It did not follow suit regarding the appointment of Tripler, for reasons to be explained.

Tripler helped fulfill McClellan's vision of assembling an "efficient staff," and the commander sought to support his team in doing "good work."[20] A national periodical hailed the staff appointments: "they comprise a body of excellent and efficient officers."[21] On a personal level, Tripler's continuing service far from the Midwest lengthened separation from family. Eunice spent the Summer of 1861 in Canada with her mother and children.

Tripler set up his office in the District of Columbia in order to be close to the levers of McClellan's command.[22] The location was

---

19. *The Sanitary Commission of the United States Army: A Succinct Narrative of Its Work and Purposes* (New York: n.p., 1864), 14 [hereinafter "*Succinct Narrative*"].
20. Allan Nevins, *The War for the Union: The Improvised War, 1861-1862*, Vol. I (New York: Charles Scribner's Sons, 1959), 267. The title of this classic work epitomizes the situation facing Tripler upon taking his new post.
21. *Harper's Weekly*, Aug. 17, 1861, 515.
22. *Papers of Abraham Lincoln*, Series 1, General Correspondence, 1833-1916: Charles S. Tripler to John Crisfield, Friday, Dec. 13, 1861, Library of Congress.

among the "Seven Buildings" on the northwest corner of Pennsylvania Avenue NW at 19th Street, where McClellan also had his headquarters.[23] It was but steps from the War Department building at Pennsylvania and 17th Street. In November, McClellan succeeded Winfield Scott as General-in-Chief of the US Army, serving in this capacity until March 11, 1862. The headquarters of the two organizations—Army of the Potomac and United States Army—were maintained separately, with the latter located in the structure at the southeast corner of Pennsylvania Avenue and 17th Street adjacent to the White House.[24] The Surgeon-General's office was here. Not averse to course corrections where needed, Tripler "immediately began to make changes."[25]

Though not part of his assignment, Tripler paid a visit each morning to the boarding house where General-in-Chief Scott resided before attending to his regular duties. He sought to preserve a quiet atmosphere for the aged leader and interdict inappropriate visitors who might worsen Scott's infirmity. On one occasion, he sensed a contractor coming in to press Scott on a purchase order. Without looking up, Tripler told the long, straggling figure "quite sharply: 'No, Sir, no, you cannot see Gen. Scott. It cannot be. He is ill and can see no one.'" Looking up, he realized the visitor was President Lincoln, who obeyed the doctor's instruction. Tripler, however, wanted to crawl under the table.[26] As time would prove, the event did the surgeon no harm. By the time Scott retired, Tripler likely had little time to superintend the old soldier's health.

The new Medical Director set to work with vigor. No one had ever attempted to fashion a medical structure of the size and competence involved to service an American army expected to exceed one hundred

---

23. The facades of two of the row houses remain.
24. *McClellan's Own Story*, 219.
25. Schaadt, 32-33.
26. The date may have been August 10. Earl S. Miers ed., *Lincoln Day By Day: A Chronology, 1809-1865*, Vol. III (Washington: Lincoln Sesquicentennial Commission, 1960), 60.

thousand soldiers. McClellan publicly envisioned an "overwhelming" force that could move on the Confederate forces in Virginia.[27] As of August 4, the Division of the Potomac consisted of 12 brigades of 51 infantry regiments, besides artillery and cavalry.[28] How soon the Medical Department needed to be in a position to support a forward movement was unclear, except that the Army commander had vowed that an advance needed to be "prompt and irresistible,"[29] not tentative, such as the movement in July. No medical leader had been tasked with so quickly embedding a suitable medical organization within such a force.

The situation was chaotic when Tripler arrived. Three months' volunteers were being mustered out of service, and regiments with longer enlistments were arriving to be incorporated into the newly forming Army. Camps were being established on both sides of the Potomac. Tripler sought but found it difficult to determine what regiments were present and whether they had medical officers. The hospital portfolio included hotels, seminaries, and infirmaries pressed into general service in Washington, Georgetown, and Alexandria. Tripler found them managed capably but without a fully standardized system for admission or discharge of patients. Each regiment's surgeon "sent what men he pleased to the general hospitals, without knowing whether there was room for them or not, and men were discharged from the hospitals with no means provided to insure their return to their regiments." Ill soldiers sometimes had to seek admission by "wandering about the streets from hospital to hospital." Much better organization was needed, starting from the ground up.[30] As one historian has summarized, "for the most part Tripler was besieged on all sides by obduracy and incompetence."[31]

---

27. *OR*, V, 6.
28. Id. 15.
29. Id. 6.
30. This and related material derive from Tripler's 42,000-word report published in the *Official Records. OR*, V, 76–77.
31. Andrew M. Bell, *Mosquito Soldiers: Malaria, Yellow Fever, and the Course of the American Civil War* (Baton Rouge: Louisiana State University Press, 2010), 23.

The new Director began by obtaining an order requiring each medical officer in every regiment and hospital to report to him, in person, without delay. They were to provide him with data: how many of the men were sick and what the prevailing diseases were, plus how the hospital departments were supplied. This inquiry revealed something more alarming than irregularities in supply or improper hygiene in the camps.

First, the competency of some personnel to act as medical provisioners was substandard. Each regiment of volunteers was to be mustered into Federal service with a qualified surgeon and assistant surgeon included among the officers. To ensure competence, each Governor was to appoint a board to examine qualifications to hold the two positions. The findings were to be supplied to the War Department.[32] Many States "had entirely neglected" to follow this procedure, Tripler discovered, and nothing had been done by the Secretary of War to enforce it. Moreover, the Department had accepted "independent" regiments into US service without a Governor's official approval, and those commanders "asserted a right to appoint their own medical officers" without a board of examination and to reject others, in defiance of every requirement. Despite Tripler's efforts to align these regiments with the rest of the Army, he was overruled by the War Department.[33] As one rather inexperienced doctor put it, "People sometimes imagine that a practising physician can be transformed into an army surgeon merely by putting a uniform on him."[34]

The second issue was the absence of medical officers in certain regiments. Some infantry units had no physician on staff; similar were all the artillery units and cavalry regiments. In the latter case, neither the law nor the Department had provided for such an arrangement.

---

32. General Orders No. 25, May 25, 1861, Adjutant General's Office, *General Orders Affecting the Volunteer Force, 1861* (Washington: Government Printing Office, 1862), 7-8; *Statutes at Large*, 318.
33. *OR*, V, 77.
34. Keen, 99.

Tripler improvised by arranging for these units to receive interim care from the medical officers in the regiments closest by.[35]

Motivated by a desire primarily "to give the troops confidence in their medical officers," Tripler did not merely accept this patchwork situation. He took advantage of authority conferred by General Orders No. 35 issued on June 20, 1861, and assembled a board of examination to inquire into the credentials of any doubtful physician. He began by ordering twelve officers to appear before it; any subsequent complaint about a suspect doctor was handled similarly. These boards took their task seriously, and, in many cases, officers were discharged for lack of qualifications.[36] Some States like New York imposed rigorous requirements, involving five series of questions by which over one hundred applicants were not passed.[37] Other States were not as diligent.

Tripler also devised an ingenious solution to dealing with regimental commanders who sought to overbear their medical officers on how to conduct their affairs. Tripler knew the importance of having physicians exercise independent professional judgment, not simply take orders from a superior officer on matters beyond his competence. The act of July 22, 1861, had provided for the brigade organization and spelled out its officer complement, including the medical officer.[38] Neither the statute nor an Army regulation had enumerated the duties of this brigade surgeon, so Tripler filled the vacuum. He assigned the doctors reporting for duty with the Army of the Potomac to the staffs of each Brigadier-General, and he procured a general order from headquarters that detailed their duties:

---

35. *OR*, V, 77-78.
36. *General Orders Affecting the Volunteer Force*, 8-9; *OR*, V, 77-78.
37. Sylvester D. Willard, *Conservative Surgery, with a List of the Medical and Surgical Force of New York in the War of the Rebellion, 1861-2* (Albany: Charles Van Benthuysen, 1862), 7-11.
38. *Statutes at Large*, 269: "each brigade shall have ... one surgeon ...."

The following regulations respecting the duties of brigade surgeons, are published for the government of all concerned:

I. The brigade surgeons will frequently inspect the police, cooking, clothing, and cleanliness of the camps and men in their respective brigades; the position and condition of the sinks, the drainage of the camp grounds, the ventilation of the tents, &c.; making written reports to the brigade commanders whenever, in their opinion, any errors in these respects require correction, and sending duplicates of these reports to the medical director of the army.

II. They will see that the medicines, hospital stores, instruments, and dressings of the several regimental surgeons are kept constantly sufficient in quantity in good order, and always ready for active service.

III. They will collect from the several regimental surgeons and transmit every Saturday morning to the medical director a copy of their morning report made to the commanding officer of their regiment, and will accompany these with remarks showing the character of the principal diseases prevailing.

IV. They will promptly report to the medical director all changes in station or location of themselves or of any of the medical officers in their brigades, with the number, date, and authority of the order by which such changes were made.

V. They will inspect carefully all men receiving certificates of disability for discharge, and if they approve, they will countersign such certificates.

VI. The hospital attendants, to the number of 10 men to a regiment, and the regimental bands, will be assembled under the supervision of the brigade surgeons, and will be drilled one hour each day, except Sunday, by the regimental medical officers, in setting up and dismantling the hand-stretchers, litters, and ambulances; in handling men carefully; placing them upon the litters and ambulance beds; putting them into the ambulances, taking them out, &c.; carrying men upon the hand-stretchers (observing that the leading bearer steps off with the left foot and the rear bearer with the right); in short, in everything that can render this service effective and the most comfortable for the wounded who are to be transported.

VII. Brigade surgeons will see that the orders of the commanding general in relation to the uses to which ambulances are to be applied are strictly obeyed, and they will report promptly to the brigade commanders all infractions of these orders.

VIII. Whenever a skirmish or affair of outposts occurs in which any portion of their brigades is engaged, they will see that the ambulances and stretchers, properly manned with the drilled men, are in immediate attendance to bring off the wounded, and that the regimental medical officers are at their posts, with their instruments, dressings, and hospital knapsacks in complete order and ready for immediate use, so that no delay may occur in rendering the necessary surgical aid to the wounded.

IX. They will report in writing to the medical director, within twenty-four hours after any affair with the enemy, the name, rank, and regiment of each of the wounded, the nature and situation of the wound, and the surgical means adopted in the case.

X. Brigade surgeons will be held responsible that the hospital service in their brigades is kept constantly effective and in readiness for any emergency. No remissness in this respect will be tolerated or overlooked.[39]

In addition to this thorough plan, Tripler added a surgical note. He desired "that exsection[40] of the shoulder and elbow joint shall be

---

39. General Orders No. 20, Army of the Potomac, Oct. 3, 1861, *OR*, V, 93-94.
40. An operation to remove a portion of a limb, especially a bone in the vicinity of a joint.

resorted to in preference to amputation in all cases offering a reasonable hope of success; further, that Pirigoff's operation at the ankle[41] should be preferred to Chopart's[42] or to amputation above the ankle, in cases that might admit of a choice." If surgery were advisable, in other words, it ought to be the least radical procedure possible.

Here is a quintessentially capable chief medical officer: seeking both to develop the best overall organization, in compliance with all mandates and—where none exists—to fill gaps where necessary, while parlaying his own unique surgical knowledge to others who could benefit from his experience. Tripler fashioned a structure that overrode the vagaries of State regimental cultures and increased the efficiency of his arm within McClellan's force.

While he was endeavoring to raise the professionalism of the Army of the Potomac medical staff, Tripler also sought to directly improve conditions in the camps of the soldiers. After less than a month at this post, Tripler secured issuance of General Orders No. 9, devoted exclusively to medical matters. It covered a wide gamut of problems:

> I. The attention of brigade and regimental commissaries of subsistence and of officers acting as such is directed to paragraphs 20, 21, and 22, Subsistence Regulations, or paragraphs 1073, 1074, and 1075, Army Regulations, 1857. Subsistence officers must make issues to the hospital, and keep the accounts of the hospital funds in strict conformity with the requirements of the regulations cited.
> II. All changes of station of medical officers are to be promptly reported to the medical director at these headquarters, and the authority given by which the change was made.
> III. Leaves of absence to medical officers are prohibited, unless granted at these headquarters.

---

41. Named for its originator, Nikolay Ivanovich Pirogov, a Russian surgeon in the Crimean War.
42. A surgical procedure involving the ankle, named for French surgeon François Chopart.

...

VIII. Medical officers joining this army for duty, with or without troops, will report promptly to the medical director in person. If with troops, they will report the number of men, the state of their supplies, and ambulance transportation.

IX. Ambulances will not be used for any other than the specific purpose for which they are designed, viz, the transportation of the sick and wounded, except by the written authority of the brigade commander, the medical director of the army, and the quartermasters in charge of them in the city of Washington. The provost-marshal is directed to see that the provisions of this order are carried out, and will arrest every officer and confine every private and non-commissioned officer who is found violating it.

X. All Government ambulances now in possession of regiments or separate corps will be turned in to the chief quartermaster, with the exception of 1 two-wheeled ambulance to each regiment. One two-wheeled transport cart will be allowed to each general hospital for the conveyance of marketing and hospital stores.

XI. The reveille will not be beaten until after sunrise, and hot coffee will be issued to the troops immediately after reveille roll-call, as a preventive of the effects of malaria.[43]

Similar to the *Hand-Book*, the routine and discipline of Army procedure is specified for the novice. Matters under the control of other departments (Subsistence; Quartermaster) are regulated thanks to Tripler securing McClellan's approval. And no detail is too small: "hot coffee will be issued," thanks to the Director's concern for the health of the men in the ranks. In an age long before operation of the US Food and Drug Administration or the National Institutes of Health,

---

43. Issued Sept. 9, 1861, *OR*, V, 94-95.

the benefits of a daily morning coffee ration were being preached and instituted in the Army of the Potomac.[44]

Tripler's efforts to establish the primacy of the medical fraternity were unflagging. He sought to build a relationship with each brigade surgeon and explain "[e]very item of the order" of October 3. He "endeavored to impress upon them the importance of the trust confided to them" for, in his view, the Army's fighting fiber depended upon its good health. They were to raise the level of performance of the surgeons in their regiments. And he backed his physician subordinates in conflicts with line officers, seeking to stiffen their resolve by reminding them that their commission had been signed by the President of the United States and did not require deference to any individual officer.[45] At the same time, Tripler did not brook unprofessionalism. He sought court-martial of Dr. William Gardiner, a Pennsylvania regimental surgeon. The charge: "being drunk on November 19, 1861, in the office" of the Medical Director. At trial in January, the tribunal found him not guilty, but higher review disapproved the outcome. He was subsequently charged with engaging in a week of drunkenness during the same month and would not serve out the War.[46]

The Medical Director also sought to exert management control over hospital procedures. Four provisions of General Orders No. 9 dealt with that subject:

> IV. Patients will not be sent from the regimental to the general hospitals without the authority of the medical director. Applications for this authority must be made in writing, specifying the names and diseases of the patients, and be handed

---

44. For example, a July 2021 study by the Northwestern University Feinberg School of Medicine showed coffee consumption was associated with a decrease in risk of COVID-19.
45. *OR*, V, 78-79.
46. Thomas P. Lowry & Jack D. Welsh, *Tarnished Scalpels: The Court-Martials of Fifty Union Surgeons* (Mechanicsburg: Stackpole Books, 2000), 163-165.

in to the office of the medical director between the hours of 9 and 10 a.m.

V. When a soldier is sent to general hospital, his company commander shall certify and send with him his descriptive list and account of pay and clothing.

VI. Male nurses and cooks for general hospitals are to be detailed from the privates of the army, regular and volunteer. The allowance will be 1 nurse to 10 patients, and 1 cook to 30. Where women are employed, the number of men to be called for will not exceed the number sufficient to make up the whole force to the allowance above authorized. Hired nurses and cooks will be forthwith discharged.

VII. Men reported at the general hospitals for duty will be sent by the surgeons in charge to the office of the medical director at 10 a.m. for the passes necessary for them to rejoin their regiments.[47]

It is notable that the Medical Director took note of, and relied upon, the employment of female nurses.

In addition to attacking the irregularities in hospital admission and discharge, Tripler sought to minimize frequenting of general hospitals. He thought it more conducive to "speedy recovery" for an ill soldier to be closer to his unit than at a more distant facility. General hospitals were sometimes necessary, but they should be used only "when they are absolutely necessary, as, for instance, when an army is put in motion and cannot transport its sick." Abuse of the system by those seeking to avoid their duty had to be curtailed. Tripler was especially proud of how he had ended the "promiscuous" dispatching of soldiers to the hospital "and thus kept a healthy army in the field."[48]

An important part of the Army's health involved medical provisioning—the supply of instruments, equipment, medicines, stores,

---

47. *OR*, V, 94-95.
48. Id. 79.

and tents. The "confusion then reigning in Washington" led to many problems in this area, and Tripler waded into the morass. He offered help to civilian contractors in procuring medical supplies. Initially, his offer was declined, but eventually turf issues were put aside and Tripler's aid accepted. Despite his fidelity to regulations and procedure, he bent the rules "to give the surgeons articles of medicine and hospital stores to suit even their caprices, if in my judgment such articles could be of any avail in the treatment of disease." Tripler ran into opposition from Surgeon-General Finley, who directed him "not to issue anything not allowed by the supply table without his sanction, previously obtained." Instead of rote obedience, Tripler implemented a work-around when the Quartermaster Department gave priority to other supplies by directing the medical officers to call for and transport supplies to their camps. A special effort had to be made to ensure each regiment "had its full supply of hospital tents"—one per thirty soldiers, though shortages in canvas production made this troublesome. By March 1862, Tripler's reports indicated he had achieved his goal.[49]

Paralleling Tripler's work to improve the medical condition of the rapidly growing army was a civilian effort. On September 13, McClellan sent Cameron a letter enclosing a report of the Sanitary Commission, with his commentary:

> Proper arrangement in field and hospital for the sick and wounded of an army is one of the most imperative, and has always been found one of the most difficult, duties of a government. From its very nature it should be under the immediate direction of the commanding general, and the whole organization intrusted to him, free from the tedious delays, inconvenient formalities, and inefficient action incident to every bureau system, however ably administered.

---

49. Id. 79-80.

The Medical Bureau of the United States, like every other branch of the military service, was organized in reference to a very small army, operating generally in small divisions, and in time of peace, and hence it could not fail to be inadequate to the sudden and enormous exigencies of the present war, while its failure affords no ground of imputation or reproach against the distinguished medical officers intrusted with its administration. By no administrative talent can a system devised for the purposes of small divisions of an army (not exceeding in the whole 12,000 men) be adapted to the necessities of an army of 100,000, actively operating upon a great theater of war. To meet their wants, there must be a medical system commensurate with the army, and the nature of its operations so organized as to be in harmonious action with every other branch of service and under the same military command. The humane and disinterested services of the Sanitary Commission have enabled them to make several judicious suggestions, and their labors entitle them to the gratitude of the Army and of the country.

The following suggestions by them are worthy of approval and immediate adoption:

1st. The appointment of a medical director of the Army of the Potomac by its commanding general, with such powers as he may deem proper from time to time to commit to such director.

2d. The immediate organization of an ambulance corps, to act under the medical director's command.

3d. The employment of an adequate corps of male and female nurses by the medical director, to act under his supervision.

4th. That "the relations of the Sanitary Commission and the Medical Bureau be placed on a basis of entire confidence and co-operation; that their disinterested counsel be received without jealousy."

These suggestions of the Commission merit and receive the cordial sanction of the Commanding General. He concurs with them in their judgment "that they have earned the right to the confidence of the Department which originally, with generous reliance, called them into being, and does not doubt that they still enjoy this confidence"; and he agrees with them in the wish "to see it extended fully from the Medical Bureau."[50]

McClellan likely expected Cameron—former US Senator and experienced politician—to bow to the necessity of pleasing the civilian entity. The Secretary could claim credit for having given official endorsement to the Commission soon after taking office. He had appointed Surgeon-General Finley after Lawson's death, and the latter owed something to the Secretary much more so than the other way round. McClellan had his own political ambitions—he would tender political advice to the President, make public pronouncements about war aims, and run against Lincoln in 1864. As for Tripler's position here, a lack of clarity adheres. Surely he would embrace having greater authority as recommended by this eminent private organization that reached from New York, Philadelphia, and Washington into the offices and drawing rooms of powerful people. But precisely what was the "brief" of this official-sounding commission?

The founding of the Sanitary Commission suggests an intent not to compete with, or undermine, the US military but, instead, to work alongside its counterparts in uniform. No better source exists than the Commission's own authorized history, from which the following chronology is taken.

- April 29, 1861. A number of prominent women in New York signed an open letter calling upon disparate efforts on behalf of aiding the Union military in its care of ill and wounded

---

50. Id. 598-599.

soldiers to unite. A meeting was called for the Cooper Institute in order to organize this joint and collective program.[51]

- May 18, 1861. A petition for creation of a national sanitary commission was tendered to Secretary of War Cameron, who had served in that position since March 5, 1861.[52]
- May 22, 1861. A letter is sent to Cameron from Robert C. Wood, Acting Surgeon-General, recommending formation of a commission "of Inquiry and Advice." Part of the rationale: "This Commission is not intended to interfere with, but to strengthen the present organization ..." of the Army's medical bureau.[53]
- June 9, 1861. Cameron tenders official approval of the recommendations.[54]
- June 13, 1861. President Abraham Lincoln appends his signature to Cameron's document, giving it formal Administration approval.[55]
- June 13, 1861. The Commission's organizing document is tendered to Secretary Cameron, who approves it the same date. The lengthy "Plan of Organization" of the Commission

---

51. Charles J. Stille, *History of the United States Sanitary Commission, Being the General Report of Its Work During the War of the Rebellion* (Philadelphia: J.B. Lippincott & Co., 1866), 523-526. The key role of women in the organizing and conduct of the affairs of the Commission is an important story. There are fascinating first-person accounts such as Mary A. Livermore, *My Story of the War* (Hartford: A.D. Worthington & Co., 1889). The Cooper Institute's Great Hall, located in the lower level of the school's Foundation Building, had been the location of a famous address in February 1860 by Abraham Lincoln that helped propel him to the Presidency.
52. Stille, 526-530. He would leave the post on January 14, 1862.
53. Id. 530-531; Lewis H. Steiner, *A Sketch of the History, Plan of Organization, and Operations of the U.S. Sanitary Commission* (Philadelphia: Jas. B. Rodgers, 1866), 3-4. Wood had been called to the sickbed of President Zachary Taylor, his father-in-law, in 1850.
54. Stille, 532-533. See Appendix for text of the official document.
55. Id. 533.

divides the entity into two branches, one for "Inquiry" and the other for "Advice."[56]

One of the principal employee-volunteers of the organization caught the theme: "an organization, through which the people could supplement" the Army—not "supplant" it.[57] Missing from these communiques is the notion that the Commission would circumvent, undermine, or in any way—to use McClellan's phrasing—exhibit a failure of entire confidence and cooperation delivered without jealousy. As early as August 24, 1861, however, the Commission was going rogue. It secured publication of "Rules for Preserving the Health of the Soldier," in which it appealed directly to "their brethren of the volunteer and militia to adopt and carry out" practices advanced by the Commission. The three-column document had been adopted on July 12, a fortnight before the Bull Run defeat. Although many points had value, some betrayed less than professional medical judgment, e.g., that "[s]leeping upon damp ground causes dysentery and fevers."[58]

The state of medical knowledge in 1860s America was in transition. Traditionally, disease was laid to an imbalance in the physical "system" of the patient; a growing view held that an outside agent (pathogen) was responsible. Pharmaceuticals, whether from natural or other sources, were the subject of exploration. Training of physicians was irregular, with no common standards and heavy reliance on schools that shaped education to attract fee-paying students. The AMA was a nascent entity without wide influence; the 16,000-man US Army was served by just over 100 doctors. But their on-the-job experience would prove invaluable as thousands were added to their ranks.[59]

Coincidentally, a publication in the first calendar year of

---

56. Id. 533-538.
57. Lewis Steiner, 5.
58. *Harpers Weekly*, Aug. 24, 1861, 542.
59. Freemon, *Gangrene and Glory*, 24-26. A fine summary of the situation is at https://www.ncbi.nlm.nih.gov/pmc/articles/PMC4790547/

America's fratricidal conflict provided the first key to unlocking the mystery of infection. Hungarian physician Ignaz Philipp Semmelweis had discovered that using chlorine on a surgeon's instruments and hands reduced the rate of death in hospital wards. It would be years, however, before the work was translated and available in America. In 1863, French doctor Jules Lemaire wrote of the efficacy of carbolic acid. His countryman, Louis Pasteur, began writing of the benefits of using heat to kill micro-organisms in certain beverages. After the War, British surgeon Joseph Lister published results of using carbolic acid as an antiseptic technique. Heinrich Hermann Robert Koch graduated from medical school in 1866, positioning him for discoveries in microbiology during the next decades. Not until much later, however, did the germ theory of the origin of disease become mainstream. It was later in the 19th century that malarial infections were understood as related to insect transmission. Evaluating Civil War era policies on the basis of later knowledge is akin to presentism.

Regardless of politics and politicians, Tripler's actions kept pace with good health for an ever-increasing force. By mid-October, the brigades of the Army of the Potomac had been organized into 11 divisions of 30 brigades for better organization and command of 132 infantry regiments. Additional units included artillery, cavalry, garrison, and guards. The grand total of all troops under McClellan's command equaled 152,051—an astonishing aggregation.[60] Tripler faced the need to ensure the health of an army practically tripled in size after only a couple of months. By March, when active campaigning began, the total of troops present and absent under McClellan numbered 221,987. The Army then had a corps structure—five, led by two Major-Generals and three Brigadier-Generals—for its 14 divisions. The behemoth that began its campaign up the James Peninsula consisted of some 150 infantry regiments besides various other units.[61]

What proportion of these totals consisted of ill soldiers? On

---

60. *OR*, V, 12, 15-17. An additional eleven regiments were in a Division at Baltimore.
61. Id. 12, 18.

October 15, roughly 6.4 percent of the aggregate present were reported as "sick." The number on the first day of December was 8 percent and, immediately prior to the Peninsula Campaign, was 6.3 percent.[62] On the last days of April and May the number was closer to 5 percent.[63] The Medical Director would seem to have provided his commander an armed force in fairly fine fettle, not sapped by disease. The Sanitary Commission's own December 1861 report to the Secretary of War concurred. It indicated that during the summer, after First Bull Run, "a very marked and gratifying improvement" in the policing of camps had taken place, and "faults" in such matters that had formerly been deemed unworthy of attention by regimental officers "are now considered disgraceful."[64] Who deserved credit? The Commission pointed to itself, even though "the chief part of the value" it delivered "cannot be specified and recorded" but surely was due to the advice contained in its informative publications that soldiers had perused and pursued[65]—informative, but "often erroneous."[66]

Hygiene was as important to Tripler as it was to any doctor. One of his first acts was to direct that inmates at the Capitol Prison[67] be vaccinated, provided a bath, and allowed outdoor exercise. On August 22, he recommended that troops encamped "upon the flats near Arlington"[68] be relocated to higher ground. Whenever "an undue

---

62. Id. 12.
63. *OR*, XI, pt. III, 130, 204.
64. *Succinct Narrative*, 20. "Policing" here means cleaning and putting in order.
65. Id. 19-21. Steiner, *Disease in the Civil War*, 103-116, argues that Tripler understated the seriousness of disease during his tenure with the Army of the Potomac. His study reveals, however, that half of the incidences of disease from April-August 1862 occurred in July and August when Jonathan Letterman was Medical Director. Id. 124.
66. George W. Adams, "Caring for the Men" in William C. Davis ed., *The Image of War: 1861-1865*, Vol. IV: Fighting for Time (Garden City: Doubleday & Co., 1983), 233.
67. Located at 1st and A streets N.E., it was the structure in which Congress met while awaiting reconstruction of the US Capitol after the War of 1812.
68. Home of Robert E. and Mary Custis Lee, later a city, in Virginia immediately across the Potomac River from Washington.

proportion of sick was reported in any regiment," Tripler called for a special report in order to ascertain the underlying causes. He lacked competent inspectors and, accordingly, spent "much labor and anxiety" doing inspections himself. In November 1861, he obtained the assistance of three officers to act in that capacity, issued them instructions, and set them at work "at once" examining the troops "from Budd's Ferry to Cumberland."[69] From their reports, Tripler was able "to correct many errors in hygiene, as well as to improve the discipline of my department and to keep it always in readiness for an advance." He reported shortcomings promptly to the Adjutant-General. Tripler recognized that some men were "predisposed to disease" from lack of prior exposure or to army life. A large cause, then, was not in the condition of the camps but the soldiers themselves. Despite his admonitions in the *Manual*, many recruiting officials had enlisted men who were infirm and ineligible—some 60 to 70 years old. In the final quarter of 1861, almost four thousand discharges were processed on account of disability, and most existed at enlistment. Tripler directly faced this issue, which would not plague successors nearly as much.

Other diseases were caused by factors that no 19th century medical expert could prevent. The virus that causes measles was not identified until the mid-20th century, and a vaccine first came on the market in 1963. Tripler dealt with the effects of this malady by seeking greater attention to policing grounds, good cooking, appropriate clothing, ventilation of tents, attention to personal cleanliness, and necessarily regular habits—all of which aided general hygiene. No occasion passed where Tripler failed to urge "upon both commanders and surgeons their obligations in this respect."

Tripler was a smallpox survivor. He knew from personal and professional experience that it could be ameliorated and overcome.

---

69. I.e., from the site of a Union battery on the Potomac River in Charles County, Maryland, across from Quantico Creek in Virginia, *Atlas to Accompany the Official Records of the Union and Confederate Armies, 1861-1865* (Washington: Government Printing Office, 1891-1895), Plate VIII [hereinafter "*OR Atlas*"], to western Maryland.

The influx of individuals from both urban and rural environments increased the likelihood that the disease would be spread. He recommended issuance of an order requiring that all recruits for the Army of the Potomac be vaccinated before departing their mustering point and for their careful re-inspection immediately upon arrival. Not satisfied with what had been done, he obtained another order in December 1861 requiring division and brigade commanders "to cause the brigade surgeons to reinspect all the men, vaccinating such as were still unprotected, and to report the results to me." As a result of his vigilance, "small-pox, though rife in the community, never gained any foothold in the army," and no major epidemic befell it.[70]

This topic revealed perhaps the first real divergence of views between Tripler and the Commission. An "eruptive-fever hospital"[71] had been established without its input. The Commission issued "[a]n alarming report of the dangers to which the army was exposed from the system adopted at the hospital." Tripler "inquired into the statistics of the disease in our army up to that time, and found that in seven months we had had but 168 cases, the majority of whom were ill with the disease when they reached Washington." Despite the overblown rhetoric from the Commission, he nonetheless adopted such of its recommendations "as were not already in use, but with no perceptible effect. In fact, the precautions always adopted had made the cases, considered in reference to the size of the army, too insignificant to give the least uneasiness to any one at all informed on the subject."

In September, Tripler departed from a Sanitary Commission recommendation on the construction of hospitals for a capacity of 15,000 patients. After attending a meeting of the Commission where wood frame buildings were endorsed, he pushed the idea of temporary frame huts as a cheaper, healthier, and more efficacious alternative. He

---

70. Judkin Browning & Timothy Silver. "Nature and Human Nature: Environmental Influences on the Union's Failed Peninsula Campaign, 1862" in *Journal of the Civil War Era*, Vol. 8, No. 3 (Sept. 2018), 35. The smallpox vaccine had been proven effective around 1800.
71. I.e., to treat disease marked by skin "eruptions" or blisters.

also advocated a capacity for 20,000. "If the matter were in my hands, I should recommend the building of these huts at once."[72]

Another example of Tripler's willingness to learn and experiment came with attempts to ameliorate malaria. Despite the silence of Army regulations, leading the bureaucratic-minded to hide behind a lack of authority, Tripler reached out to the Sanitary Commission for a supply of quinine and whisky to use prophylactically.[73] As always, he insisted on receiving reports on effects. Finding those to be generally favorable, he secured approval from the Surgeon-General to issue the elixir "in reasonable quantities to regiments whose condition seemed most to demand it." As further reports continued to be generally favorable, the Medical Director made sure it was "constantly on hand."

This resourcefulness marks Tripler as a disciplined scientist. He demonstrated familiarity with the literature on malaria and quinine, and his open-mindedness was worthy of praise. According to a leading journal article on July 20, 1861, "What malaria is nobody knows. It may consist of organisms, either animal or vegetable, too minute for even the microscope to detect or it may be some condition of the atmosphere in relation to electricity, or temperature, or moisture; or it may be a gas evolved in the decay of vegetable matter." Quinine—derived from bark of the cinchona tree—seemed efficacious. So, Tripler tried it, in the absence of affirmative permission, and made it available based on data.[74]

He also exhibited initiative in launching brigade hospitals where zealous surgeons pressed the matter. Army regulations did not recognize such a facility, but Tripler put them into operation when he could

---

72. *OR*, V, 100-101.
73. "Whisky" is the Old English spelling. Tripler did not drink alcohol, according to his spouse, but he "never opposed" it in moderation for others. *Heart in Tatters*, 53-54; see Megan Leigh Bever, *War Is A Terrible Enemy to Temperance: Drinking, Self-Control, and the Meaning of Loyalty in The Civil War Era*, Ph.D. Dissertation, University of Alabama (2014), 113, 187, 190-191, published as *At War with King Alcohol: Debating Drinking and Masculinity in the Civil War* (Chapel Hill: University of North Carolina Press, 2022).
74. *Scientific American*, Vol. V, No. 3 (July 20, 1861), 42.

make arrangements for suitable buildings and personnel (including stewards, cooks, and nurses). Their proximity to the camps enabled the men to readily return to duty when sufficiently recovered.[75]

On one particular subject—ambulances—Tripler's record showed mixed results. Recall, first, that Tripler had sought to bring order out of chaos in General Orders No. 9 and No. 20 regarding the dispersal of ambulances. Recall also that McClellan had endorsed the creation of an ambulance corps. Such a proposal was necessary since the antebellum Army had only experimented with specifically designed transportation devices. A board had recommended 2-wheeled devices in a 5 to 1 ratio over 4-wheeled wagons, and the Quartermaster-General placed orders in that proportion. Tripler had made his own design for a 4-wheeled transport, and he regarded the other as unfit for its purpose. He observed misuse of these carriages for pleasure or for transportation of officers as "cabs." He stopped such practices. Many had broken down or were missing. Rather than seek identical replacement, he thought the use of *cacolets*—a seat, like a saddle, or prone litter, attached to the side of a horse or mule—would better aid the transportation of wounded. The Quartermaster had engaged in their procurement, and Tripler sought improvements in their design. Ultimately, he secured more than 200 *cacolets* from that Department but, despite the support of McClellan, horses were not trained to carry them.[76]

In December 1861, the Quartermaster-General signed a contract with the W.W. Woods Company providing for acquisition of one hundred four-wheeled "Tripler Ambulances" as per detailed instructions for construction, along with litters and "springs to cushion the journey for sick and wounded." The cost of each vehicle was set at $140, and they were to be delivered by the end of January.[77] This initiative came at Tripler's urging. He did not receive pecuniary benefits.

---

75. The foregoing treatment is largely based on *OR*, V, 80-86.
76. *Medical and Surgical History*, Part III, Vol. II, 930 n.3.
77. Jonathan D. Hood, *Jonathan Letterman and the Development of a Battlefield Evacuation System*, Ph.D. Dissertation, Texas Tech University (Dec. 2004),

Tripler estimated a need for 250 four-wheeled ambulances in order for the Army of the Potomac to be ready for battle, plus other vehicles. The Quartermaster-General did not reach this goal, and the Medical Director "was obliged afterwards to contrive the best I could to make the number actually furnished go as far as possible." A kind of dress rehearsal occurred when some 35,000 troops were advanced to Fairfax Court House after the abandonment by the Confederates of their positions at Manassas. On March 10, 1862, having received orders to move ambulances to accompany the advance, Tripler called upon General Van Vliet of the Quartermaster Department to distribute the inventory according to his plan. He moved with the headquarters to Fairfax the next day.[78] When the Army assembled there, the ambulances were not in position. McClellan quickly fell back to the vicinity of Washington, from which he would begin his real campaign. Tripler hastened to gain assurances of better performance by the Quartermaster and received from Van Vliet an expectation of furnishing 177 for the whole Army—"too few, but it was the best that could be done with the number reported on hand." Not until May 1 did Tripler receive the final batch to make up the "best available" ambulance fleet.

The Medical Director endorsed the concept of a corps that would control its own performance in attending to the wounded, rather than be under the direction of regimental officers. He supported a specific proposal to Secretary Cameron, "but no action was taken on it." What Tripler considered "an elaborate project for an ambulance corps" was submitted to the Surgeon-General by a private individual and referred to Tripler for examination in March 1862. No matter its merits, Tripler lamented, "it is now too late to raise, drill, and equip so elaborate an establishment as this for our service" with the Peninsula Campaign

---

51-52; 1861 contract, W.W. Woods & Co., Entry 1246, Box 236; Record Group 92, Records of the Quartermaster General, National Archives and Records Administration, Washington.

78. McClellan accompanied the movement and established his headquarters at Fairfax. *McClellan's Own Story*, 224.

looming. He was encumbered by "the then existing laws" and sought to effectuate the best training for the personnel available. He worked with line officers to "be drilled regularly every day by the medical officers under the superintendence of the brigade surgeons."[79]

During the Army's winter quarters, Tripler was joined by his wife in Washington. When he was quickly summoned east in April, she had packed up the children and possessions on her own. Eunice and children passed the Summer and Fall in Ontario, Canada, with her mother. In December, she came to be with him in his small, one-room accommodation. Her days were spent seeing to the progress of the medical reform bill, which she believed would advance her husband's career. In the evenings, she joined him at the office:

> I soon found I could be of real help. He had to affix his signature to about eighty discharges of soldiers each day, and I could and did write his name on these papers so that no one could tell his signature from mine.[80]

On Sundays, he would go off to work until time for them to attend church services; afterward, he returned to the office. She remained until the end of March when the Army of the Potomac, and Dr. Tripler, shipped off to the James Peninsula. Though she would recall how his duties meant "little time for rest in those days," not every moment was consumed with official business. In December, Eunice Tripler gave birth to their ninth child—their final offspring.[81]

The summary reports out of Army Headquarters portray a force not at all ravaged by illness. On February 28, the total present for duty strength of the Army of the Potomac amounted to 177,556.[82] Its total complement of troops numbered 221,987.[83] The data show

---

79. The foregoing treatment is largely based on *OR*, V, 87-89.
80. *Heart in Tatters*, 65.
81. Id. For a full description, see p. 122, *infra*.
82. *OR*, V, 732.
83. Id. 12.

the number of diseased soldiers out of the ranks to be 6.3 percent—a rather positive statistic given the size of the Army and the impediments to such a state of health. Tripler's own data tracked these reports. For example, as of January 1862, among 181,082 troops, he recorded 11,225 as ill, for a percentage rate of 6.18.[84]

Before the Army's first move in the forthcoming campaign to the tip of the James Peninsula, Tripler and his medical team had yet to experience a major battle. Skirmishes were not infrequent but easily handled with few wounded. In the highly publicized Battle of Ball's Bluff on October 21, 1861, 158 men were reported wounded. On December 20, a relatively small battle occurred at Dranesville, Virginia. The Union force under Brigadier-General E.O.C. Ord clashed with Confederates commanded by General J.E.B. Stuart. Rebel losses were around 200; the Union casualties amounted to 61.[85] At Ball's Bluff, the number of ambulances provided by the Medical Director was sufficient to evacuate the wounded—though a deficit "was misrepresented by some volunteer philanthropist to the Sanitary Commission." At Dranesville, ambulances were not in sufficient supply to bring off, in addition to Union wounded, the Confederate captives.[86] Did capacity exist for a bloody battle once the Army of the Potomac actively campaigned? Only time and circumstances would tell.

Contemporaneous observers in the medical community gave Tripler positive marks for his work. The *Medical Times* praised his efforts to increase hospital resources over the opposition of Finley:

> Dr. Tripler, Medical Director of the army of the Potomac, has made arrangements for the care of a large number of patients, whose condition may permit their removal from Washington and Baltimore to Philadelphia. A friend in the latter city writes: "The military hospitals here are now ready

---

84. Id. 92.
85. Id. 308, 489. Tripler reported 280 wounded at Ball's Bluff and 34 at Dranesville. Id. 93.
86. Id. 93, 476.

for the reception of patients. There are five of them, with an aggregate capacity for 1500 beds (640, 250, 275, 250, 80). The buildings, leased for the purpose, have been judiciously arranged." This provision for the removal and proper care of patients at a distance from the crowded hospitals on the Potomac, is an act of prudent foresight ...."[87]

In expanding the supply of hospital beds and systematizing admissions during his first several months, Tripler had achieved an enormous task. Arranging for patients to be taken in at hospitals in nearby East Coast cities, including Annapolis, shortened the distance to others, such as New York City.[88] Clearly, he had substituted organization for what had previously been "hastily extemporized."[89] Other medical periodicals also were monitoring the situation and advising the profession of positive military developments. The *Medical and Surgical Reporter* had told readers that Tripler "will soon issue an order to the surgeons of the various hospitals" requiring a weekly report in place of a quarterly system on deaths, a great and compassionate improvement.[90]

The concept of establishing fixed rather than field hospitals was new to the Army and the medical community at large. Civil hospitals consisted of "one tier of wards piled over another in a solid and permanent structure." The initial military facilities in Washington were in hotels, churches, warehouses, schools, private houses, and similar permanent buildings. Even the US Capitol was pressed into service.[91] Tripler regarded this arrangement "to be totally inadequate." In early September 1861, he began lobbying for rapid construction of relatively inexpensive "frame buildings."[92] Although the Sanitary Commission

---

87. *American Medical Times*, 419 (Dec. 28, 1861).
88. Id. 166-168.
89. *American Medical Times*, 127 (Aug. 24, 1861).
90. Volume 7, January 4, 11, 1862, 357. The *Reporter* largely published factual events without commentary.
91. *Medical and Surgical History*, Part III, Vol. I, 896-897.
92. OR, V, 89-91. Tripler's contributions were ignored in the official postwar history. Instead, William A. Hammond and Jonathan Letterman were given

initially thought the surgeon's request for 20,000 beds 400 percent too high, it came around to endorse 15,000—but "Washington's hospital capacity did not reach the level of Tripler's recommendation" until late 1864 thanks to War Department short-sightedness.[93]

Tripler spent much energy ensuring that medical personnel were adequately trained. One physician testified to the diligence employed and the results achieved:

> For six months, these soldiers, by the direction of the Medical Director of the Army, have been thoroughly trained to the performance of those duties which are expected of hospital attendants on the field of battle, and I venture nothing in saying that the hospital under their care will show that they are second to no corps on the Potomac.[94]

While respective of Army requirements, Tripler had shown a willingness to exploit loopholes when it appeared to benefit patients. Charging him with too rigid an adherence to red tape seems misplaced. A prominent modern historian attached a more positive

---

first mention in opting for temporary wooden structures that served as hospitals, *Medical and Surgical History*, Part III, Vol. I, 908, as was the US Sanitary Commission, 917. A modern history criticizes Tripler, *inter alia*, for opposing general as opposed to regimental hospitals, Alfred J. Bollet, *Civil War Medicine: Challenges and Triumphs* (Tucson: Galen Press, 2002), 17-18, citing his statement that they were "general nuisances." Tripler did write that, but the words are taken out of context: he spoke of the practice "of sending men promiscuously and without restraint to the general hospitals," and his actions belie the charge of indiscriminate opposition. General hospitals were (and are) not immune from disease themselves; for example, Union hospital gangrene cases increased dramatically after July 1, 1862. Id. 202 (Table 7.1).
93. Kenneth J. Winkle, *Lincoln's Citadel: The Civil War in Washington, DC* (New York: W.W. Norton & Co., 2013), 223.
94. Alfred L. Castleman, *The Army of the Potomac: Behind the Scenes; A Diary of Unwritten History* (Milwaukee: Strickland & Co., 1863), 88. This same physician would throw shade on Tripler in late April 1862 when the supply chain controlled by the Quartermaster Department did not furnish needed stores and supplies. Id. 129.

attribute to his approach: Tripler was "reform-minded."[95] The reality is that he sought to obey the laws and regulations that governed the Medical Department but, where not a violation of such mandates, to take steps that ran afoul of higher-ups, or of bureaucratic and turf sensibilities, in the cause of patient care. The matter came to a head when Finley sought to bully Tripler in a meeting with another officer present, accusing him of seeking to humiliate and embarrass the Surgeon-General. Tripler did not accept the insult. He placed charges, and a court-martial was convened to try Finley for conduct unbecoming an officer and a gentleman. The matter was resolved by a retraction of the criticism of Tripler.[96] According to one historian, Finley's antipathy to Tripler arose from jealousy over the successful organization of the medical operations of the Army of the Potomac.[97] Whatever the cause, the colloquy between the two reveals Tripler's ability to avoid insubordination while sticking to his guns:

> Tripler: I have here, in my memorandum book, data concerning buildings in Philadelphia suitable for hospitals.
> Finley: In making such a visit to Philadelphia, you have undertaken to do what I have already done. ...
> Tripler: I acted under orders from General McClellan.
> Finley: This order was of your own suggestion and you went to Philadelphia without conferring with the head of your own department.
> Tripler: I went by orders of the general and had not a moment to spare after its reception.

---

95. Stephen W. Sears, *George B. McClellan: The Young Napoleon* (New York: Ticknor & Fields, 1988), 127. McClellan used Tripler to work "around the incompetent surgeon general," Finley. Id.
96. Mary C. Gillett, *The Army Medical Department, 1818–1865* (Washington: Center of Military History, 1987), 168-169; Lowry & Welsh, 174-175.
97. McGaugh, 58.

Finley: Do you pretend to say that you had not time between the order and your departure to communicate with me upon the subject.

Tripler: I acted under orders.[98]

Tripler had bucked the Army bureaucracy and a Surgeon-General whose conduct resembled that of a "martinet"[99] and was unafraid of dealing with commanders in the field. He faced down superior officers when appropriate, as when he assured one of his doctors that "when he needed the interference of my General in his hospital, he would let him know it."[100] He was no inflexible martinet.[101] Unlike McClellan, who "liked everything to proceed in accordance with a careful plan" and could not adapt when situations changed, Tripler exercised flexibility. He had to, as a physician and surgeon repeatedly being confronted with new cases.[102]

To sum up Tripler's first phase as Medical Director, "the paramount importance of hygienic morality" had been his operative watchword during the build-up and the launch of McClellan's great offensive.[103]

---

98. Lowry & Welsh, 174-175.
99. Pilcher, 46.
100. Castleman, 147.
101. The prime antebellum example being Braxton Bragg, later a Confederate general, who acted as company commander in submitting a requisition; then, acting as quartermaster, he declined it; followed by an appeal as company officer and a repetition of the denial. *Personal Memoirs of U.S. Grant*, Vol. II, 86-87.
102. Kevin Dougherty & J. Michael Moore, *The Peninsula Campaign of 1862: A Military Analysis* (Jackson: University Press of Mississippi, 2005), 13-14. This insightful work treats logistical considerations without analysis of Union army medical matters.
103. Hood, 51-52.

Prelude to the Peninsula Campaign: War Department and Sanitary Commission

Statistics proved, indeed, that the Army of the Potomac would enter into its first great campaign in a much healthier condition than during the early days of its formation. Medical Director Tripler deserved credit for helping spur its readiness. He introduced an improved daily report to record each day's sick call to meet the exigencies of the War.[1] He increased the rate of smallpox vaccination. He purged the ranks of incompetents. He increased the number of inspectors and charged them with integrity in reporting on the conditions in field hospitals. He sought changes when the Army went into Winter quarters in the design and construction of tents and shelters in order to increase hygiene. He banned "indiscriminate amputation."[2] He worked with the Sanitary Commission to provide quinine to deal with malaria, then persuaded Surgeon-General Finley to change its role in policy. To the extent other steps might have been taken by Tripler and his medical staff, one evidence-based conclusion is that "they were handicapped in their attempts by factors beyond their immediate control."[3]

Two of those impediments, it seemed, were removed during the early months of 1862. On January 7, the President nominated Edwin M. Stanton to succeed Secretary of War Cameron; the Ohioan was confirmed on January 15.[4] Cameron left without remorse, distancing

---

1. *The Medical and Surgical Reporter*, Vol. IX, No. 4 (Oct. 25, 1862), 100.
2. Id., Vol. IX, Nos. 21, 22 (Feb. 21, 28, 1862), 377.
3. Gillett, 171.
4. *Journal of the Executive Proceedings of the Senate of the United States*, Vol.

himself from the bureaucracy he had struggled to lead for just over nine months: "I found scarcely a man throughout the whole War Department in whom I could put my trust."[5] His departure pleased the Sanitary Commission, for in their view Cameron "did nothing" to implement their suggestions beyond signing onto the initial agreement.[6] Perhaps Stanton would be more open to advancements on the medical front.

The second encumbrance fell when Finley was officially replaced on April 14. It was a move that came after Stanton had effectively exiled him. A friend of Stanton's wrote what he intended to be a confidential letter criticizing Finley's choice of a supervising physician for the general hospitals in Philadelphia. Stanton referred it to Finley, who referred it to the supervisor—who instituted a libel suit against the confidential correspondent. Stanton summoned Finley, who asserted he had only followed regular protocol. The explanation did not placate the Secretary, who transferred Finley to Boston. Excluded from his post and prerogatives, and eligible for retirement, Finley stepped down.[7] A new Surgeon-General, William A. Hammond, took office. Hammond was a thirty-three year-old who had a degree in medicine from New York University, had served at western frontier outposts, and had resigned from the Army in 1860 for a position at the University of Maryland School of Medicine in Baltimore. A short biography and sketch appeared in *Harper's Weekly*, reporting that he had experienced "a functional disorder of the heart" in the early

---

XII (Washington: Government Printing Office, 1887), 73, 75, 76-77. See Frank A. Flower, *Edwin McMasters Stanton, The Autocrat of Rebellion, Emancipation and Reconstruction* (Boston: Geo. M. Smith & Co., 1905), 116-117.

5. John S.C. Abbott, *The History of the Civil War in America*, Vol. I (New York: Henry Bill, 1863), 92.

6. Allan Nevins, "The United States Sanitary Commission and Secretary Stanton" in *Proceedings of the Massachusetts Historical Society*, Third Series, Vol. 67 (Oct. 1941-May 1944), 402, 407. The article is an encomium of the Commission and does not discuss whether it exceeded its agreed-upon role with the War Department.

7. Pilcher, 44-46. He died in 1879, age eighty-two.

1850s, followed by "a somewhat disordered constitution" requiring a sojourn in Europe. When recovered, he spent a year "at Mackinaw in the service" before resignation.[8] Perhaps he would sustain Tripler better than his predecessor.

One thing Hammond would likely do is please the Commission. As early as October 1861, the brain trust of the Commission met to plan for and "reinvigorate" the process of replacing Finley. They had then settled on their candidate:

> Dr. Hammond, U.S.A., of Baltimore, is in town. Only as Assistant Surgeon, but he has had intimations from the War Department that the last may be first, and that he may take Dr. Finlay's [sic] place. ... Dr. Bellows thinks well of him.[9]

The "intimations" came from Assistant Secretary of War Thomas A. Scott, for Cameron categorically opposed Hammond's appointment. Scott, a railroad executive, had been appointed to his post in order to promote Union capabilities in railroad transportation. Henry W. Bellows was a Harvard graduate, clergyman, editor, lecturer, and president of the Commission.[10] Neither had any medical credentials. When the Commission secured introduction on December 10 of a bill to reform the Medical Bureau, it was Hammond who had authored the draft.[11]

The backdrop for Finley's replacement took place at both ends

---

8. November 21, 1863, 748.
9. Nevins, "The United States Sanitary Commission and Secretary Stanton," 407-408.
10. Id. 408.
11. Jane T. Censer ed., *The Papers of Frederick Law Olmsted: Defending the Union*, Vol. IV (Baltimore: Johns Hopkins University Press, 1986), 17-18 [hereinafter "*Olmsted Papers*"]. A recent biography contains interesting revelations. Justin Martin, *Genius of Place: The Life of Frederick Law Olmsted* (Boston: Da Capo Press, 2011); see Appendix. An earlier effort relies uncritically on Olmsted and Sanitary Commission-originated material. Laura Wood Roper, *F.L.O.: A Biography of Frederick Law Olmsted* (Baltimore: Johns Hopkins University Press, 1973).

of Pennsylvania Avenue, as well as at 244 F Street NW where the Commission's secretary, Frederick Law Olmsted, had established its offices. Olmsted would gain fame for another proficiency, landscape design, and its manifestation in places such as New York City's Central Park, the National Zoological Park in D.C., Detroit's Belle Isle, and at Pinehurst, North Carolina. In January 1862, the New York leadership of the Commission authorized a committee "to visit Washington and press passage of the Medical Reform Bill." Other delegations would descend on the capital as well to form "a strong lobby there in favor of reforming the Medical Bureau." On January 29, the lobbyists met with new Secretary Stanton and General McClellan to gain assent. Not confident of their promises and assurances, the Commission mounted public opinion as well. The Senate soon passed the Commission-supported bill, and in early March the House committee on military affairs gave approval to the measure.[12]

On April 16, the President signed into law "An Act to reorganize and increase the Efficiency of the Medical Department of the Army." It sought to achieve these two ostensible purposes by: adding additional personnel in the form of cadets and hospital stewards to the Medical Bureau; creating eight medical inspector positions; adding surgeons and assistant surgeons; imposing obligations on and giving recognition to medical purveyors regarding the sick and wounded; and, perhaps most significant, elevating the top echelon of the Bureau within the Department. The office of Surgeon-General "to be appointed under this act" achieved the rank of Brigadier-General, and the Assistant Surgeon-General and Inspector-General of Hospitals held the rank of Colonel.[13]

But had the War Department only come to support improvements with Stanton's arrival? The President had not called for it in his first "State of the Union" address in December 1861, but he had endorsed Cameron's recommendations here:

---

12. Nevins, "The United States Sanitary Commission and Secretary Stanton," 409-410.
13. 12 Stat. 378-379.

> I respectfully refer to the report of the Secretary of War for information respecting the numerical strength of the Army and for recommendations having in view an increase of its efficiency and the well-being of the various branches of the service intrusted to his care. It is gratifying to know that the patriotism of the people has proved equal to the occasion, and that the number of troops tendered greatly exceeds the force which Congress authorized me to call into the field.

Lincoln also expressed satisfaction—not irritation—with the state of hygiene in the armies of the Republic:

> I refer with pleasure to those portions of his report which make allusion to the creditable degree of discipline already attained by our troops and to the excellent sanitary condition of the entire Army.[14]

In effect, the President's assessment formed a rebuke to the view that the Medical Bureau had utterly failed in its duty.

Cameron's report had incorporated one from Finley that was tendered on November 13, 1861. The Surgeon-General actually did recommend organization change, to some extent. Ten assistant surgeons should be promoted to full surgeon, and thirty additional assistant surgeon positions should be authorized. Perhaps most important, Finley complained about the disparity in rank, and thus in the level of respect, for the medical officer corps "compared with other branches of the general staff."[15] Here, his views and the Commission's were in sync.

Had Finley lobbied Congress successfully on behalf of what took effect on April 16? According to one history, he "gave considerable

---

14. *Message of the President of the United States to the Two Houses of Congress, 37th Congress, Vol. II, Report of the Secretary of War*, Senate Ex. Doc. No. 1 (Washington: Government Printing Office, 1861), 60.
15. Id. 62.

time" to dealing with members of Congress "and others from whom advantages of legislation ... might be hoped for." The bill to change up the Medical Bureau embodied Surgeon-General recommendations. But it was said he could be counted "only indirectly responsible" for the full program in the legislation.[16] Since the bill mandated retirement for those over sixty-five years of age, it benefited him—but also ended his career. The Commission, rather, had been the prime mover of the measure. It had made "numerous suggestions" for reorganizing the medical structure.[17] Olmsted led a "carefully orchestrated" campaign on behalf of the bill, calling upon public opinion as well as Commission personnel and sympathizers to do lobbying.[18] Cameron had not helped, and perhaps neither had Stanton. The Commission's clout on the Hill proved enough "being in a position to confer advisedly with the Military Committees of Congress." It is not a shock, then, that the group openly claimed credit for securing passage and signing of the bill.[19] Olmsted was triumphant: "Our success is suddenly wonderfully complete."[20]

Having carried out "the responsible duty of aiding in the preparation and advocacy of the New Medical Act," a title itself reflective of sentiment for a new kind of medical bureau, the Commission came away with even more. It felt a proprietary interest in the candidates for the new and enhanced positions adopted in the act: "The Sanitary Commission had clearly won the right to a preponderating opinion in the choice of candidates, and when consulted, it unhesitatingly expressed its preference, and gave good reasons for such choice."[21] That term—"preponderating"—is key, for it means nothing less than exceeding any other force in influence, power, or importance.

---

16. Pilcher, 43-44.
17. Id. 44.
18. *Olmsted Papers*, 17-19.
19. *Succinct Narrative*, 24-25.
20. Elizabeth Stevenson, "Olmsted on F Street: The Beginnings of the United States Sanitary Commission" in *Records of the Columbia Historical Society, Washington, D.C.*, Vol. 49 (1973/1974), 134.
21. *Succinct Narrative*, 25.

The Commission had months before settled on Hammond for the newly enhanced top post, and Bellows personally lobbied Lincoln for his appointment.[22] It would become common knowledge that the Commission "took a hand in affairs" and pushed for his elevation.[23] Confirmation of Hammond as the new Surgeon-General at Brigadier-General rank only reinforced the confidence of the Commission's leadership in its preeminence. Finley was out, and Hammond was in—and so was the Commission. This achievement was another part of Olmsted's "wonderful" success, that "the very man whom, eight months ago, we picked out" was set in the place they had envisioned and created for him.[24] As for Tripler—another strategy was in play.

It is thus anti-historical to maintain that the Commission refrained from seeking to "supplant" Army ways and means and, with purity of motive and deed, "maintained its subordination to army rules and regulations."[25] The heightened role of women in seeking formation of the Commission, and in playing a major role in its relief work on the ground, was an important contribution to Union victory that should not be downplayed.[26] But the leadership of the Commission was, typical of the era, a male-dominated contingent. The Commission's public posturing that it was merely a loyal partner to the Army apparatus—revealing, in that it had to be stated on more than one occasion—protesteth too much. It cloaked its full program by dissembling statements, such as: "To every unbiassed [*sic*] and discerning mind, whether in the medical profession, or the army, the Sanitary Commission has manifestly been, from its organization until now, the most unfaltering and faithful friend and ally of the Medical

---

22. Nevins, "The United States Sanitary Commission and Secretary Stanton," 412. Much of the inside story is derived from George Templeton Strong. More on him *infra*.
23. Pilcher, 47.
24. Stevenson, "Olmsted on F Street," 134.
25. Pam Tise, *A Fragile Legacy: The Contributions of Women in the United States Sanitary Commission to the United States Administrative State*, Masters Thesis, Texas State University-San Marcos, 2013, 4.
26. Id. 11.

Department, and of all that is good and faithful in it."[27] Indeed, the Commission could not restrain itself, and it came out from behind its cloak in certain statements: "It fearlessly attacked the policy of *perpetual succession by seniority alone* in the medical service of the army."[28] In seeking a higher posture for the Medical Bureau within the War Department, the Commission had not limited itself to advising and counseling. And it said so: "[w]hatever and whoever stands in the way of this, the Commission wants put out of the way." Overzealousness? No, claimed the Commission's own narrative; "that impression is without the smallest foundation of truth." Why not? Because Union soldiers were due the best medical care—a point on which no one disagreed—and "it must be given them, let who will stand in the way."[29] With this self-justification, the Commission's leadership saw its "official" duty subsumed making and unmaking individual Army officer careers.

An official mid-war history of the Commission reveals much. Entitled *The Sanitary Commission of the United States Army: A Succinct Narrative of Its Work and Purposes*, the title itself—that the Commission was "of the" Army—portrayed a hand-in-glove approach, rather than an iron fist when it came to personnel and policy. Equally telling were such disavowals as that the organization was "in the way of obtaining rights, privileges, or opportunities for itself" or "of making itself more active, important and influential." Rather, its one goal was "always in the way of stirring up the [Medical] Department to a larger sense of its own duty," such that the Commission would be rendered "unnecessary." On May 23, 1861, the representatives who sought official sanction for the Commission pledged it had been organized "for the purposes only of inquiry and advice" and sought "no legal powers." It would work with the War Department and its "Medical Bureau," not against it, refraining from "impertinent and offensive

---

27. *Succinct Narrative*, 22.
28. Id. 23 (emphasis in original).
29. Id. 24.

interference."³⁰ The quarters promised by the Administration were made available in the Treasury Building, where the Commission's "Central Office" was set up.³¹ It gave up this free space for new quarters in the "old three-story, rambling Adams house at 244 F Street." It was a house purchased by John Quincy Adams—a New Englander like the Commission's leadership—when serving as Secretary of State. Its closer proximity to Capitol Hill than to the environs of the White House spoke volumes.³²

And what of the Commission's position vis-à-vis Stanton? He had no ties to Finley, so when the time came and "the Commission had to demand the wholesale reorganization of the Medical Bureau and the ousting of Surgeon General Finley,"³³ he could be expected to act as its ally. Since Finley had fallen out of Stanton's favor independent of the Commission's input, the objectives of both seemed in harmony. Indeed, the appointment came with initial approval by the Secretary of War, since the Commission "consisted of some powerful celebrities whom Stanton hoped to win over."³⁴ It appears, though, that Stanton's "cantankerous anger" and "unsleeping hostility" had been aroused by the group.³⁵ He came to consider them "meddlers in his affairs."³⁶ How had this happened?

For one thing, Stanton really had his own preferred candidate, which he had to forego once it became clear how much sway the Commission held.³⁷ He also denigrated Hammond's pick for a main assistant—who had himself been a candidate for the post—pointedly

---

30. Id. iv, 5-6.
31. Id. 13-14.
32. Stevenson, "Olmsted on F Street," 125, 129.
33. Nevins, "The United States Sanitary Commission and Secretary Stanton," 402, 405.
34. William Marvel, *Lincoln's Autocrat: The Life of Edwin Stanton* (Chapel Hill: University of North Carolina Press, 2015), 156.
35. Nevins, "The United States Sanitary Commission and Secretary Stanton," 405.
36. Stevenson, "Olmsted on F Street," 132.
37. Pilcher, 49.

saying, "I did not before think you a weak man."[38] Stanton had promised the post to Robert C. Wood, and he found himself outrun.[39]

For another thing, Hammond was to blame. He did not curry favor with Stanton through Wood's appointment. He owed his own elevation to the Commission and to McClellan—so he thought, and so he admitted in writing. From the first, Hammond worked closely with the Commission and earned its "enthusiastic support"—but regarded it as more important than those within his chain of command.[40] He was "so low in rank" as a 1st Lieutenant compared to other qualified candidates,[41] and jumping over so many officers who thought themselves to be a better choice produced "angry feelings."[42] Hammond had left the Army before the Civil War; those "who deemed themselves outraged"[43] were aggrieved by the law and by its implementation in affirmatively disrespecting the financial sacrifice they had made by remaining in uniform. The Commission praised his patriotism for leaving "the tempting professional relations of civic [sic] life" for a second stint in the Army.[44] As for those physicians who had resisted such temptations while continuing to serve (and Tripler fit this bill), they were denigrated as career hacks.

Although the pay rate for a surgeon or assistant surgeon appeared significant, the net effect of Army service proved far from lucrative. At the grade of Major, a surgeon's monthly pay and allowances were $165; assistant surgeon, at Captain, $130. The officer, however, was responsible for his own subsistence. From his pay each month, he had deductions ranging from $75 to $125 for the necessities associated

---

38. Id. 50.
39. William A. Hammond, *A Statement of the Causes Which Led to the Dismissal of Surgeon-General William A. Hammond from the Army* (New York: n.p., 1864), 4.
40. Gillett, 177-178.
41. Pilcher, 47.
42. Hammond, 4.
43. Id.
44. Pilcher, 25.

with uniform, horse, servant's pay, and so forth.[45] None became rich on such remuneration. By contrast, private practice could be more lucrative—and Tripler's experience in California proved so.

Nearly all of this background, legislative history, and personnel intervention has been ignored or downplayed by histories. Regardless of Hammond's achievements, his unqualified endorsement by the Commission has infiltrated the memorializing of his service, as witnessed by the history of Surgeon-Generals published by the Association of Military Surgeons in 1905.[46] Hammond's only halfhearted acceptance of females in the medical service, and undermining of Dorothea Dix, belies the notion that he was utterly forward-thinking and reveals an arrogance that characterized his behavior.[47] The Commission had sought his elevation "after careful consideration of the claims of all the medical officers then in the service"—a startling assertion given its official status, lack of medical expertise, duration in existence, and the facts. Additionally, attention has focused quite naturally, given the competing subject matter, on a parallel congressional vehicle enacted on April 16, 1862. This measure dealt with an overarching subject that underpinned the entire conflict. Slavery in the District of Columbia was abolished in section 1 of "An Act for the Release of certain Persons held to Service or Labor" in the district, signed into law by the President on the same date as the Medical Bureau reform bill. It provided remuneration to former owners (in some circumstances), but the action amounted to the first sea change in Federal policy since the Northwest Ordinance of 1787 forever banned slavery within its

---

45. Albert G. Hart, *The Surgeon and the Hospital in the Civil War* [reprint from Papers of Military Society of Massachusetts] (n.p.: 1902), 236. This retrospective by a physician is revealing as to the learning curve experienced by a volunteer medical staffer.
46. One of those achievements was the *Medical and Surgical History*.
47. Jane E. Schultz, *Women at the Front: Hospital Workers in Civil War America* (Chapel Hill: University of North Carolina Press, 2004), 15, 18, 111. Although Dix had been appointed by the War Department as superintendent of women nurses, the Sanitary Commission overrode and arrogated her authority. Winkle, 220-222.

borders.[48] From the standpoint of the issues for which the Civil War was being fought, the abolition of slavery meant much more than bureaucratic reform. For individuals impacted by the other law, however, the importance was keenly felt. And here is another aspect of the Commission's full record.

Among its initiatives, the Commission would end up engaged in a "large-scale endeavor to identify and catalog anatomical and physiological evidence of racial inferiority in the bodies of African American soldiers."[49] The Commission "played a particularly important role" in seeking to undergird racial stereotypes. It was "central" to affirmance of racial hierarchies by "insisting" that race differences were based on real facts—and no less than President Bellows held this work "the most important literary and scientific result" of the Commission's labors. The group was "[e]ver in competition with what they saw as the misplaced rival authority of the army's Medical Department." Investigating and publishing data on different racial characteristics "would set them apart—and above—the army's research and publishing agenda."[50]

The Commission's inquiry into the "Physiological Status of the negro as compared with white soldiers" produced information tainted by the racial attitudes of the examiners. Hammond expressed views supportive of racial hierarchy, including the belief that those

---

48. 12 Stat. 376–378.
49. Leslie A. Schwalm, "A Body of 'Truly Scientific Work': The U.S. Sanitary Commission and the Elaboration of Race in the Civil War Era" in *Journal of the Civil War Era*, Vol. 8, No. 4 (University of North Carolina Press, Dec. 2018), 647. This article points also to the Army Medical Museum—Hammond's claim to fame—and the Smithsonian Institution, American Freedman's Inquiry Commission, and other organizations as contributing to "racialized" medicine. Id. 649. It also lists in this racialized approach noted astronomer Benjamin A. Gould, author of *Investigations in the Military and Anthropological Statistics of American Soldiers* (New York: Hurd & Houghton, 1869), "published for the U.S. Sanitary Commission." See also ch. 6 of Jim Downs, *Maladies of Empire: How Colonialism, Slavery, and War Transformed Medicine* (Cambridge: Belknap Press, 2021).
50. Schwalm, 650–651, 655.

of European origin were "pre-eminent" and possessed "great superiority" for war, while those of African descent were "altogether incapable of attaining to the highest point" of intellectual or physical development.[51] Years later, W.E.B. Du Bois spent much of his early career seeking to refute the pseudo-science that justified segregationist policies.[52] Contrary to the notion that "all men are created equal," the United States Sanitary Commission sought a natural law basis to differentiate those of African origin. Thanks in substantial part to those efforts, "the notion of mean differences between racial groups" in physical capabilities "became deeply entrenched in the popular and scientific imagination in the nineteenth century."[53] Some claim that the undermining of Reconstruction, the rise of segregation, and the imposition of Jim Crow policies can all be tied to this pseudo-science.

The Sanitary Commission—beyond dispute—could not legitimately make a claim that it acted with clean hands. Uncritically approaching its legacy, and accepting its claims at face value, histories have white-washed its less than sterling record. As a result, confirmation bias infiltrated literature on the Union medical front.[54]

---

51. *A Treatise on Hygiene, with Special Reference to the Military Service* (Philadelphia: J.B. Lippincott, 1863), 62–76.
52. Schwalm, 659–661.
53. Lundy Braun, "Spirometry, Measurement, and Race in the Nineteenth Century" in *Journal of the History of Medicine and Allied Sciences*, Vol. 60, No. 2 (Oxford University Press, Apr. 2005), 135.
54. In law (pun intended), the doctrine of unclean hands bars a court from affording relief to a party who has engaged in inequitable behavior (e.g., fraud or deceit) related to the subject of that party's claim.

The Peninsula Campaign, March-July 1862

As of the first of March 1862, the Army of the Potomac had become the nation's largest, most imposing, and most publicized armed force. Its commander, nicknamed the "Little Napoleon" for his stature and expected brilliance, brimmed with self-confidence to the point of arrogance. The War had been going well for the North during the previous months. In November 1861, the US Navy, aided by an Army landing force, took command of Port Royal Sound and nearby Beaufort and Hilton Head Island in South Carolina. Fort Pulaski and control of the Savannah River had been taken. In February 1862, Rebel Forts Henry and Donelson had fallen in Tennessee, leading to Union advance and capture of the capital at Nashville. On March 9, the first naval conflict between ironclads had resulted in withdrawal of the Confederate *Virginia* and control maintained over the Hampton Roads and lower Chesapeake Bay thanks to the USS *Monitor*. New Orleans would be in Union hands in April; major portions of the Mississippi River thereafter would fall under Federal control.

The defense by the *Monitor* of Chesapeake Bay would enable McClellan to proceed with his plan to capture the Confederate capital of Richmond. He eschewed a purely overland campaign, convinced it would take too long and be too costly. Instead, his first iteration involved a water transport of the great portion of his force to Urbanna on the Rappahannock River, to cross over the York River at West Point in Virginia, and to reach the environs of Richmond, a march of only fifty miles. The rest of the army would have gone to Point Lookout in Maryland, shipped across the Potomac onto the Northern

Neck, then proceed to Urbanna and follow in the wake of the advance. McClellan's plans were fluid: he might then proceed across the James River and attack Richmond from Petersburg, a rail hub.[1] But "McClellan was a secretive man" and did not begin to share his plans with the Administration until early February.[2] On March 8, Lincoln approved the waterborne route. Ironically, the Confederate force at Manassas began withdrawing from its positions that very day. As it moved southward, it rendered a landing at the Rappahannock problematical. McClellan now needed to disembark his army farther south. He still intended to make White House his base for the close advance on Richmond, but the Peninsula route would not "cut off the Confederates" and would involve more fighting.[3] McClellan told Tripler none of this.

Plans were set in motion for the Army of the Potomac to board ship for a destination at Fort Monroe on the east end of the James Peninsula.[4] From there, the distance to Richmond remained much shorter than from Washington, only eighty miles or so. On March 17, with "the stride of a giant," the massive Army began its trans-shipment from the vicinity of the capital. The officer in charge of its transport would detail the results: delivery at Fort Monroe of 121,500 men, 1,224 ambulances and wagons, artillery, animals, and an equivalent required amount of equipment.[5] The grand aggregate of the infantry, artillery, and cavalry components in the Army equaled more than 200,000 soldiers, which *inter alia* included troops in the Shenandoah

---

1. *McClellan's Own Story*, 227.
2. Dougherty & Moore, 37-41, 147.
3. Id. 46.
4. The initial idea was to land troops between the Rappahannock and York rivers and "move thence on West Point." George B. McClellan, "The Peninsular Campaign" in *Battles and Leaders of the Civil War*, Vol. II (New York: Century Co., 1887), 167. McClellan's forces did not reach that location until May 7, six weeks after the landings at Fort Monroe. The health impact was correspondingly lengthened.
5. Stephen W. Sears, *To the Gates of Richmond: The Peninsula Campaign* (Boston: Houghton Mifflin Co., 2001), 22, 24. McClellan's plan was for a contingent of 155,000 troops. McClellan, "The Peninsular Campaign," 168.

Valley, at Manassas, and in garrison around Washington.[6] The movement of the army, while impressive, "was also time-consuming and at times chaotic."[7] McClellan traveled aboard the *Commodore* and arrived on April 2 at Fort Monroe. Tripler went along. He had accompanied the Army on its expedition to Mexico a decade and a half earlier; he would do so here. His duty lay at the front.

Other changes had affected the Army. The President had ordered the divisions of the army organized into five corps for better battlefield coordination. Although McClellan said he favored the move as an abstract principle, "I did not desire to form them until the army had been for some little time in the field" and he had weighed capabilities based on performance.[8] Consequently, Tripler had no real warning when the Corps structure was created. He reacted by seeking to assign an experienced medical officer from one of the Washington area hospitals to each corps as its medical director; doing so would facilitate the provision of care within each new organization.[9] He also found impediments within the Army bureaucracy. Although Tripler intended to transfer everyone and everything in Washington to Fort Monroe, Surgeon-General Finley asserted control over the hospitals, instructed Tripler to use inspectors as the corps medical directors, and refused to allow the bulk of medical supplies to be shipped from Washington. Instead, Tripler "could take part of what was there, and that the remainder of what I wanted would be ordered from New York to meet me at Fort Monroe." He accordingly wrote a formal letter to Finley:

> Sir: I have the honor to request that field supplies for 140,000 men may be put up by the medical purveyor immediately,

---

6. *OR*, XI, pt. III, 26, 53. On April 13, aggregate present for duty on the Peninsula equaled slightly over 100,000. Id. 97. Same, April 30, over 112,000; the sick, in arrest, and on special duty numbered 5,850—5 percent. Id. 130. The percentage in the Washington garrison was 7 percent. Id. 60.
7. Dougherty & Moore, 57.
8. *OR*, V, 18.
9. *OR*, XI, pt. I, 178-179.

to be transported with Major-General McClellan's army wherever it may be ordered. I have appointed Assistant Surgeon Bartholow medical purveyor for this army. He has been ordered by telegraph to report to me without delay. General McClellan has directed his chief quartermaster to furnish the transportation for these supplies as soon as they are ready.

The general intends to move in from forty-eight to seventy-two hours.[10]

Tripler prepared for transport by moving to the new Army headquarters at Alexandria, one of the embarkation points, in the nearby Theological Seminary.[11] When McClellan and his staff, including Tripler, boarded the *Commodore* on March 29, representatives of the Sanitary Commission met them at the wharf and requested that three representatives be permitted to accompany the Army and that facilities be provided to transport "such supplies as they might think proper to send." The requests were referred to Tripler. He assented upon agreement to certain conditions: "provided their agents shall consult with me before making issues to the troops, and that their reports shall be submitted to my inspection before they are transmitted for publication." Tripler wanted to "economize" resources and collect them centrally for "when they could be commanded in any emergency, such as a battle." He would find that the Commission would not abide by the provisos.[12]

The *Commodore* pushed off on April 1 and arrived at Fort Monroe the next evening. The massive fort provided "a protected landing site and a stable base of operations" for the launch of the campaign.[13] On April 3, Tripler met with Major Cuyler, who agreed to move his ill patients into tents and accept one thousand wounded from the Army

---

10. Id. 196 (letter dated March 15, 1862).
11. Id. 197; XI, pt. III, 13, 15, 33
12. *OR*, XI, pt. I, 180.
13. Dougherty & Moore, 58. The US Army had additional forces at Camps Butler and Hamilton on the mainland. Id. 59.

into the Fort Monroe facilities. As the Army moved up the Peninsula, Tripler expected six times that number from an effort to break through Confederate lines that had appeared at Yorktown. He began to plan for contingencies; these would be the largest losses, by far, in the war. He ensured use of meeting-houses and private dwellings, as well as newly constructed huts at Yorktown and Ship Point.[14] He also discovered that the countryside "was but a succession of swamps, that in warm weather would be too prolific of malarial poison." Concluding that a severe action would overwhelm the field hospitals, Tripler arranged for the handling "at some of the hospitals North" of the overflow. He also reached an agreement with the Quartermaster's Department of the Army "to transport my men from any point on York River to such hospitals as I might indicate."[15]

The phrase "my men" signifies the degree of attachment Tripler felt. Army headquarters had been established at Camp Winfield Scott, a tent encampment near Yorktown.[16] He did not content himself with sitting at McClellan's camp city, instead conducting inspections of facilities and checking on practitioners to ensure care was being properly provided to the troops. First-person testimony corroborates that he engaged in field travel: "Was visited to-day by Medical Director Tripler, with whom, after inspecting my own hospital, I went to General Hospital, at Whittaker's."[17] Hospitals were established fairly quickly; an image of one in existence on April 12 appeared in a post-war account.[18]

---

14. *McClellan's Own Story*, 308. Ship Point was at the confluence of Cheeseman's (Chisman) Creek and the Poquosin River. *OR Atlas*, Plate XVIII-1.
15. *OR*, XI, pt. I, 181, 198.
16. *OR*, XI, pt. III, 93.
17. Alexander M. Stewart, *Camp, March and Battle-field; or, Three Years and a Half with the Army of the Potomac* (Philadelphia: Jas. B. Rodgers,1865), 140. The location is likely the Whitaker House, headquarters of Brigadier-General William F. ("Baldy") Smith during the Battle of Williamsburg on May 5, commemorated by a Virginia Historic Landmarks Commission marker on Pocahontas Trail (Route 60) just miles east of Route 199 in York County. McClellan also used it as a command post. *McClellan's Own Story*, 330-331.
18. McClellan, "The Peninsular Campaign," 172.

As of April 20, Tripler had not received confirmation from the acting Surgeon-General on specifics of the hospital arrangements in the "North." So he made arrangements for a steamship to be moored and available "constantly" at Cheeseman's Landing, reserved for wounded soldiers.[19] Soon afterward, the *Commodore* was assigned to Tripler by the Quartermaster's Department. With the aid of Pennsylvania Surgeon-General Henry H. Smith, the two physician leaders "had her ready to receive 900 wounded." Tripler cheerfully accepted other voluntarism. Smith had "arrived with the steamer *Wm. Whildin*, completely fitted up with bedding, stores, instruments, a corps of 18 surgeons and dressers, and a full complement of Sisters of Charity for nurses." A half-dozen "eminent surgeons, deputed by the Governor of Massachusetts by authority of the Secretary of War, arrived in camp and offered their services." The Medical Director pressed them all into service in addition to continuing his reliance on the supplemental resources of the Sanitary Commission.[20]

Tripler did not overlook the sick lists. He regarded the initial numbers of those falling ill to be small "considering the strength of the army, the wretched weather, the character of the country, &c."[21] but made arrangements to send North "those too ill to move" forward with the Army. He arranged for the *Massachusetts* to take on the sick and transport them to the hospital at Annapolis.[22] He also worked with Olmsted to make use, for this purpose, of the *Daniel Webster No. 1* and the *Ocean Queen*, which Tripler procured and turned over to the Commission. Olmsted committed to fitting out the ship within forty-eight hours. Tripler reported that "[i]t took rather longer than that, however, and then she carried but about three-fifths of the number she

---

19. Perhaps, Ship Point, or Belvin's Pier. *OR Atlas*, Plate XVIII-2.
20. *OR*, XI, pt. I, 181, 198.
21. Id. 182.
22. The vessel was "an iron screw steamer" built in 1860, purchased by the US Navy in 1861, and first assigned to blockade duty. It was fitted out as "a transport and supply ship" and commissioned for this duty on April 16, 1862. US Navy Department, *Dictionary of American Naval Fighting Ships*, Vol. IV (Washington: Government Printing Office, 1969), 263-264.

should have carried."[23] The *Webster* had come into the Commission's control on April 25.[24] The readiness of the *Queen* suffered from shifting plans within the Quartermaster Department.[25]

New ground was being broken here. The Peninsula Campaign was the "first use of such hospital transports in the war on a daily basis," and leeway for the absence of precedent ought to be given.[26] Cooperation that Tripler sought from the Quartermaster and Subsistence Departments fell short; both gave medical supply a lower priority than food or armament and, in at least one case, buried it within and below foodstuffs being delivered.[27] Olmsted found difficulty in procuring crews for the growing fleet of Commission-operated vessels, both on account of fear from contracting disease and the voluntary nature of personnel who could not be ordered about.[28]

Rather than assault Rebel fortifications at Yorktown along the Warwick Line, McClellan ordered siege operations. Although he had revealed it to perhaps no one, a "slow and strangulating siege" had been his real intent all the way to Richmond.[29] The month-long effort, from April 5 to May 4, resulted in five hundred Union casualties. An action on April 17 involved 32 men reported as killed and 100 wounded, the latter group being sent to the hospital ships. On April 26, "12 men of a Massachusetts regiment were wounded and sent to the ships. In irregular firing during the siege several more of our men were wounded, and disposed of in the same manner."[30] The Confederates withdrew from Yorktown on May 4, the day before the planned Union attack.

In a new development in the annals of warfare, the Rebels had left

---

23. *OR*, XI, pt. I, 181-182.
24. *Olmsted Papers*, 27.
25. Id. 28.
26. Id. 27.
27. *OR*, XI, pt. I, 183.
28. *Olmsted Papers*, 28.
29. Judkin Browning, *The Seven Days' Battles: The War Begins Anew* (Santa Barbara: Praeger, 2012), 41; Dougherty & Moore, 81-83.
30. *OR*, XI, pt. I, 182.

behind what they referred to as "torpedos." Unlike other meanings for the term, the concept here was akin to the later use of a contact explosive device. An artillery shell was placed inside a box with a system for detonation. Since such contraptions had not been seen, nothing was suspected. A small number of Union soldiers suffered wounds from these devices.[31] Tripler might have confronted a much larger and more devastating type of casualty.

It was not until the first major hostile action of the Campaign, the Battle of Williamsburg on May 5, that Tripler's planning was put more fully to the test. This triumph's cost in casualties was higher[32] than at First Bull Run: just over 2,000 in killed, wounded, and missing (presumed captured). Some 1,400 Union soldiers suffered wounds. The Medical teams did their job well, according to McClellan. He reported that "[s]teps were at once taken to care for and remove the wounded,"[33] a far cry from the disorganized response at First Bull Run. Tripler also had responsibility regarding care of nearly five hundred Confederate wounded prisoners. Those in either uniform with slight wounds were not transferred to hospital. Tripler reported: "Eight hundred of our men and 100 prisoners were sent to Fort Monroe on the Commodore, and 427 of our men and 273 prisoners on the Wm. Whildin and other transports," with the latter sailing for Philadelphia where capacity for 600 patients had been arranged. Other hospitals and their patient numbers included: Albany, 1,500; Alexandria, 400; Annapolis, 250; Baltimore, 700; Boston, at least 260; Georgetown, 400; Washington, 1,500; New York, 2,000. On May 11, the embarkation of Union wounded was completed, and prisoners were loaded

---

31. Six soldiers were wounded in the 22nd Massachusetts Volunteer Regiment, Porter's Division; the 52nd Pennsylvania, Casey's Division, suffered 1 killed, 6 wounded. Id. 400, 560.
32. A tactical draw, but the Confederate withdrawal enabled continued Union advance.
33. Id. 23, 450.

and transported the next day.³⁴ Confederate medical aid was offered but not accepted.³⁵

Another "enemy" appeared. Tripler saw an article out of New York City that asserted, in his words, "no provision was made for the shelter or professional care of the wounded at Williamsburg except by the Sanitary Commission." He responded, on behalf of the "medical officers of the army and volunteers," that such a report was slanderous. In fact, he maintained, no agent or member of the Commission had been involved until all the wounded were aboard the transports.³⁶

The Army of the Potomac continued its ponderous advance toward Richmond, fighting skirmishes and minor battles until the last day of the month. The day-to-day issues on the Peninsula did not translate into easy understanding in Washington or at homes throughout the North. Having only eighty miles to traverse, the Army carried huge expectations of rapid victory. As dissatisfaction grew, some publications took to defending "Little Mac." One was the national periodical *Harpers Weekly*, which editorialized: "With regard to the course pursued by Major-General McClellan, there is but one principle which can be safely adopted by good citizens, and that is, to trust him until the proofs of his incapacity are so flagrant as to be obvious to every one."³⁷ A week later, under the headline "On to Richmond!," the paper triumphantly reported: "It is at last safe to say in print what every one has been whispering to his neighbor for some days past—that McClellan has started on his march to Richmond."³⁸ Understanding was lacking, however, that the route required traversing marshes, swamps, and flooded lowlands on rudimentary roads that became quagmires, producing delay and disease.³⁹

As the Army proceeded, it secured a new base of supply much

---

34. Id. 184-185, 203.
35. *McClellan's Own Story*, 338.
36. *OR*, XI, pt. I, 185.
37. Issue of April 12, 1862, 226.
38. Issue of April 19, 1862, 242. The weather, terrain, and condition of roads, combined with inadequate maps, contributed to the pace of advance.
39. Dougherty & Moore, 60-63, 68-69.

closer than Fort Monroe. McClellan sent a force up the York River to West Point; Union troops next occupied New Kent Court House and Cumberland. Headquarters moved progressively to four miles west of Williamsburg, to Roper's Church fifteen more miles on, then to Cumberland on May 13.[40] Located at a bend of the Pamunkey upriver from West Point, the landing at Cumberland Plantation represented a colonial river port and trading center and provided waterborne access only thirty miles from Richmond. It soon became the site for a burgeoning tent city, crowded wharf, and growing number of escapees from slavery. On May 16, McClellan established his headquarters on the grounds of White House plantation, a Custis family property connected to George Washington.[41] Located farther upriver from Cumberland, securing the grounds again narrowed the distance to the Confederate capital and—most important—opened use of the Richmond & York River Rail Road.[42] Several stations along the route provided locations for supply and storage, including Tunstall's and Savage's. The latter was but seven miles from Richmond.

Two months had elapsed since the first elements of the Army had left the Washington area. For McClellan, "[t]he question was now to be decided as to the ultimate line of operations of the army." Should he continue, or abandon this line of operations and switch its base to somewhere on the James River? Continuing this line meant the provision of medical supplies and the transport of the sick and wounded could be most efficient.[43] It meant no change to the Medical Director's

---

40. *McClellan's Own Story*, 341.
41. Id.
42. The process McClellan followed of changing bases is now referred to as "logistics over the shore (LOTS)." White House Landing, located just upriver from the house, served as the Army of the Potomac's major supply base after May 10. Richard E. Killblane, *White House Landing: Sustaining the Army of the Potomac during the Peninsula Campaign*, 1-2. [https://transportation.army.mil/historian/documents/White%20House%20Landing%20paper.pdf] See Robert H. Rhodes ed., *All For the Union; The Civil War Diary and Letters of Elisha Hunt Rhodes* (New York: Vintage Books, 1992), 58.
43. *McClellan's Own Story*, 342-346.

expectation of a great battle to take Richmond where, presuming success, "we should have the whole city, if necessary, for a hospital."[44] Perhaps, had McClellan taken advantage of the situation along the James River and provided infantry for a combined operation on May 15 to take Drewry's Bluff, the only major impediment to a water threat to Richmond, the course of the campaign would have altered.[45]

Tripler had his own issues; he lagged behind headquarters in order to settle matters at Williamsburg. He left there on the evening of May 13 and camped on the road during the night. At noon on the 14th, he reached Cumberland to discover "a number of sick, reported as unable to go on." The Director demonstrated his fortitude and resourcefulness, with rain rendering roads impassable. That night, he boarded a small tug to reach the *Commodore* and bring it back as a hospital ship. When the ship's master refused, and the provost-marshal was no aid to finding a pilot, Tripler located "the mate of a brig about sailing for home who was said to know the river." He ordered him, using McClellan's name, to steer the vessel to the Army base. Successful in providing a hospital ship for these ill soldiers, he moved on to headquarters on the 16th.[46] Here, he established a general hospital comprised of 100 tents, which increased over time to 170.[47]

To ensure the wounded could be treated, Tripler rode herd. At one point, he found 900 of 1,020 in the hospital tents to have "trifling ailments." They were sent back to the ranks. When he heard that scurvy cases were increasing, he attacked the issue by securing lemons and other remedial items. He also requested the men be compelled to not avoid desiccated (dried) vegetables and to make and consume soup daily, along with prohibiting fried meat in favor of boiled or

---

44. *OR*, XI, pt. I, 202.
45. Emory M. Thomas, "The Peninsular Campaign" in William C. Davis ed., *The Image of War: 1861-1865*, Vol. II: The Guns of '62 (Garden City: Doubleday & Co., 1982), 115-116.
46. Id. 185-186.
47. Id. 186, 205-206.

roasted beef. His first priority was to "at all events" be prepared for the outcome of armed conflict.[48]

Tripler traveled frequently away from headquarters, moving to Tunstall's Station on the Richmond & York, then to Cold Harbor, to Dispatch Station,[49] to the rear hospitals at Yorktown, and to the supply depots at White House. His official report carries the impression of a peripatetic officer, inspecting facilities, procuring supplies, asking the Sanitary Commission to furnish needed items, and personally giving examinations to ill soldiers in order to separate the seriously sick from mild cases who could be returned to the front lines. He ensured hospitals had the necessary supplies, finding them "generally in good order and well arranged" and publicly praising the facility managed by Dorothea Dix, Superintendent of Army Nurses, as particularly well-kept.[50] Some of his rides put him within reach of Confederate cavalry raids and infantry skirmishers. He must have, like his fellow veteran from Mexico, experienced how his "heart kept getting higher and higher until it felt to me as though it were in my throat" with danger lurking. Like Grant, he put fear aside.[51]

The Army's approach toward the capital city meant its right flank followed the Pamunkey River to cut the Rebel supply line of the Virginia Central Railroad.[52] On May 27, the resulting Battle of Hanover Court House was a Union victory. Losses were 62 killed and

---

48. Id. 186-187, 203, 207-210. "Desiccated vegetables became an important tool in the arsenal of nutrition" in seeking to prevent vitamin deficiency that could lead to chronic diarrhea. John Lustrea, "How Civil War Cooks Kept Soldiers Healthy with History's Worst Vegetables," Aug. 11, 2022, at https://www.historynet.com/civil-war-desiccated-vegetables/
49. On the Richmond & York River in the vicinity of Bottom's Bridge. *OR Atlas*, Plate XIX-1. *McClellan's Own Story*, 360-362.
50. *OR*, XI, pt. I, 186-187.
51. Grant, *Memoirs*, Vol. I, 249-250.
52. Fitz John Porter, "Hanover Court House and Gaines's Mill" in Robert U. Johnson & Clarence C. Buel eds., *Battles and Leaders of the Civil War*, Vol. II (New York: Century Co., 1887), 319. Porter had served as chief of staff to General Patterson when Tripler had been the chief medical officer. Dougherty & Moore, 16.

223 wounded, of which "138 only went into the hospital." Care was extended to 123 wounded Rebels, and arrangements were made for all to be succored at William Gaines's and Hogan's houses and outbuildings on the north bank of the Chickahominy River not far from the action. Tripler requested that two Sanitary Commission-controlled vessels, the *Knickerbocker* and the *Elm City*, transport wounded and ill to facilities in the rear. Unfortunately, he reported, "[n]either of them were ready," so he "directed our own boat, the Commodore, to be placed in position to receive the wounded" and substituted the *Daniel Webster No. 2* as well.[53]

On May 31 and June 1, the Confederates went over to the offensive in the Battle of Seven Pines (or Fair Oaks).[54] More than five thousand Union casualties were the toll, largest in the campaign and three times the number at First Bull Run. The total of wounded approximated 3,600, for the first time approaching Tripler's largest anticipation.[55] The medical staff coped well with such a "heavy" loss.[56] The medical director of one Corps published an account revealing that "so terrible a conflict had not been anticipated," but, with supplies forwarded by Tripler and the Commission, those wounded in the battle were able to receive the care due them.[57] Tripler's report stated:

> Immediately upon the commencement of the battle the boats at White House were ordered to be in readiness to receive the wounded. Surgeons were placed on board those in need of them. Other surgeons, volunteer and contract, of whom I had a supply at White House, were brought up to the field depots.

---

53. *OR*, XI, pt. I, 187, 685; *OR Atlas*, Plate XX-1. Annie Etheridge of Michigan served as a nurse aboard the *Knickerbocker*. Frank Moore, *Women of the War: Their Heroism and Self-Sacrifice* (Hartford: S.S. Scranton & Co., 1868), 426-427.
54. The latter was a station on the Richmond & York rail intersecting the Nine Mile Road (VA-33).
55. *OR*, XI, pt. I, 754, 762.
56. McClellan's own words, id. 751.
57. *American Medical Times*, 117 (Aug. 30, 1862).

> The transportation of the wounded was begun that night and steadily kept up till completed. This was accomplished by the 7th of June. ... The whole number sent from White House by the steamers was 3,580.[58]

In contrast to statements that the Army, prior to this action, was rife with illness, the official return for the end of May showed 5,374 "on special duty, sick, and in arrest." Another 23,784 were reported "absent."[59]

On June 15, "the roads then for the first time admitting of it," Tripler transferred the remainder of the Hanover wounded to the floating hospitals at White House.[60]

As elements of the Army of the Potomac moved to within four miles of Richmond,[61] Tripler anticipated even more costly fighting was imminent. He asked that leaves of absence for medical officers be rescinded; he directed enlargement of the Yorktown facilities to the capacity of 2,500-3,000 beds; he had 100 new tents pitched at the White House hospital and at Fair Oaks station; and he maintained a reserve of three wagonloads of medical supplies in his own camp. At Savage's Station, he established a receiving hospital for wounded under the direction of a civilian surgeon, Dr. John Swinburne of Albany, N.Y.:

> Every facility was given ... large details of men, all the tents we could command, abundance of subsistence, &c. There were several outhouses at the Station that were directed to be vacated; some sick in them belonging to Keyes' corps were transferred to White House. An ice-house near Savage's house was filled with ice. In twelve days, with a detail of 100 men, or as many of them as chose to report to Dr. Swinburne,

---

58. *OR*, XI, pt. I, 187-188.
59. *OR*, XI, pt. III, 204.
60. *OR*, XI, pt. I, 189.
61. *Harpers Weekly*, June 14, 1862, 370.

succeeded in getting the buildings cleaned, 25 tents pitched, two or three caldrons for making soup in position, water-casks prepared and filled with water, hospital stores and dressings, and was prepared to receive the wounded.[62]

The location was less than ten miles from the center of the Confederate capital city.

Rain had plagued the Campaign, and it continued to do so in June. But McClellan promised Washington that he would "move forward and take Richmond" as soon as the ground permitted and reinforcements arrived. Both occurred by the 13th. Headquarters were advanced on June 12 to near Dr. Trent's house.[63] On the 25th, McClellan advanced his pickets on the left, preparatory to the long-awaited ultimate battle, producing some 500 casualties.[64]

Frustration plagued Tripler over the Sanitary Commission. He had noted several instances of unreadiness; as June progressed, relations continued to deteriorate. When he had substituted one Commission vessel for another, his action "was met by further objection, and I was obliged to reiterate the order peremptorily." Some 450 ill soldiers were transported to Boston by the Commission, "contrary to my orders"[65]—which were in compliance with an order from the Surgeon-General.[66] The decision to violate the directive was made by Olmsted; he disliked how the wounded were being loaded aboard ship and "felt obliged" to send the *Daniel Webster No. 1* to Boston.[67]

---

62. *OR*, XI, pt. I, 189-190. Swinburne served after the War as mayor of Albany and Republican Member of the US House of Representatives.
63. Near the Grapevine Bridge over the Chickahominy. See *OR Atlas*, Plate XX-1. The headquarters site before here was at Dr. William Gaines's near New Bridge. Edwin C. Bearrs, "'… Into the very jaws of the enemy…': Jeb Stuart's Ride Around McClellan" in William J. Miller ed., *The Peninsula Campaign Of 1862: Yorktown to the Seven Days*, Vol. One (Campbell: Savas Woodbury, 1997), 125. A Civil War Trails sign/marker denotes the location.
64. *OR*, XI, pt. I, 46-47, 49, 189.
65. Id. 188.
66. *Olmsted Papers*, 367 n.19.
67. Id. 30-31.

Despite such insubordination, Tripler authorized Olmsted later in the month to proceed with patients from the White House and Yorktown hospitals aboard two vessels to New York. He understood that the Commission secretary had only a limited viewpoint of the overall medical program.[68]

For Olmsted, his part of the relationship was marked by a growing appreciation for his counterpart. In September, he had concluded that Tripler ought to be replaced—after literally days on the job. On May 3, the secretary wrote that the Medical Director "seems to have been badly used" by the Army's Surgeon-General "and by the Q.M. Dept." Serious "deficiencies" thus were not his fault.[69] Both men recorded how supplies for the Campaign had been left inexplicably behind, and how new shipments to the Peninsula were delayed.[70] On May 18, Olmsted noted that "I found him, as I always do, when I came to reason with him, very sensible." Olmsted had come to recognize that unfolding events deranged his careful plans and urged his fellows to appreciate the need for flexibility—a recognition of how the conduct of a war is not the same as implementing a plan for, say, a park.[71] The two jointly wrote recently appointed Surgeon-General Hammond for approval and creation of a hospital for six thousand at White House to be "sent here from Washington."[72] In reply, Hammond scolded Tripler instead of providing support—something he would extend without quibbling to the next Medical Director of the Army of the Potomac.[73] Olmsted's conclusion: "I believe that the Surgeon General

---

68. *OR*, XI, pt. I, 188. Tripler's exact words: "if civilians are allowed to have anything to do with military matters confusion cannot be avoided. They see things only from their own limited standpoint, will form and act upon their own opinions, and in ninety-nine cases in one hundred go wrong."
69. *Olmsted Papers*, 317.
70. Id. 334; *OR*, XI, pt. I, 199-200.
71. *Olmsted Papers*, 340, 349-350,
72. Id. 335, 337 n.4, 344. Later, breakdowns in the telegraph between the front (Tripler) and the receiving points (Olmsted) led to confusion and misunderstanding. Id. 362-363.
73. Id. 341-342 n.2.

is wrong."⁷⁴ He hoped that Hammond would show better judgment and concomitant action "pretty soon."⁷⁵

The situation proved several hard truths. McClellan had not made plans carefully enough or communicated them appropriately as to the medical aspects of his Campaign. The quickly made arrangements to ship an army of over one hundred thousand men, with all of its support, fell short of arranging for waterborne transportation of the sick and wounded. And the Washington bureaucracy, whether led by Finley or Hammond, was not fully sympathetic to conditions at the front. The Commission had been authorized to aid the Army, whose central leadership allowed more and more responsibility to be thrust upon the volunteers.

A special case concerned the Custis-Lee plantation house on the Pamunkey. According to one contemporary, "[t]he young gentlemen of the Sanitary Commission coveted the house, and complaints were made because they could not get it for a hospital."⁷⁶ That complaining made its way to Washington, and the Commission's friendlies in Congress and the media made hay with McClellan's protection of the property: he was coddling secessionists, not preserving a historic property meaningful for posterity. On June 16, the US House of Representatives passed a resolution demanding Stanton explain why the structure had been placed off limits.⁷⁷ Tripler was assigned to prepare a report for McClellan, involving an inspection on June 20 and a letter submitted on June 22. His assessment: it was not worth the investment, and it might be unhealthy:

---

74. Id. 344.
75. Id. 351, 353-354. His complaints about Hammond continued well into June. Id. 369-370.
76. F. Colburn Adams, *The Story of a Trooper, With Much of Interest Concerning the Campaign on the Peninsula, Not Before Written* (New York: Dick & Fitzgerald, 1865), 457-458. Adams observed: "The good intentions of these gentlemen were not always advanced with good judgment." Id. 458.
77. *Congressional Globe*, 37th Congress, 2nd Session, 2738-2739. The sponsor was Congressman John F. Potter of Wisconsin, whose wife served as a hospital volunteer at the nation's capital in conjunction with the Sanitary Commission.

The cellar is dark, damp, and foul, and, in my opinion, should of itself forbid the occupation of the house as a hospital. The greatest number of sick the house can accommodate is, then, 24, leaving no room for the nurses. The outbuildings are entirely unfit for hospital purposes.[78]

This vignette, by itself, should have endeared the Medical Director to McClellan.[79] It also demonstrated Tripler's lodestar: not political considerations, but good medicine.

On the same day that Tripler visited the White House, the Adjutant-General recorded the strength of the Army he served. The "present for duty equipped" total was 114,691. The difference in the numbers of sick and otherwise not available, compared to April 1, had increased by only 3,377.[80] By then, Olmsted had arrived at a new opinion. "The horror of war," for which his civilian life left him unprepared, had proven "far beyond all imagination." His level of anxiety had grown to be, candidly, "almost beyond endurance." He feared the outcome of the next battle—perhaps ten thousand would bleed or starve to death before aid arrived. He despaired of both Hammond and Tripler. Olmsted longed for order.[81]

By contrast, the Medical Director showed his openness to opportunities for improvement. He sought the opinions of subordinates via issuance of a circular on June 18. He asked "the whole body of the medical officers for their opinions and advice" on whether anything else needed to be done for the condition of the Army. The replies he received were gratifying: "nothing of any consequence had been left undone that the medical department could do. Better shelter for the men, less work, and in a few instances new clothing, were all

---

78. *OR*, XI, pt. I, 186, 190, 205–206.
79. Another accrued from Tripler's commendations of the General's cousin, Dr. Ely McClellan (1834–1893) who served as aide. Id. 196. He was son of Dr. Samuel McClellan (1800–1854), the younger brother of Dr. George McClellan (1796–1847).
80. *OR*, XI, pt. III, 238–239.
81. *Olmsted Papers*, 368–370, 375.

that seemed to be wanting."[82] A visitor reported being "pleased with what he saw" upon a medical survey trip of the Army: physicians and nurses ("both male and female") were competent, camps were sanitary, drainage was appropriate, and the ten general hospitals needed little improvement.[83]

A neutral observer, the *Medical and Surgical Reporter*, provided a running account of efforts by medical personnel to provide care on the Peninsula. In its June 7th edition, it opined that Tripler's "care of the sick is deserving of the highest commendation."[84] His attention to the wounded also showed keen concern for their welfare and "evinced the highest degree of administrative ability."[85]

McClellan appeared to have led his Army to the brink of victory, despite criticism over the pace of its overall movement. The Rebels had withdrawn into their defensive works, and he was on the verge of taking Richmond. McClellan seemed, however, to be unprepared for the human cost of this war. Perhaps such an aversion influenced his approach to military medical matters. In letters to his wife, candid thoughts revealed a General hopeful of a fairly bloodless culmination:

> It is possible that yesterday's victory will open Richmond to us without further fighting. (June 2, 6:30 p.m.)
>
> I am tired of the sickening sight of the battlefield, with its mangled corpses & poor suffering wounded! Victory has no charms for me when purchased at such cost. (June 2, 8:00 p.m.)
>
> Have been as usual very quiet today—lying down almost all the time & leaving my tent scarcely at all. ... I can't afford to have any more men killed than can be avoided. (June 6, 10:00 p.m.)

---

82. *OR*, XI, pt. I, 189.
83. Gillett, 184.
84. *Medical and Surgical Reporter*, Vol. XIII, No. 10 (June 7, 1862), 255.
85. Id. 303–304 (June 21, 1862).

>Whenever I feel discouraged by adverse circumstances … the sight of poor human suffering—all these things *will* force the mind to seek rest above. (June 10, 7:30 a.m.)
>
>I feel too that I must not unnecessarily risk my life—for the fate of my army depends upon me and they all know it. (June 22, 3:00 p.m.)
>
>You may be sure that no man in this army is so anxious as its General to finish the campaign—every poor fellow that is killed or wounded almost haunts me! (June 23, 10:30 p.m.)[86]

The commanding General's reaction is surprising for a military man who had already seen the effects of combat. It would be completely understandable of a civilian, like the Commission volunteers. Casualties were "the dark side of glory, the not-so-thrilling aspect of battle." Scenes near the action could repel those unaccustomed to their horror: "degraded are the wounded as they lie shattered and helpless on or near a festering battlefield, immobilized in pools of hardening blood and vermin-filled bodily excrements."[87] Bearing responsibility to care for a multitude of "soldiers who had been cut and maimed and crushed" by battle, with "each man's wound bleeding like that of his suffering neighbor, and each demanding the attention of the overwrought surgeons," could overwhelm the unprepared. Just as were the maimed men who had fought, those who administered care—the doctors and nurses especially—were heroes in their own way, writing in blood a testament to selflessness:

>It is a story of Americans coping against almost insurmountable odds for the common good. It is the story of hundreds

---

86. Sears, *The Civil War Papers of George B. McClellan*, 287-306. The General's health is touched on in the Appendix.
87. Gregory A. Coco, *A Vast Sea of Misery: A History and Guide to the Union and Confederate Field Hospitals at Gettysburg, July 1-November 20, 1863* (El Dorado: Savas Beatie, 2017), viii.

and thousands of acts of individual kindness, of bravery and courage, of charity and love, faithfulness and patriotism.[88]

As one novice surgeon put it: "Since coming here death has faced me at every turn and in every conceivable form ...."[89]

Perhaps the expectation that the Army could proceed to and capture Richmond via siege operations had led McClellan to underestimate the need for a plan to handle large numbers of wounded. Up to June 25, Tripler had to deal with casualties on the following order of magnitude, per reports:

April 17 and 26: 32 killed, 112 wounded
May 4: 3 killed, 28 wounded
May 5: 460 killed, 1,474 wounded
May 9: 49 killed, 131 wounded
May 27: 62 killed, 210 wounded
May 31: 3,500 wounded
June 8: 4 killed, 23 wounded

These patient counts, though each individual held importance, had proved manageable. As Tripler would later summarize, though, "from this time events hurried on with great rapidity" in the aftermath of Seven Pines.[90]

Time ticked away against the Union juggernaut. On the 26th of

---

88. Kathleen Georg Harrison, "Foreword," id. vi-vii. An account of several weeks of nursing work by a famous female author in a Washington hospital records treatment of Union wounded from the Battle of Fredericksburg—described as "wrecks of humanity"—requiring her to "cork" up her courage. Louisa May Alcott, *Hospital Sketches* (Boston: James Redpath, 1863), 34. She also wrote of the professionalism of surgeons, id. 42-43, 45, 56, 96-101, of the use of ether, id. 96, of a case of PTSD, id. 51, of a soldier's dying, id. 54-65, and of grief, id. 92-93.
89. Martha Derby Perry ed., *Letters from a Surgeon of the Civil War* (Boston: Little, Brown & Co., 1906), 6. John G. Perry was a volunteer contract assistant surgeon stationed at Chesapeake Hospital in Hampton, Va., near Fortress Monroe.
90. *OR*, XI, pt. I, 190.

June, the Rebels took the initiative under a new commander, Robert E. Lee, who attacked on the very day McClellan "had decided as the time for our final advance." The turnabout, said Little Mac, "turned my attention to the protection of our communications and depots of supply."[91] Over the next week, in the Seven Days Battles, practically each set of daylight hours brought fierce fighting. Lee sought to destroy, not merely defeat McClellan. He drove the Union commander into, rapidly and under duress, a change of base from White House on the York/Pamunkey rivers to the James.[92] Although none of the battles involved a disgrace such as First Bull Run, and only the Battle of Gaines Mill could be tallied in the Confederate win column, McClellan continued to retreat regardless of each day's outcome. In particular, his Army's overwhelming success at the Battle of Malvern Hill on July 1 failed to alter his flight to the safety of a new base behind entrenchments at Harrison's Landing.[93]

The casualty count might have been quite different. At Gaines's Mill, McClellan essentially left his V Corps to fend for itself against the bulk of Lee's army. He sent minimal reinforcements, retaining four corps on the south side of the Chickahominy. He had several options, one of which being to "hold with his right and attack to capture Richmond" now that all his forces were on the same side once V Corps came over. Lee's army was divided; he was on exterior lines; his force in front of the capital was outnumbered. Instead, with a "defense-retreat state of mind," McClellan forsook possibilities that might have retrieved the initiative and, through a turn of events,

---

91. Id. 51.
92. Very early on, critics asserted that McClellan should have planned for such a change. E.g., William Swinton, *Campaigns of the Army of the Potomac* (New York: Charles B. Richardson, 1866), 140-141. The earliest he appears to have taken steps to achieve it is as a result of Stuart's ride around the Union Army between June 12 and 18. Bearss, 142. Abandoning the York River line also lengthened the distance of McClellan's army and separation from the Union Army of Virginia under Major-General John Pope.
93. Eunice Tripler's cousin, Henry J. Hunt, first came to real prominence here.

compacted casualties into a single thrust at Richmond.[94] Indeed, some highly capable officers believed McClellan intended such a gambit.[95] Confederate President Jefferson Davis feared and expected McClellan to attack the "small force" that was "too weak" to defend Richmond during Lee's advance.[96] Confederate trenchworks around Richmond "at that time were very slight."[97] In that case, Tripler would have been attending to casualties in a diametrically different context. Had the Army of the Potomac gained Richmond through the "sacrifice at Gaines' Mill of 7,000 men," such losses were warranted.[98]

It was a startling turn of events. Hearing no update from McClellan, the President and the Secretary of War believed on June 29 that he "will probably be in Richmond within two days."[99] Even along the James River route, Northern papers still expected McClellan to move on Richmond.[100] The outcome launched Lee's reputation as the preeminent Southern commander. It contributed to McClellan's downfall, especially when his raw emotions came to light. At noon on the 26th, he had telegraphed Stanton that "you may not hear from me for several days," that he would need to resort to "desperate measures," yet not to despair if Yorktown was reoccupied by Rebels.[101] A message at 9:00 p.m. ended with: "I almost begin to think we are invincible."[102] At 8:00 p.m. on the 27th, his communique contained ominous

---

94. Matt Spruill, *Decisions of the Seven Days: The Sixteen Critical Decisions That Defined the Operation* (Knoxville: University of Tennessee Press, 2021), 46, 49-50, 96-97.
95. Alexander S. Webb, *The Peninsula: McClellan's Campaign of 1862* (New York: Charles Scribner's Sons, 1882), 187.
96. Jefferson F. Davis, *The Rise and Fall of the Confederate Government*, Vol. II (New York: D. Appleton & Co., 1881), 132.
97. Daniel H. Hill, "Lee's Attacks North of the Chickahominy" in *Battles & Leaders*, Vol. II, 362.
98. Webb, 187.
99. *OR*, XI, pt. III, 274-276. Stanton even believed the war could soon be over. Id. 277. He soon revised his estimate but continued in the belief that Richmond could be taken. Id. 281.
100. *Harpers Weekly*, July 12, 1862, 435.
101. *OR*, XI, pt. I, 51-52.
102. *OR*, XI, pt. III, 260.

overtones: "attacked by greatly superior numbers in all directions," with "the odds" being "immense."[103] From Savage's Station at 12:20 a.m. on June 28, he telegraphed Stanton perhaps the most insubordinate conclusion to an Army commander's message in American military history:

> If I save this army now, I tell you plainly that I owe no thanks to you or to any other persons in Washington.
> You have done your best to sacrifice this army.[104]

On the 30th, McClellan posited that "none of us" might escape.[105] The mindset reflected "a commander thinking solely of defense" and retreat,[106] who had no awareness of the effects of his loss of will on an increasing casualty tab requiring the emergency provision of medical care.

Events did hurry on, but the change of base could have been planned and implemented in a much more coordinated manner, one that would have conserved medical supplies and preserved health and lives better. Evidence is absent that McClellan brought the Medical Director into his thinking. He had "made arrangements" as early as June 18 to "have transports with supplies of provisions and forage" shipped up the James River to Harrison's Landing.[107] But for someone so acclaimed as an organizational expert, the lack of foresight caused 100,000 soldiers, 300 artillery pieces, 4,000 wagons, 2,500 head of cattle, and tens of thousands of horses to wind their way over narrow,

---

103. Id. 266.
104. *OR*, XI, pt. I, 51-52; 61. The sentences were deleted by the military supervisor of the telegraph from the copy delivered to the Secretary of War; this edit came to light once McClellan's official report became public in mid-1863.
105. *OR*, XI, pt. III, 280.
106. Spruill, 46.
107. *OR*, XI, pt. I, 52. The main supply wharf was actually located at Westover Plantation to the east. John M. Coski, *The Army of the Potomac at Berkeley Plantation: The Harrison's Landing Occupation of 1862* (self-pub., 1989), 28, inside back cover.

muddy, swamp-fringed, and crooked roads to the new base—which would house not just the Army's supplies but its men as well. The consequence for the medical staff: "It is no wonder that rates of illness rose dramatically during the Seven Days' campaign."[108]

The week of battles proved bloody; Union losses totaled 15,855: 1,734 killed; 8,066 wounded; 6,055 missing or captured.[109] These figures were on a par with the Battle of Shiloh, which had shocked the North with its two-day butcher's bill. McClellan had convinced himself of being overwhelmingly outnumbered, estimating Lee's force in the vicinity of 180,000 present for duty equipped.[110] The Confederates had half that force; on the south bank of the Chickahominy, the Union forces grossly outnumbered the enemy. Another outcome was abandoning the wounded who were incapable of evacuation, plus their caregivers, relegating them to prisoner of war experiences.

Where was Olmsted? Understandably, he took shelter aboard a stateroom in one of the Commission vessels, the *Wilson Small*, moored at Hampton Roads at the east end of the James Peninsula. He described the departure from White House as "the skedaddle of the Pamunkey," descriptive of a sudden, unplanned, disorganized affair.[111] Olmsted did not blame McClellan; instead, he adopted the General's complaint that insufficient strength, compared to Lee's numbers, had led to the situation. The Commission representative soon turned his principal energies to the political arena, seeking to lobby all the way up to the President for reinforcements to the Army of the Potomac that he saw necessary to enable resumption of the Campaign. In this, he concurred with the incoming Medical Director of that Army in estimating total Union casualties at 30,000 during the Seven Days. All three held to the view that the Rebels outnumbered McClellan's Army, which was false.

---

108. Browning, *The Seven Days' Battles*, 86.
109. Sears, *To the Gates of Richmond*, 344-345; *OR*, XI, pt. II, 24-41.
110. *OR*, XI, pt. I, 51. In some writings he asserted Lee had a force of at least 200,000.
111. *Olmsted Papers*, 381-384.

Like Olmsted, a civilian, McClellan's locations during the Seven Days were not at the front, not always with his headquarters. At one point he rode off to scout for a new base along the James, reaching Haxall's Landing from which he boarded the USS *Galena*.[112] He again took shelter on the ship early in the day on July 1, departing Haxall's to steam down to Berkeley Plantation at Harrison's Landing where he found the environs more suitable for the terminus of the retreat.[113] The *Wilson Small* made its appearance there on July 3.[114] Tripler had no similar sanctuary. He accompanied the move of headquarters to Savage's Station on the 28th, where the wounded from Gaines Mill had been brought via ambulance. All who could help were pressed into service to attend to the wounded, some 2,500 in number at "the great hospital."[115] In the afternoon, Tripler was ordered to abandon the post and go overland to Harrison's. Only about half of the patients were capable of moving on their own, and orders were to leave behind those not able to walk. One soldier described the Army's action as "[t]urning their backs upon the battle-field and the hospital camp"—leaving the Union casualties, along with "medical men, surgeons, and attendants, who remained behind, to the number of 500," to be captured by the Confederate advance.[116] Because of the hastened retreat, a less than appropriate supply of hospital stores existed; the rest, an immense quantity that a Rebel officer characterized as "hard to realize" in its volume, fell into enemy hands.[117] McClellan's "failure

---

112. A location on the James River east of Turkey Island Creek and due south of the Malvern Hill battlefield. *OR Atlas*, Plate XIX-1. The *Galena* was an armor-plated screw steamer; McClellan's shipboard time included a meal with fine wine. Browning, *The Seven Days' Battles*, 106; Sears, *To the Gates of Richmond*, 280, 283; *OR*, XI, pt. I, 67.
113. Browning, *The Seven Days' Battles*, 132. The channel at Haxall's was narrower and on the southern, more exposed side of the river. Coski, 3.
114. *Olmsted Papers*, 384.
115. Webb, 141.
116. Warren L. Goss, *Recollections of a Private: A Story of the Army of the Potomac* (New York: Thomas Y. Crowell & Co., 1890), 62; Webb, 141.
117. *OR*, XI, pt. III, 272-273; Terry L. Jones, "Down the Peninsula with Richard Ewell: Captain Campbell Brown's Memoirs in the Seven Days Battles" in Miller, *The Peninsula Campaign*, Vol. II, 57. Other field hospitals besides Savage's were abandoned. Id. 59.

to evacuate large stores of supplies"—including numerous "stockpiles" of medicine—unnecessarily jeopardized the preservation of his force.[118] Tripler had stockpiled those stores, and the hasty withdrawal destroyed any chance to secure them.

A contemporaneous description of the rail station field hospital tracks a famous photo:

> Savage's Station is a point on the Richmond and York river railroad, about seven miles from Richmond, within a few yards of which Mr. Savage has a fine dwelling house, surrounded by a beautiful sloping green sward, shaded with large oaks, and inclosed by a paling. There are in addition, adjoining the family residence, negro quarters, barns, and sheds, twelve or fourteen in number; all together being sufficient to accommodate 500 men. Within a short distance is an ample supply of water.[119]

The image was snapped by one of Matthew Brady's photographers, James F. Gibson. How many of these wounded warriors ended up as prisoners-of-war—or the additional number that were left "by the road-side" during the hurried and disorganized retreat—can only be imagined. But it was not Tripler who bore responsibility for their fate.[120]

Here, surgeons sought to save the lives of mangled Union soldiers. One account regards Swinburne, who had received responsibility for the hospital and aid from Tripler for its staffing. The doctor in charge identified the team of doctors who aided him personally "in my surgical labors"—including Tripler himself, among several who "assisted me very materially in the necessary surgery." Swinburne was hailed

---

118. Dougherty & Moore, 159-160.
119. *American Medical Times*, 117 (Aug. 30, 1862).
120. Swinton, 156; https://www.battlefields.org/learn/articles/through-cameras-lens-savage-station ; *OR*, XI, pt. II, 469, 556, and another 350 sick and wounded were captured at White Oak, id. 557, 627. See Appendix.

as a hero for his conduct.[121] Concerned about the welfare of those to be abandoned by the Army, Tripler—with McClellan absent—wrote a letter directly to the "Commanding General Confederate Forces" about the situation. Addressed from "Headquarters Army of the Potomac," the communication appealed to the better angels of Lee's nature:

> Dr. Swinburne, a volunteer surgeon, with a number of other surgeons, nurses, and attendants, have been left in charge of the sick and wounded of this army who could not be removed. Their humane occupation commends itself under the law of nations to the kind consideration of the opposing forces. It is requested that they may be free to return as soon as the discharge of their duties with the sick and wounded will permit, and that the same consideration shown to the Confederate sick, wounded, and medical officers that have been captured by our forces may be extended to them. A large amount of clothing, bedding, medical stores, &c., have been left both at Savage Station and Dr. Trent's house.[122]

The fluid nature of the situation complicated Tripler's duties on the retreat. He then followed with the Army to Haxall's Landing before finally reaching the James River base. On July 2, Tripler began loading the wounded aboard the hospital vessels that had arrived. The operation was ordered to cease so that supplies for the Army—subsistence and ordnance—could be brought ashore. Still, Tripler worked to ensure everything possible was done for the comfort of the wounded, including provision of tea, coffee, soup, and stimulants. His own reserve supplies, which he had brought with him during the withdrawal, proved sufficient until the stores aboard ship could be

---

121. *American Medical Times*, 151 (Sept. 13, 1862).
122. *OR*, XI, pt. I, 191. Notably, Tripler did not refer to the "Confederate States of America."

unloaded.[123] There would have been no need for concern as to medical supplies, patently close enough to the frontlines that many went up in smoke, had a more orderly withdrawal been ordained.[124] Watching their own pillars of smoke as they trudged away from the very outskirts of Richmond sapped the spirits of many below McClellan. They did not understand why repeated repulses of the Confederates translated into continuous retreat, and their dispiritedness made them more susceptible to disease. The retreat after Malvern Hill especially demoralized the army, and a pouring rain exacerbated this effect:

> Upon arriving at Harrison's Landing, the army occupied a four-mile-wide and one-mile-deep position backed up to the James River. ... Ninety thousand troops, 288 guns, 3,000 wagons and ambulances, 2,500 beef cattle, and 27,000 horses and mules were packed into this space. This crowding would soon cause sanitation and medical problems.[125]

Was the condition of the Army of the Potomac on the Peninsula dire? One Commission leader personally visited a "full" regiment "upon the Chickahominy, during the severest" days of the Campaign, to find "but four men sick in general and regimental hospitals." To be fair, the observation likely predated the Seven Days. The credit for health was claimed by the Commission, of course, because in July 1861 it had embedded two staffers to teach this regiment "the art of preparing

---

123. *McClellan's Own Story*, 423; OR, XI, pt. I, 191.
124. Brian K. Burton, *Extraordinary Circumstances: The Seven Days Battles* (Bloomington: Indiana University Press, 2011), 203, 225.
125. Spruill, 83. Tripler could well have expected a successful outcome to the operation; at the commencement of the Peninsula Campaign, "the rebel cause was at its lowest ebb" over the preceding twelve months, and until the end of June "there were few commanding officers of the Army of the Potomac who did not expect to be led offensively against the enemy." So said the Chief Engineer of the Army of the Potomac. OR, XI, pt. I, 129; John G. Barnard, *The Peninsular Campaign and Its Antecedents* (New York: D. Van Nostrand, 1864), 43, is an even more unvarnished view of McClellan's leadership by this observer. See n.418 *infra*.

army rations."[126] The broader *programme* instituted by the Medical Bureau during the next year apparently counted for little. The month of June may have been the "sickliest" of the Campaign, compounded by the Army's "supply nightmare, which prevented adequate amounts of quinine from reaching regimental surgeons" despite Tripler's advocacy within the War Department since May 29.[127]

A total of 8,000 wounded in a single week would not be the largest set of casualties during the War. A comparable total happened in the two days at Shiloh. More than 9,000 wounded would be produced by the single bloodiest day at Antietam. The three days of Gettysburg would yield some 15,000 wounded. The Seven Days involved a different set of circumstances: the Army of the Potomac retreated on successive days, adding to its casualty list on each, shifting its location, and requiring adapted procedures to handle the wounded. The morale of the Army reached its nadir on the bank of the James River, with many—officers and enlisted—still holding the conviction that McClellan's force had the capability to take Richmond, if only its leader agreed.

Just what was the proportion of sick after the Seven Days? It was the highest during all of the months of the Army's existence, more than 15 percent. The number had increased by a half in only three weeks, likely due to almost daily fighting and the crowding into a narrow, confined, and swamp-fringed space.[128] The figure had been under 10 percent on June 20.[129] Still, McClellan retained nearly 90,000 soldiers under his command who were healthy and could again be roused for

---

126. *Succinct Narrative*, 17–18.
127. Bell, 73-74. Had McClellan "moved more quickly or begun his campaign earlier in the year, it is unlikely that his army would have suffered as many disease casualties as it did." Id. 74.
128. *OR Atlas*, Plate XIII-3. This image is worth many words.
129. *OR*, XI, pt. III, 238–239. Miller's article on logistics (see n.585) incorrectly states that over 25,000 men were on the sick list before the Seven Days (at 166) but correctly cites 16,619 on the sick list as of July 14, when the Army was bottled up at Harrison's Landing.

"On to Richmond."[130] Their leader, however, had no stomach for it in those first days of July 1862.

On Capitol Hill, the reaction from members intent both on smashing the Rebellion and eradicating slavery was swift and harsh. One Republican Senator, Zachariah Chandler, ripped McClellan as an imbecile and traitor. At a Cabinet meeting at the White House, Stanton and Secretary of the Treasury Salmon P. Chase "lambasted" the "young Napoleon" and pressed Lincoln to replace him with a General of greater moral fortitude.[131] Political conflict was ever present. McClellan had courage enough to offer the Administration unsolicited advice on broad war policy, and inside of two years he would run as a Democrat against Lincoln for the Presidency.[132]

The Peninsula Campaign had been "a chapter of blunders."[133] Within a month, its chief Union strategist was withdrawing his Army north to help defend the US capital while its Medical Director confronted a sick list approaching 12,500 soldiers.[134] But it was not Dr. Tripler who faced that challenge. He had turned over responsibilities to a successor, Dr. Jonathan Letterman, on July 3-4. Unlike the

---

130. *OR*, XI, pt. III, 321.
131. Gary W. Gallagher, "A Civil War Watershed: The 1862 Richmond Campaign in Perspective" in Gary W. Gallagher ed., *The Richmond Campaign of 1862: The Peninsula and the Seven Days* (Chapel Hill: University of North Carolina Press, 2000), 16.
132. On June 20, as his concentration most likely ought to have been on taking Richmond, McClellan asked if he could set before the President his views "as to the present state of military affairs throughout the whole country." *OR*, XI, pt. I, 48. On July 7, after the retrograde movement, he proffered them in a letter to Lincoln, even though "they do not strictly relate to the situation of this army or strictly come within the scope of my official duties." Id. 73-74.
133. James F. Rhodes, "The First Six Weeks of McClellan's Peninsular Campaign" in *The American Historical Review*, Vol. I, No. III (New York: Macmillan Co., 1896), 464, 466.
134. Richard B. Irwin, "The Administration in the Peninsular Campaign" in *Battles & Leaders*, Vol. II, 435, 437; *OR*, XI, pt. I, 80-81, 191. One survivor noted that "about 15 per cent. of the duty men, were sick in the camp hospital July 24th." George L. Kilmer, "The Army of the Potomac at Harrison's Landing" in *Battles & Leaders*, Vol. II, 427–428.

temporizing engaged in by his commander,[135] Tripler again showed decisiveness. He had determined to leave his post, though not the Army, and sought transfer. His hands were clean—he would write at length about fulfilling his duties—but others' were far from sanitary.

---

135. Philippe, Comte de Paris, "McClellan Organizing the Grand Army" in *Battles & Leaders*, Vol. II, 116.

The Commission's Subversion

The Army of the Potomac stood in great shape, with excellent prospects, on May 6, 1862, the day after the Rebel positions at Williamsburg fell. Tripler's prospects also seemed bright. Even though departed to the James Peninsula, accompanying the Army and out of the Washington scene, courage in being at the front should have counted. At first, it appeared that he might benefit from the vagaries of the capital labyrinth. The passage of a bill reforming the Army medical bureau meant the Administration had positions to populate. The office of Surgeon-General had to be filled; William Hammond was nominated and confirmed. The office then submitted nominees to Stanton for remaining vacancies, but he attended to other matters before taking up Hammond's suggestions. Four months into his tenure, the Secretary got around to forwarding four of the eight men suggested. Among them was Major Tripler, advanced to the President for the new post of Inspector-General of Hospitals. Attaining such a post meant a promotion, since the new position held the rank of Colonel.[1]

From subsequent events, it is clear that Tripler knew of and supported the appointment. It meant he would be leaving the Army of the Potomac, for the inspectors' task was to examine all of the armies fighting under Old Glory. His office might remain in Washington, or perhaps he would be sent to the Western Theater, closer to home. Either way, he likely would be able to spend more time with Eunice

---

1. *Statutes at Large*, Vol. XII, 378-379 (37th Congress, 1st Session, Act of April 16, 1862).

and, perhaps, the children. She had joined him for several of the most meaningful months of their lives as a wedded couple:

> In December, 1861, I went to Washington to join Dr. Tripler, and remained there till 25th March, 1862, when the Army of the Potomac moved to the Peninsula. I left all my children with my Mother in Canada. In Washington Dr. Tripler had one room only and very insufficient accommodation generally, and when my going on was mooted he wrote me that Washington was over-crowded and stricken with small-pox and had become one great military camp, but I replied that I "could roost on a lamp-post." Nearly every day in Washington I went to the Capitol to watch the progress of legislation which might affect my husband's rank — and almost every evening I went to Dr. Tripler's office, where I soon found I could be of real help. He had to affix his signature to about eighty discharges of soldiers each day, and I could and did write his name on these papers so that no one could tell his signature from mine.[2]

On Christmas Day 1862, the ninth and last child of their marriage was born. Had Father been promoted? Henry Hunt Tripler—named for the cousin and artillery officer—made his appearance in Detroit.

The medical community regarded the choice of Tripler as among the best candidates who could have been selected:

> [T]he Medical Department is placed on a new footing. Important changes must be made to give that wider scope and efficiency to its service which the Act of Congress contemplates. ... the entire Bureau of Sanitary Inspection is to be organized ... by placing at its head as eminent a representative of the Volunteer corps as now represents the Regular

---

2. *Heart in Tatters*, 64-65.

Staff at the head of the Medical Department. Many names will suggest themselves to every reader … ; while for the eight inspectorial offices the names of Coyler, Cooper, J.H. Bailey, Tripler, Vollum, of the Regular Staff, and Dalton, Clymer, Andrews, and Suckley, of the Volunteer Corps.[3]

The post would extend Tripler's expertise to the entirety of the Union Army.

As McClellan and his Army methodically made their way closer to the Confederate capital, a communication made its way up to the Capitol:

War Department
May 21, 1862

Sir: I have the honor to propose for your approbation the following named persons for appointment to the Medical Department of the United States, to fill some of the original vacancies created by the Act approved April 16, 1862:

…
Surgeon Charles S. Tripler to be medical inspector-general with the rank of colonel."

E.M. Stanton[4]

The same day, the President signed and sent his nomination letter to the Hill.[5] Although the nomination had its basis in the Secretary's recommendation, Lincoln had met and knew his nominee. In July, apart from that embarrassing episode, Tripler happened to be in Winfield Scott's office—his "quarters" or "room," given the aged

---

3. *American Medical Times*, 252 (May 8, 1862).
4. *Journal of the Executive Proceedings of the Senate*, 305.
5. Id.

warrior's ill health. President Lincoln entered, and an earnest conversation ensued between the three men.[6]

The nomination, along with the others in the package, was received on May 28 and referred to the Senate Committee on Military Affairs and Militia. The next several days occasioned the Battle of Seven Pines, another Union victory on the Peninsula. Although much attention has been placed by historians on the Joint Committee on the Conduct of the War—the so-called "War Committee"[7]—this Senate committee also played an important role in determining the conduct of the war. Its chairman was Henry Wilson of Massachusetts, one of the so-called "radical" Republicans who favored a harsh line on the Rebels, including confiscation of their property and eradication of slavery. Six other Republicans served on the committee, with only one Democrat as an active member. Not all in Wilson's caucus held radical views, but one certainly did: Chandler's fellow Senator from Michigan, Jacob M. Howard.

Howard was older than Tripler by several months. He, too, had been born out East and come to Michigan as an adult. He had been a citizen of Detroit since 1832, and his political career launched almost immediately. As a former Whig and one of the founders of the Republican Party, Howard's views on slavery were solid abolitionist. He had served a single term in the US House of Representatives before being chosen by the Michigan Senate to fill the State's vacant Senate seat in January 1862.[8] Tripler's political views were never revealed, but nothing suggests he was pro-slavery or in opposition to the Lincoln Administration.

As of June 18, three weeks from receiving the nomination package, the Military Affairs Committee had met and considered and was

---

6. Charles S. Tripler to John Crisfield, Friday, Dec. 13, 1861, Library of Congress, #13403.
7. See, e.g., T. Harry Williams, *Lincoln and the Radicals* (Madison: University of Wisconsin Press, 1941); Bruce Tap, *Over Lincoln's Shoulder: The Committee on the Conduct of the War* (Lawrence: University Press of Kansas, 1998). For the referral, see *Journal of the Executive Proceedings of the Senate*, 310.
8. http://bioguide.congress.gov/scripts/biodisplay.pl?index=H000839

ready to bring to the Senate floor its judgment on Tripler. Chairman Wilson delivered the Committee report. The recommendation: "That the Senate do not advise and consent to the appointment ...."[9] It would later be determined that Howard had played a key role in opposing Tripler for the post. According to one historian, the Sanitary Commission opposed him for not offering aid to the wounded during the Battle of Bull Run.[10] If that was the basis for rejection, it was unfounded: Tripler was miles away near Harpers Ferry.

Tripler's reaction: give up his post with the Army of the Potomac. If Congress did not see him as qualified enough to be an inspector, it obviously regarded him as inappropriate for his present job in the field. Honor was at stake, though it had been secondary since Fort Sumter. He sought the aid of a member of Congress from his birth State, asking for another posting that would be conducive to the family. Representative John B. Steele, Democrat, managed to pull strings and enable Tripler to gain transfer back to Detroit.[11] He would only need to await his front line replacement.

That process actually had been underway. On June 19, the day after the Senate voted to reject Tripler, Hammond wrote Letterman to convey news of his elevation to Medical Director of the Army of the Potomac. He did more, claiming credit for the move: "In making this assignment," Hammond bragged, he had placed his colleague "in the most arduous, responsible, and trying position you have yet occupied."[12] Hammond clearly had inside and accurate information, for not until June 23 did Special Orders No. 142 issue from the Adjutant General's office in the War Department relieving Tripler and putting

---

9. *Journal of the Executive Proceedings of the Senate*, 361.
10. Freemon, *Gangrene and Glory*, 37. A citation in this text at this place regarding Tripler erroneously provides information on Hammond. Id. 236 n.8. Elsewhere, his record receives mixed reviews. Id. 67-71, 73.
11. Steele (1814-1866) was a law graduate of Williams College in Williamstown, Massachusetts, who had served as a district attorney and judge before election to the 37th and 38th Congresses (March 4, 1861-March 3, 1865). https://bioguide.congress.gov/search/bio/S000833
12. Stouffer, 8.

Letterman into the spot.[13] The Assistant Surgeon "had apparently already formulated plans to improve the efficiency of the Medical Department," a task made productive in light of inside knowledge.[14] On June 28, Letterman arrived at McClellan's base of operations at White House.[15] The Army, however, was engaged in abandoning that facility. Not until after Malvern Hill, and the Army's retreat to Harrison's Landing, did Letterman show up at the wharf. The Seven Days Battles had run their course, and Tripler had borne the brunt. On the Fourth of July, Letterman officially relieved Tripler.[16] Entering the Army upon graduating medical school in 1849, Letterman was too late to participate in the Mexican-American War, and his posts were to various forts from Florida to California. His lack of battlefield experience might have disqualified him.[17] It paid to have allies in high places.

The announcement to the troops of Tripler's replacement issued from Army headquarters in a Special Order on July 4. It referenced the precipitating order issued by the War Department and took the occasion for a personal note:

> In carrying out the provisions of this order, the General commanding cannot omit the expression of the high appreciation in which he holds the services rendered to this army by Surgeon Tripler, and of his thanks for the zeal, energy and ability displayed by that officer in the discharge of the arduous and responsible duties of his position.[18]

---

13. ¶ 6, p. 2: Assistant Surgeon Letterman "will report in person to Major General McClellan, as Medical Director of the Army of the Potomac, to relieve Surgeon Tripler, who will then repair to Detroit for duty in that city."
14. Gillett, 190.
15. Jonathan Letterman, *Medical Recollections of the Army of the Potomac* (New York: D. Appleton & Co., 1866), 5.
16. *OR*, XI, pt. I, 191, 210.
17. Stouffer, 5.
18. *Detroit Free Press*, July 24, 1862, p. 2.

McClellan did not stop there. He also wrote Tripler a personal letter under the same date:

> My dear sir: It was with much regret and surprise that I learned you had been relieved from duty with this army, and this regret is not diminished now that the hour of your departure has arrived.
>
> It is but a matter of duty that I should express to you my entire satisfaction with the manner in which your arduous and most important duties have been performed.
>
> I am satisfied that every arrangement possible, under the circumstances, has been made to insure the comfort, safety, and recovery of the sick and wounded of this army. I doubt much whether any army, situated as this has been, was ever as well taken care of in these respects. I am confident, also, that such is the feeling of the mass of those interested, viz.: the men themselves.
>
> I know that everything possible has been done to insure the prompt care of the wounded on the field, and their rapid and comfortable removal to the rear.
>
> I regret to learn some accusations have been made against you of cruelty to the sick and wounded of certain States. This charge is simply absurd, for the reason that the nature and extent of your duties rendered it impossible for you to be brought into personal contact with individual sick, or to know any distinction of States.
>
> Regretting much that there can have been on the minds of any an impression so unfounded as that the performance of your duties has been otherwise than most creditable to yourself and beneficial to the service,
>
> I am, my dear sir,
> Ever your sincere friend.
> George B. McClellan[19]

---

19. Id. Although his sentiments appear to have been genuine, McClellan

Tripler's comrades took a similar step. A circular letter dated July 4 advised Tripler of the signatories' regret over his departure from the Army of the Potomac. Putting their names to it were Chief Engineer Barnard,[20] Seth Williams, Henry Hunt, Andrew Humphreys, Colburn, Van Vliet, Alexander S. Webb, and fifty-five other officers.[21] Webb's autograph is especially significant: an erudite eyewitness, he would write a sagacious analysis of the Campaign in which, *inter alia*, he criticized McClellan for an inadequate personal staff but complimented "the special staff departments at the army headquarters."[22]

Notice of Tripler's "retirement" from the post appeared in medical journals. One surveyed his work:

> Since the unfortunate battle of Bull Run Dr. Tripler has held this most important and responsible post, and has given to the discharge of its duties the well directed energies of an experienced mind. To arrange and systematize the medical affairs of this large department, both in camp and in field, has required constant and excessive labor amid a thousand annoyances and perplexities. But these difficulties have all been overcome, and to-day the Army of the Potomac has a better medical provision than any army in the world. In retiring from this position, we believe Dr. Tripler will carry with him the warm sympathies and kindest wishes for his future happiness of the

---

might have been dissembling. His father had been an instructor at Jefferson Medical College in Philadelphia; Letterman had received medical training there. Stouffer, 5.

20. Brigadier-General John G. Barnard (1815-882), West Point 1833 (graduated second in class, age 18), served in the Mexican-American War, as Superintendent of the US Military Academy, as key designer of the Washington defenses, and, after McClellan, as a chief aide to Grant.

21. Id. Also signing was a hero of Fort Sumter, Norman J. Hall, 1st Lieutenant of the 5th US Artillery, serving as Assistant Chief Engineer. *American Medical Times*, Aug. 2, 1862, 70.

22. Webb, 182-183.

Medical Staff of the Army, and of the volunteer surgeons who have served under his orders.[23]

Another reported his retirement from the Army of the Potomac and published "complimentary correspondence" on his tenure.[24] It also published accounts by volunteer surgeons on the cordial reception they received from Tripler and his staff, and the type of collegiality they felt and witnessed:

> We are under great obligations to Drs. Tripler and Smith. They were ceaseless in their activity. Possessing, in addition to medical skill, that energy, system, and business capacity, without which the operations of an army must be delayed, by the disorder which, to a greater or less extent, is consequent upon every battle, they provided for the disabled, sent those that could be removed in safety to the transports in the river, promptly brought order out of confusion, and yet had time to appreciate our services, and to consult for our comfort.[25]

Ironically, a post-war publication of the Commission would be in accord with these encomiums, characterizing Tripler as "one of the oldest and most experienced army surgeons."[26]

Meanwhile, Hammond was running afoul of Secretary Stanton. Part of the conflict between them arose because Hammond had recommended Letterman for the post for which the Administration had nominated Tripler. The two doctors had served together in West Virginia during the first months of the war, and Hammond had campaigned for his associate to get a plum assignment "as soon as

---

23. *American Medical Times*, 360 (June 29, 1862).
24. *Medical and Surgical Reporter*, Vol. VIII, No. 15 (July 12, 1862), 371.
25. Id., Vol. VIII, No. 19 (Aug. 9, 1862), 441-442.
26. U.S. Sanitary Commission, *Surgical Memoirs of the War of the Rebellion*, Vol. II (New York: Hurd & Houghton, 1871) (by John A. Lidell, Frank H. Hamilton ed.), 101.

I was appointed Surgeon-General."²⁷ Letterman's appointment to the Army of the Potomac had been made over Stanton's objection and "only after some correspondence"—highly suggestive of Sanitary Commission influence.²⁸

The role of the Commission bears inquiry. Publicly, it did not pillory Tripler. Privately, and in the power avenues of Washington, its posture was altogether different. As early as the Fall of 1861—when Tripler's many changes were just getting underway—the Commission leaders, Olmsted included, were already seeking his transfer. The Commission's Secretary wanted Tripler "shipped off to Missouri" so that none other than Hammond could take his job.²⁹ The Commission had gotten the Surgeon-General post for Hammond, and it eventually got Tripler. Nothing else explains how his home Senate delegation had come to block a fellow Detroiter's advancement.

And so Tripler went home. He could have treated the assignment as nothing more than a sinecure, but it was not his nature to cheat the Government, or the public, for the compensation and benefits he received in military service. His community welcomed him home, and his cause was not laid aside. On July 24, under the headline "The Attack on Dr. Tripler," the *Detroit Free Press* expressed surprise at the outcome of the appointment process:

> …it is passing strange that his friends in the Senate should have allowed him to be rejected upon the false charge that he was not attentive to the sick and wounded of the army.³⁰

Such a sentiment accorded with its judgment when news of Tripler's rejection had come. On June 18, the *Free Press* had first expressed its shock. Though it was no fan of the President, it praised Lincoln for

---

27. Hammond, 8.
28. Id.
29. Ira M. Rutkow, *Bleeding Blue and Gray: Civil War Surgery and the Evolution of American Medicine* (New York: Random House, 2005), 92.
30. *Detroit Free Press*, July 24, 1862, 2.

sincerely discharging his duty to appoint a highly capable surgeon for Army Inspector-General:

> His qualifications are undoubted. For more than thirty years he had been connected with the army, had served in every campaign and under every General of distinction in the army during that long period. So pre-eminently fitted is he for the place, that as soon as the act was passed creating the office all eyes were turned to him as the person best qualified to discharge the duties required of the Inspector General.[31]

At that juncture, the newspaper found it strange that the Senate had turned down his appointment. "Why?" it asked; the nominee "and his friends and the public have in vain endeavored to ascertain what reasons influenced the Senate to reject him." It did have a clue: "all that is known is, that one of our Senators was engaged in a crusade against General McClellan, the other, Hon. Jacob M. Howard, made it his special business to procure the rejection of Surgeon Tripler."[32] If, indeed, Howard had become "the chief actor in this drama," the paper questioned both his motives and the source of whatever justification he had to squash the nomination.

A year later, the drama came to light in detail. Howard wrote to the other newspaper, the *Detroit Advertiser & Tribune*, an outlet more in tune with his politics. On July 2, 1863, the *Free Press* reacted to his explanation. Howard had revealed (1) the source of his "facts" had been within the Army itself, and (2) Sanitary Commission members had lobbied against the appointment. The *Free Press* published in full Tripler's reply to Howard's letter. He had quoted the Senator as having alleged: "The sickness and sufferings of the troops before Yorktown, were notorious, and everything betokened from the first the necessity of the utmost care and foresight of the Medical Corps." But that

---

31. Id. June 18, 1862, 2.
32. Id.

had not transpired. Instead, "the Sanitary Commissions of the various States were active, devoted and energetic in their humane efforts to alleviate the sufferings of the sick, who were dying by hundreds daily in the damp mud and malaria of that ill starred siege." There it was: Tripler had been one of McClellan's own during the too-slow campaign. He was guilty by association. And by fake news: "dying by hundreds" was patently false, but it was information Howard received from what he thought was a reliable source: "he obtained his information direct from the Surgeon General's office"—from Hammond, the Commission's agent.[33]

What role had F.L. Olmsted played while he and Tripler were on the Peninsula? On Wednesday, April 30, 1862, Olmsted reported to his colleagues from Cheeseman's Creek, Virginia. His party had arrived on Sunday the 27th: "I went ashore to report our arrival to the Medical Director." It was not immediately easy to locate Tripler, for he was not sitting in camp at the York River: "…we landed on a large meadow where were a number of wall-tents, one labelled 'Office of Quartermaster's Department' &c." Apparently, the tent of the Medical Director was closer to the front. Olmsted went to Colonel Rufus Ingalls of the Quartermaster's, who got them horses, and off they rode. Arriving at Army headquarters, they were obliged to tie up their horses and proceed on foot. "We walked to the tent of the Medical Director, and just then there came another of those crashing reports [artillery]. 'They have been keeping that up all night,' said the Doctor. 'That isn't the enemy?' "Yes." "Is he so near?" "O yes! we are quite within range here." Olmsted's team had not the same familiarity with hostile fire. At this point in his correspondence to the office, Olmsted focused on general matters: "The medical arrangements seem to be deplorably insufficient. The Commission is at this time actually distributing daily of hospital supplies much more than the government.*" When later published, the added asterisk was significant; it would point to a correction: "* See Appendix A."

---

33. Id. July 2, 1863, 2; Oct. 19, 1863, 2.

Despite the "deplorable" situation, the Medical Director was not unfriendly to the Commission representatives. Olmsted recorded cordiality in dealing with "Dr. Tripler, who dined with us." Tripler aided Olmsted in the latter's dispute with a brigade surgeon. Such events suggested something other than conflict. Instead, Olmsted reported on how Tripler sought to work with the Commission:

> I saw the Medical Director at head-quarters. He seems to be in a worse boggle than ever as to the disposition of his sick. There are a great many still at Yorktown to be removed, but the work is now fairly systematized there, and the sick begin to collect here by hundreds, with a prospect of thousands, and no thought of system in disposing of them, as far as I can see. The Director has ordered us to take on men at once, but our bunks are not up, and I have promised him the Daniel Webster and Elm City, which should be here to-morrow, and can take six hundred. B. has gone down to bring up our boats from Yorktown, with all the stores that can be spared from our supply-ship. I shall try my best here to carry out the plan I have always wished to have pursued,—namely, the establishment of a large receiving hospital, from which those who really need to be sent away may be deliberately selected and transferred to proper vessels, properly equipped. During my visit this morning to the Medical Director's tent, four persons reported their arrival with sick, and were informed that there were no accommodations for them. Tents had been received, but there was no detail on hand to pitch them, and if they were pitched, there were no beds to put in them. Sickness was increasing rapidly, every case showing the influence of malaria. The Medical Director said, apparently with justice, that he had anticipated all this waste and confusion, and had made ample provision against it, but that almost none of his ordered supplies had reached him.

> By night the Daniel Webster and Elm City had come up from Yorktown, and I went up with the first, securing with some difficulty a berth for her, and began taking on the sick at once, the Medical Director being present and superintending the embarkation. He seemed to have entirely lost sight of the plan about determined upon the day before, to establish the shore receiving hospital, and was only anxious to get the sick off his hands as rapidly as possible, being appalled by their accumulation ....

Tripler even let Olmsted take control on occasion: "I wrote a memorandum of what we expected to be able to do, and got the Director to sign his approval of it."

The Commission Secretary became more sympathetic to the point of view of his counterpart: "Dr. T. says that he is pestered by volunteer surgeons, who leave their business at home to have a short holiday professional excursion, and who always expect to be put in the 'imminent deadly breach' at once. He has not tents, horses, forage, nor table-room for them. Don't let any more *surgeons* come here, if you can help it."[34] When Hammond pressed Tripler to do more in sorting out ambulance issues, Olmsted understood that the Medical Director was dependent on the Quartermaster. Even McClellan could not surmount every obstacle.[35] After Letterman replaced Tripler, "the supply and transportation problems remained" that both Hammond and Olmsted had criticized.[36]

Tripler would be forced out, and the Commission helped see to that. But Olmsted was too honorable to let history draw the wrong conclusion. He did not directly and overtly admit error, but the concession is there for any who would seek it, in the aforesaid *asterisk:

---

34. *Olmsted Papers*, 340 (emphasis in original).
35. Blustein, 61.
36. Id. 62.

APPENDIX A.

See page 23.

"The Commission is at this time actually distributing daily, of hospital supplies, much more than the government."

This refers to a temporary emergency alone, for, notwithstanding the recognized necessity for volunteer aid, it is believed that the aggregate of all hospital supplies voluntarily furnished by the people through the Sanitary Commission and otherwise, great and unparalleled as this gratuitous supply is, is but about one tenth as much as is furnished by government. This fact ought to be kept in mind, as there is a natural tendency on the part of those who are rendering volunteer aid to exaggerate the relative magnitude of their own labors, while the permanent and vastly larger provisions of government are underrated, and a habit of unjust censure indulged in, in speaking of deficiencies which have to be supplied. The character of this censure generally indicates complete ignorance: the failures of other governments when engaged in war and a careless estimate of the immense labors involved, and difficulties which invariably have to be overcome, in providing for the constant necessities and exigencies of a great army. It is the opinion of those whose sympathies with the suffering of the soldiers on the one hand, and whose careful study of facts on the other, ought to give weight to their judgments, that never before, in the world's history, was an army so well cared for in all its departments, Quartermaster's, Commissary, and Medical, and that never before, when deficiencies were discovered, were they, on an average, as speedily remedied. In every great trial, by war, of a nation, it has been found necessary to employ a very large number of men in positions of the gravest responsibility, for which they were not adapted by nature or by training. This involves, of course, not only incompetency for duties assumed, but necessarily opens a door to continued neglect of trusts, frauds, and peculations, which, under ordinary circumstances, would seem to be of stupendous magnitude. This is always a part of the cost of war, and, so far from being the peculiarity of a republican form of government, or of the present occasion, in no modern war have frauds and in efficiency of administrative service been anything like as slightly manifested in the condition and efficiency, under all circumstances, of the troops in the field; and this, whether we have regard to their food, clothing, equipments, transportation, or, finally, to the provision which has existed for the sick and wounded. The sustained average health, vigor, and good spirits of our several grand armies, in the great variety of circumstances in which they have been placed, tells of a virtue and a vital force in our people and in our institutions, which, rightly understood, should put to shame much customary cavilling of flippant critics.

...

F.L.O.[37]

Although his role as Secretary had been important, Olmsted's attention—unlike Tripler's—was not solely devoted to military medical matters. He unsuccessfully sought positions at Port Royal, South Carolina, aiding the newly freed, and as street commissioner of New York City.[38]

The attitude of other Commission personnel did not mature as did Olmsted's. Twenty-five years later, one of its prime movers published a volume of her letters during the Peninsula Campaign. She entitled one section of the book: "Powers granted to Sanitary Commission by President Lincoln and Secretary of War."[39] A "power granted" to a

---

37. *Hospital Transports: A Memoir of the Embarkation of the Sick and Wounded from the Peninsula of Virginia in the Summer of 1862* (Boston: Ticknor & Fields, 1863), 20-23, 25, 56-57, 73-73, 76, 94, 139-140.
38. *Olmsted Papers*, 20-25.
39. Katherine P. Wormeley, *The Other Side of War with the Army of the Potomac* (Boston: Ticknor & Co., 1889), v.

person or an organization typically carries with it the ability to compel, to direct, to force. The Commission's formative charter had no such contents.

Nurse Wormeley arrived off Ship Point on May 10. She first provided direct aid to soldiers, when moored off Yorktown, who were suffering from typhoid fever. Word got around that many wounded in the Battle of Williamsburg had not been treated at the front, based on the assertion of a Commission representative. When her vessel ran up the York River to West Point, it was "in obedience to a telegram from the Medical Director of the Army, requesting the Commission to take off two hundred wounded men immediately." It would appear a partnership was at work in which Tripler relied on the Commission to supplement the Army's efforts—not the other way around. The Army's morale was "splendid," she observed. She did excellent work; she also had times of "sitting idly" or "loafing," a situation not enjoyed by uniformed medical staff. On May 16, she appeared to be taxed by the previous six days, asking whether one week, or five, had passed since she left New York. Two days later, she wrote home to advise that the Army was "unprepared" and so had "flung itself" upon the Commission.[40] Wormeley concluded: "[w]hen the Peninsular campaign in Virginia opened, in 1862, it was found that the Medical Department was unable to meet the needs of an army actively employed in a low, swampy, and malarious region."[41] Statistics belied this conclusion—a letter of hers on May 24 contradicted this judgment,[42] and Olmsted's admission rebutted it. But criticism of the Medical Director did not abate, since the Commission "does all" (to quote her assertion).[43] When the Commission received harsh judgment, Wormeley bemoaned such "unjust" treatment.[44] Like Olmsted, her position during the Seven Days Battles was off Hampton Roads

---

40. Id. 16, 20, 22, 28, 30, 32, 36, 41, 55
41. Id. 13.
42. Id. 72-73.
43. Id. 101-102, 124.
44. Id. 147-148.

and Norfolk.[45] She, too, justified McClellan's retreat, and she immediately became a Letterman fan.[46]

By contrast, the judgment of an impartial observer published soon after the Campaign held to the opposite viewpoint. A Pennsylvania chaplain wrote a memoir of his experience and asked a friend, John Swinburne, to write the introduction. The frontline caregiver treated the purported ineptitude of the Medical Director and categorically rejected the calumny. Completed on July 23, 1863, Swinburne effectively penned his own memoir of medical care on the Peninsula:

> It will be recollected that the celebrated Dr. Tripler, an old army surgeon, whose most valuable works upon military surgery have justly attained a fame as world-wide as the subject itself, was Medical Director of the Army of the Potomac at that time. It has been charged that, by reason of his neglect, the Army of the Peninsula was left without many things which were absolutely requisite for the proper administration of the medical department of that army; and that thus the soldiers, worn out by the fatigues of the march, weakened by exposure to severe storms, and the dangerous miasmas of the swamps, and brought down to the hospital by disease, were literally allowed to die from want of these necessaries, when they could have been promptly obtained at any time, as it is said, upon proper call. This charge, it has occurred to me, is grossly unjust to one whose highest aim in life has been to serve his country faithfully, and make himself a useful and a shining ornament to the glorious profession he has adopted, and a lasting benefit to the human race. The office and duties of a faithful surgeon, even in civil life, is no sinecure; and when a surgeon of noblest mind and purest purpose, impelled by love of country, has chosen to abandon even the emoluments

---

45. Id. 175-176.
46. Id. 181. Wormeley's work with the ill and wounded, unlike her general observations, cannot be praised too much.

to be derived from the practice of his profession as a civilian, and is willing, for the paltry pittance allowed by Government, to assume the responsibilities and devote his utmost energies to the duties of Medical Director of an army so large as that over which Dr. Tripler had charge, it seems to me that even the pardonable anxiety of the friends of those dying under his charge is not excusable for a violation toward him of the ordinary rules of charity which are, in the "Book of Books," laid down for our conduct toward all men. It has been made apparent to me, as well by the declarations of men who were in position to know the facts, as by my own experience in the matter, that the lack of proper materials in the medical service of the army, at that time, was caused, not by the neglect of Dr. Tripler to call for them at the proper places under Government, but by the failure or inability of the Government to supply the articles he ordered.

In my own experience in the Peninsular campaign, many incidents of which are referred to in this work, by the author, in terms of praise which have afforded me the most ample and gratifying reward for all I there endured, I found it at all times difficult to obtain a sufficient supply of many materials which were absolutely necessary for the proper care and cure of the sick and wounded, and, in fact, I was many times utterly unable to obtain articles most needed; and yet I have had the most convincing proof that the Medical Director cannot be justly held responsible for this. The fault, I am convinced, laid nearer to the Government at Washington. To my mind the Surgeon-general (superior officer to the Medical Director) having the means at hand at Washington for ascertaining, if he did not know, the proportions of war the campaign was assuming,—and knowing, as he must have known, the size of the army, the dangers by which that army were beset from the effects of the climate, the character of the country, and the probabilities of battle,—was in duty bound to see that all necessary material was provided for the medical department of the service; and it would be but a sickly compliment (as it is an illy-consoling excuse) for that officer to say that, perhaps, he did not realize all the necessities of the case. And yet the fact is patent, that there was, during the whole of this campaign, a lack of supplies for the medical and hospital departments, which, without doubt, was the cause of more deaths than occurred by the other and more direct casualties of war.

It may be remarked here, in defence of Dr. Tripler, that although he has not, for a long time past, filled the office of Medical Director, yet at every battle since the removal of the army from Harrison's Landing (as I have been informed by a number of returned surgeons whose capacity and credibility cannot be questioned), the same lamentable defects in the medical service of the army have existed to a greater or less extent; as, for instance, in the location of, and supplies for, the hospital at Windmill Point, where days are said to have elapsed before necessary food and medical supplies were obtained, and a great number of our men actually died from lack of them; the medical history of the battle of Antietam, at which it is charged, by Dr. Agnew, that at least five hundred men died from the want of medical supplies; the late battle of Chancellorsville, where thousands were, it seems to me, needlessly left in the hands of the enemy, when they might and should have been transferred to the other side of the river, and there received proper surgical attendance. It is said that, after this battle, our brave wounded soldiers, in many instances, laid for days without proper (and in some cases without any) food, and with no medical relief, many of them left to the mercies of the enemy, a large number dying from sheer neglect, and many more were buried alive in fires occasioned by the contending armies in shelling the woods, and in burning the Chancellor House.

Where now rests the responsibility for all these incidents of lack of proper care and exertion in providing for the medical department of the service? Not on Dr. Tripler, certainly. If there were any faults in that gentleman's administration of the medical department of the Army of the Potomac, it seems apparent at a glance that those above him at the time, and yet in office, have not profited, or at any rate have not, for the advantage of the soldiers (who are, after all, most interested), availed themselves of and acted upon the instruction which should have been derived from the development of such faults.

Swinburne stood convinced that not one of the civilian surgeons he had served with on the ground would dispute his assessment.[47]

Ultimately, few historians have argued that the Army of the Potomac held insufficient numbers to defeat its opponent. Hardly any make the argument based on the effects of illness and disease. McClellan insisted on the numbers argument up until his death, even after it was conclusively proven that he did not confront superior numbers. But his focus was on how the Administration failed to provide him with sufficient reinforcements to overcome the odds of facing Lee's army of 200,000 effectives. He was cognizant mid-campaign that disease could sap his strength: "Delays on my part will be dangerous. I fear sickness and demoralization. This region is unhealthy for Northern men …."[48] Indeed, "the Virginia Peninsula … offered

---

47. Found in James J. Marks, *The Peninsular Campaign in Virginia* (Philadelphia: J.B. Lippincott & Co., 1864), xiii-xvi. Marks held a D.D. and served as a chaplain with the Army. His account of the scenes around Savage's Station is poignant to the extreme. Id. 189-193. Swinburne biographers extol his virtues and self-effacing grace. The Citizens' Association, *A Typical American; or, Incidents in the Life of Dr. John Swinburne* (Albany: n.p., 1888); *The National Cyclopaedia of American Biography*, Vol. VII (New York: James T. White & Co., 1897), 33. See also John Swinburne, *Reports on the Peninsular Campaign, Surgical Experience, &c.* (Albany: C. Van Benthuysen, 1863). One regimental surgeon who was a Tripler critic was George T. Stevens, *Three Years in the Sixth Corps* (Albany: S.R. Gray, 1866), 53.
48. *McClellan's Own Story*, 349.

ideal environmental and geographical conditions" for bacterial contagions.[49] The Chickahominy swamps—were they the Confederates' unseen ally, a critical factor in the failure of the Union campaign?

If so, the mastermind behind the decision to attack Richmond and its defenders via the Peninsula should have incorporated such factors into his plan. But "McClellan apparently gave little thought to the peninsula's geography and climate" and betrayed "unfamiliarity with the terrain."[50] Bad roads, wet weather, and the Chickahominy River caused the Army of the Potomac to slog its way to the gates of the Confederate capital until, on June 26, Lee turned the tables with the advance against the Union right. It was not until this point, however, that sickness diminished the capabilities of McClellan's men. When the commander penned his defense twenty years later, he did cite geography and terrain—and meddling from Washington—as crucial factors leading to the failure of his plan. If sickness had been a contributing cause, he would have mentioned it.[51] Because of the retreat to Harrison's Landing, a chaotic "rough slog" without proper food and water, many of the Union army "were on the verge of collapse."[52] As it holed up in its confined defensive position along the James River—"not a particularly healthy place"—the army in blue became more ill than it had ever been, with one in five soldiers incapacitated.[53] The same environmental conditions had plagued the Confederate army, and it did not possess the supply and medical resources that McClellan enjoyed.[54] In the end, military leaders are to be held accountable for their decisions.[55]

---

49. Judkin Browning & Timothy Silver, *An Environmental History of the Civil War* (Chapel Hill: University of North Carolina Press, 2020), 17.
50. Id. 53.
51. See McClellan, "The Peninsular Campaign", 546, McClellan mentioned how, "at the close" of the Campaign, "many thousands" were "unfitted for duty for some days by illness, demoralization, and fatigue."
52. Browning & Silver, 62.
53. Id. 64.
54. Id. 65.
55. Id. 69-70.

Plates

Charles S. Tripler, MD, Brevet Brigadier-General, US Army (posthumous).

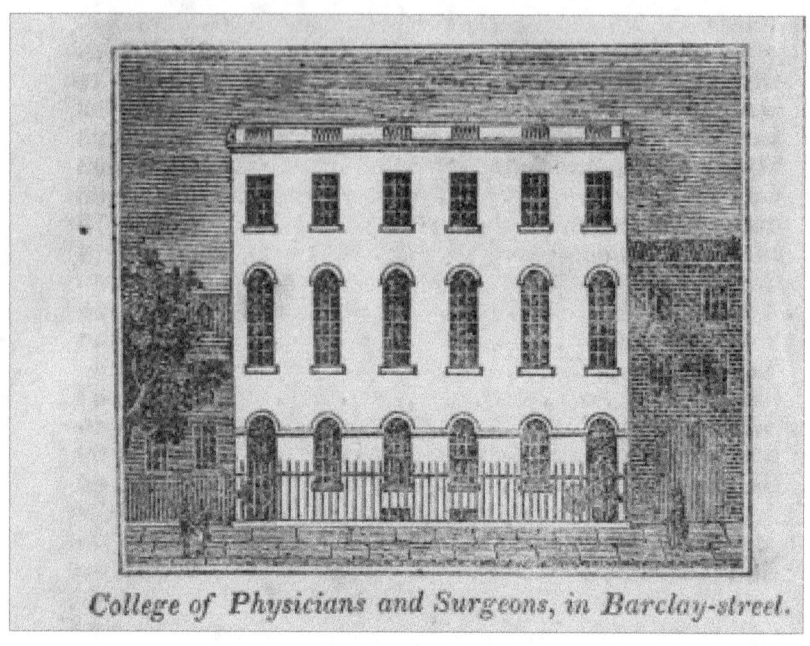

Columbia College Medical School, New York City, ca. 1828. From *History of the College of Physicians and Surgeons in the City of New York* (1888).

Dr. Tripler. From pen-and-ink sketch in the field at Sandy Hook, Md., August 9, 1861, by "Porte Crayon" (D. H. Strother).

The "Seven Buildings" Army headquarters on Pennsylvania Avenue, Washington, D.C. *Library of Congress*

Headquarters of Gen. George B. McClellan, Camp Winfield Scott, May 3, 1862, Peninsula Campaign. *Library of Congress*

Corps General Hospital near Yorktown, Peninsula Campaign. *Battles & Leaders of the Civil War*

"White House on the Pamunkey," Lee family home, converted into Union base, May 17, 1862, Peninsula Campaign. *Library of Congress*

Army of the Potomac encampment, Cumberland Landing, Virginia. *Library of Congress*

Field Hospital, James Peninsula.
The Photographic History of the Civil War, Vol. VII

View of Savage's Station area showing house and outbuildings, with barn on right where hospital was located. *Battles & Leaders of the Civil War*

Savage's Station rolling stock with hospital tents in distance, June 27, 1862. *Library of Congress*

Field hospital at Savage's Station after the battle, June 30, 1862. Close inspection reveals the brutality of war; in the foreground is an examination of a wounded soldier. *Library of Congress*

Harper Hospital, Detroit, 1865. *Burton Historical Collection*

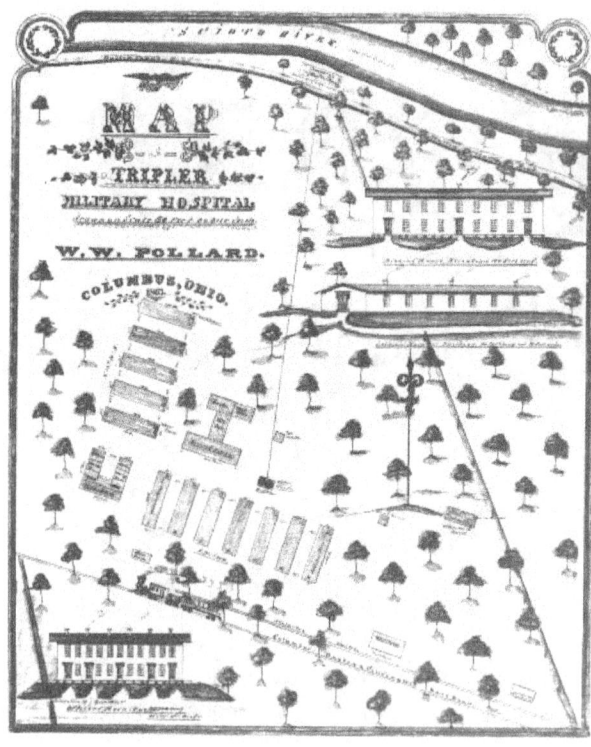

Tripler Hospital, Columbus, Ohio. *National Archives*

Tripler ambulance. *Courtesy of National Park Service*

Gravestone of Charles Stuart Tripler,
Elmwood Cemetery, Detroit. *Editor's collection*

Monument to Charles Stuart Tripler by colleagues of Army Medical Service, Elmwood Cemetery, Detroit. *Editor's collection*

Part Three
August 1862—1866

Continuing Care

Behind the Lines in the Midwest

That Tripler had not resigned from the Army underscored his commitment to soldier welfare no matter where he was assigned. He reported for duty in Detroit on August 1, 1862. His immediate charge was care of "sick and convalescents at the Hospital of Detroit Barracks."[1] Instead of a hundred thousand, his responsibility extended to a hundred or so. It left time for other activities, some personal, some official.

With a date of February 7, 1863, Tripler submitted a report on his tenure as the first Medical Director for the Army of the Potomac. The passage of seven months had enabled retrospection, review of the record, and writing. At over 40,000 words, accompanied by multiple appendices, the document was comprehensive and detailed and much more than a summary.[2] Tripler's intent was evident: this information could serve to instruct and improve medical care in the US Army. It was a candid and revealing portrayal of the problems, decisions, results, and personal challenges that Tripler experienced. He pointed to a number of achievements and relied on data to demonstrate a positive trend in the Army's health until the last week of the Peninsula Campaign. Overall, he adjudged that "the army was favored with excellent health" during the three months of his frontline leadership.

---

1. Frank B. Woodford & Philip P. Mason, *Harper of Detroit: The Origin and Growth of a Great Metropolitan Hospital* (Detroit: Wayne State University Press, 1964), 72. The Barracks were on Clinton Street just west of Elmwood Avenue, across from the historic cemetery. Id. 71.
2. Several appendices are missing in the *OR* (A-L are found in volume V; O and following in volume XI).

At the same time, he admitted falling short in certain areas. Overall, he regarded his performance as "neither a complete success nor a very decided failure." His staff had not failed.[3] He could have pointed out that Surgeon-General Hammond would give his successor "unparalleled authority" and autonomy but had denied it to him.[4]

Tripler did not refrain from criticism of the Sanitary Commission. And he was rather blunt. "Presumptuous intermeddling" driven by "uninformed zeal" had sought "to regulate" Tripler's decisions; i.e., override him. Uninvited suggestions "obtruded" on procedures that had merit and stood the test of time. The career medical officer defended Army regulations as providing needed order, rather than inflexible mistreatment of patients. Indeed, Tripler himself had shaved corners and cut "red tape" when appropriate. But the Commission higher-ups felt free to employ "a 'strong mind'" in such a way as to encourage general disregard for order. Not all of its personnel had medical training or experience, and its plans could be impractical. They also could misrepresent the state of affairs and cause unnecessary alarm. The report chided "sensation preachers, village doctors, and strong-minded women" for their overnight expertise seemingly superior to Tripler's obtained over thirty years.[5] At the same time, Tripler praised "a party of well-qualified nurses .... No more devoted band, none perhaps so much so, had ever presented themselves."[6]

Medical knowledge in 1863 did not encompass the germ theory of disease; that breakthrough would arrive later in the 19th century. Self-care and hygiene, the report argued, was the best defense against illness:

---

3. *OR*, XI, pt. I, 191-196.
4. McGaugh, 76-77.
5. *OR*, V, 89-91; XI, pt. I, 177-178, 192. Quartermaster-General Montgomery C. Meigs wrote a similar excoriation of the "[c]haritable people, men and women," who lacked experience as to scenes of horror attendant to a battlefield yet felt free to render unqualified and unjust criticisms of the War Department. *OR*, Series III, II, 698. Tripler's beloved wife ironically epitomized the "strong-minded" woman.
6. *OR*, XI, pt. I, 190.

> To bad cooking, bad police, bad ventilation of tents, inattention to personal cleanliness, and unnecessarily irregular habits we are to attribute the greater proportion of the diseases that actually occurred in the army.[7]

He acted to improve food supplies and handling, advocated for inoculation, worked hard for better conditions and better equipment. It was up to the individual soldiers, of course, whether to comply with expert advice. Sometimes, conditions might be seen to have prevented it; in one first-person account, thirst during a dusty march led soldiers to drink from a mud puddle where "in one edge of it lay a dead mule."[8]

Tripler also took steps to ensure better doctors filled the ranks of the Army medical department, and he could point to his rigorous attempts to weed out the incompetent. Some of those physicians who had given much to the service had gone even beyond. He concluded the report by commending the "conspicuous services" of aides and allies who had "well and promptly done" their duty with unfaltering zeal and unfailing ability.[9] Together, they all had sacrificed for the army.

With the report behind him, Tripler devoted attention to improving the circumstances for the care of those within his military district. In addition to those patients at the Barracks, Tripler took responsibility for the sick and the wounded at St. Mary's Hospital in Detroit. It was the city's first such institution, established in 1845 by the Sisters of Charity of St. Vincent de Paul, and located on Clinton Street near St. Antoine.[10] New wards were erected, and spare capacity was devoted to

---

7. *OR*, V, 83. Even in modern times, Civil War medical phenomena continue to be revealed, such as the account of wounded soldiers glowing after the Battle of Shiloh attributed to a parasite that is bioluminescent—not yet a completely proven incident.
8. Goss, 43.
9. *OR*, XI, pt. I, 196.
10. Later known as Detroit Memorial Hospital, the facility closed in 1987 and was demolished in 1990.

soldier care. Still, the sense was that "it could accommodate comparatively few" of those who needed to be admitted.[11] Tripler took note and forwarded to Washington a plan for a new military hospital of two hundred beds, much more accommodating to the needs of men who had served and suffered and deserved the best medical treatment then possible. The Army did not immediately act on his request.[12]

Not all of the surgeon's professional time was devoted to purely military matters. He served as a "councillor" for 1863–1864 on the board of the alumni association for his alma mater, the College of Physicians and Surgeons.[13]

In May 1863, Tripler again pressed the issue of a soldier's hospital. He wrote to Assistant Surgeon-General Wood, urging "construction of the single hospital I recommended last autumn." He noted the "good deal of feeling in this state" that Michigan had been unjustly bypassed in the creation of general hospitals. Wounded Wolverines were sent "everywhere except in Michigan." This situation undermined their recuperation since proximity to family and friends would accelerate a patient's recovery.[14]

As 1863 came to a close, regardless of the status of his hospital proposal and the war's outcome, Tripler continued to do his duty. His work on behalf of the wounded and sick was hailed as "indefatigable" and "strenuous."[15] Some observers acknowledged his continuing and unselfish service with special recognition. Before the end of the year, he was gifted with two sets of surgical instruments through subscription by admirers, who included "many of the leading citizens of Detroit" and Army comrades. The letter that accompanied

---

11. *Detroit Free Press*, Apr. 8, 1864, 1.
12. Id. Nov. 11, 1862, 1.
13. William C. Roberts, *An Address Delivered Before the Alumni Association of the College of Physicians and Surgeons, Medical Department of Columbia College, New-York, at the Spring Commencement, March 12, 1863* (New York: John A. Gray & Green, 1864), 24.
14. *Harper of Detroit*, 70-72. Not addressing the communique to Hammond speaks volumes.
15. *Detroit Free Press*, Mar. 10, 1864, 2.

the presentation was profuse in its praise.[16] It was not just hometown recognition that he received. In Spring 1864, an article appeared surveying the progress achieved in building excellence in the medical staff of the Army of the Potomac. The first Director, William King, was credited with "assiduously" laboring for an efficient operation. To the third, Jonathan Letterman, "[t]oo much praise could not be awarded" for his excellent work. What was said of the second?

> Dr. Tripler brought to the discharge of the responsible duties of reorganizing the medical department great experience, untiring zeal, and practical familiarity with every detail. He proceeded at once to introduce needed reforms, and to give them effective development. The personnel of the staff was greatly improved by the addition of brigade-surgeons, many of whom were among the most eminent civil practitioners. During the early movements of the army from Washington to the Peninsula, and onwards to the Chicahominy [sic], Dr. Tripler had to contend with and surmount obstacles of the most formidable character. At every point he met with delay and disappointment. All the appointments of this large army were then new and untried, and it required the highest order of executive ability to manage this as well as the other branches of the service. Under the circumstances, we believe, Dr. Tripler's administration was entirely successful. He received the commendation of the Commanding General, of the corps commanders, and of all who were acquainted with the details of his management.[17]

Could Tripler have served capably as the chief inspector of all US military hospitals? On December 22, 1863, he acted on a request from Lieutenant-Colonel Bennett H. Hill, the commander of the District

---

16. Id. Dec. 9, 1863, 1.
17. *American Medical Times*, Apr. 30, 1864, 211-213.

of Michigan, to look into conditions at Camp Ward. The muster location was part of the Barracks complex on the near east side of Detroit, and the troops resident there were a newly formed unit: the First Michigan Colored Infantry. Made possible by the Emancipation Proclamation and War Department orders, the regiment began recruitment in August 1863. When Tripler made his inspection, he found matters unsatisfactory—and reported so:

> The Army surgeon recommended that the sides [of barracks] be repaired with tar paper and also the roofs and then covered with sand; more windows; planed boards for the floor; brick flues for the stove pipes; decent bunks instead of bed sacks; two blankets per man because one blanket was not sufficient in this climate; and a mess room so that men will not have to eat and cook where they sleep.

The War Department responded by ordering these improvements. Tripler's role must have been gratifying to the supporters of enlisting Black troops. His conduct flew in the face of hostility to the notion of enlisting African-Americans on the part of the city's Democratic Party daily.[18]

Awaiting approval for the new hospital, Tripler pressed the matter before the Assistant Surgeon-General during a trip to St. Louis, where

---

18. Hill (1816-1886), West Point Class of 1837. *Cullum's Register*, Vol. I, 676. Norman McRae, *Negroes in Michigan During the Civil War* (Lansing: Michigan Civil War Centennial Observance Commission, 1966), 48, 58-59; Michael O. Smith, "Raising a Black Regiment in Michigan: Adversity and Triumph" in Darlene Clark Hine & Earnestine Jenkins eds., *A Question of Manhood: A Reader in Black Men's History and Masculinity*, Vol. I (Bloomington: Indiana University Press, 1999), 509, 515 n.26. Tripler's assessment was attacked by the local Army Quartermaster in the *Detroit Free Press*, Dec. 28, 1863, p. 3, referencing a letter asserting that "the barracks furnished to the colored troops are as good as the average of those" erected for white troops. Tripler's role, and other evidence of the shoddy conditions, is referenced in Sharon A. Roger Hepburn ed., *Private No More: The Civil War Letters of John Lovejoy Murray, 102nd United States Colored Infantry* (Athens: University of Georgia Press, 2023), 9.

he secured a recommendation. Still nothing developed, so Tripler went to Cincinnati and laid the issue before Major-General Ambrose E. Burnside, commanding in the Midwest, who also gave support.[19]

He also cared for the disabled. Although one historian characterized this period as one of semi-retirement,[20] the record shows that Tripler continued to serve in important capacities on both a full-time and part-time basis. The latter service included membership "on a board assembled in October 1863 that interviewed various makers of artificial limbs." He wrote the board's report, recounting interviews of various artificial limb manufacturers and supporting the provisioning at a government paid and profit-yielding price of $50.[21] The next May, Tripler recommended to acting Surgeon-General Barnes that the makers on the Army's approved list be required to sell such equipment to commissioned officers who were maimed (they were not covered by congressional authorization). "I know that very many of the officers who have lost limbs are in limited and even straitened circumstances, & they cannot afford to pay the price demanded by the limb manufacturers."[22] Once again, the sage surgeon was ahead of the curve; not until 1868-1870 did Congress act to include officers. Then, in June, Tripler called attention to the case of an Indiana private who was informed by the manufacturer that he needed to travel to Cincinnati for fitting of his artificial leg. The soldier could not afford the journey. So Tripler took a stand: he would no longer authorize

---

19. *Detroit Free Press*, Aug. 9-10, 1863, 2. Burnside (1824-1881), West Point Class of 1847, commanded the Army of the Potomac after McClellan was dismissed. Following the disastrous Battle of Fredericksburg on December 13, 1862, he was placed in command of the Department of the Ohio, serving from March 25 to December 12, 1863. *Cullum's Register*, Vol. II, 318-319.
20. Freemon, *Gangrene and Glory*, 176.
21. Guy R. Hasegawa, *Mending Broken Soldiers: The Union and Confederate Programs to Supply Artificial Limbs* (Carbondale: Southern Illinois University Press, 2012), 27-28. Since Barnes was acting Surgeon-General as of September 3, it would appear he made the appointment.
22. Id. 41-42, 101 n.21, quoting a letter in the records of the Office of the Surgeon General.

sales by this maker.²³ Of others in the Medical Bureau hierarchy, he was "especially" indignant of mistreatment of his fellow veterans.²⁴

Tripler also was on duty that Winter as head of the Examining Board for Medical Officers in New York City.

In early 1864, Tripler received appointment as Medical Director of a restructured Army organization, the Northern Department. Its new commander was Major-General Samuel P. Heintzelman, familiar from prior service together, who had been assigned to the district in January.²⁵ The Department encompassed Indiana, Illinois, Michigan, and Ohio, with headquarters at Columbus. Tripler's role was to supervise the care provided to soldiers in the hospitals within the region. The General's confidence in Tripler made appropriate his appointment over all surgeons in the four-State region.²⁶

On March 5, 1864, the trustees of the private Harper Hospital charitable organization offered up the property they owned on Woodward Avenue for the location of a military hospital. Since early 1859, the board had been seeking to erect Detroit's first general hospital. Offering the site to the War Department at nominal rent could finally launch the facility into existence; when the war ended, presumably soldier care would end and the facility converted to civilian use. Tripler was to serve as agent to convey their offer to Washington.²⁷ Whether due solely to the offer, or coupled with the surgeon's persuasiveness, within a month Detroit heard positive news when the War Department issued an order for establishment of a Military Hospital

---

23. Id. 42-43, n.23.
24. Id. 72.
25. General Orders No. 17 issued Jan. 12, 1864. He served in that capacity until Oct. 1864, being requested *inter alia* to aid the Illinois Governor during civil disturbances. *OR*, ser. 3, IV, 221-222. Their paths had overlapped in the war in Mexico, in California, and on the Peninsula where Heintzelman had commanded the III Corps and been involved in the battles of Williamsburg and Fair Oaks.
26. *Detroit Free Press*, Mar. 10, 1864, 2.
27. *Harper of Detroit*, 76.

through lease of the proffered grounds.[28] Work was to commence immediately on the facility, which would have capacity for five hundred patients, less than Tripler had sought but, still, a major step forward for the welfare of Michigan's infirm soldiers.[29] The facility had its formal dedication on October 12, 1864,[30] at noon, with many dignitaries present to open the doors to patients. (See Illustration 13) The doctor was on hand, and a newspaper account made sure to call attention to his role:

> To Dr. Tripler, whose unwearied devotion to the care of our sick and wounded men has endeared him to Michigan soldiers everywhere, are we indebted for the location of this splendid institution in our city.[31]

No doubt politics had played more than a minor role in the decision. Tripler had procured support from Republican Governor Austin Blair and his team of military authorities ranging over the State, and he was not the exclusive vehicle to obtain such endorsements. He could rely on support from his chief aide, Dr. David O. Farrand, Assistant-Surgeon in the US Army.[32] Colonel George W. Lee, chief quartermaster in Michigan and stationed at Detroit, also lent his voice to the

---

28. Id. 77.
29. *Detroit Free Press*, Apr. 8, 1864, 1. See Appendix for an excerpt from this article.
30. George S. May, *Michigan and the Civil War Years, 1860-1866: A Wartime Chronicle* (Lansing: Michigan Civil War Centennial Observance Commission, 1964), 66.
31. *Detroit Free Press*, Oct. 13, 1864, 1. The only Michigan historical marker on site commemorates a piece of 20th century history. American Academy of Pediatrics, Registered Site S534B, 3990 John R Street, Detroit. Another erroneously dates Harper's founding.
32. Farrand (1837-1883) had become one of the prominent doctors in Detroit, having graduated from the New York College of Physicians and Surgeons in 1862 and working as a partner with Zina Pitcher, M.D. (1797-1872). He "proved to be an excellent surgeon and administrator" and, as a protégé of Tripler's, a testament to the older physician's judgment. *Harper of Detroit*, 86-87.

effort and worked during its construction. What resulted could not have been anticipated at the time: the institution would become one of America's oldest and most highly regarded teaching institutions. In the 20th century, it would become a constituent of the Detroit Medical Center, and beyond the millennium it would function as part of the Wayne State University School of Medicine.

The constitution and rules, together with the report and statement of the trustees published in 1866, were colorblind. The principal, detailed study of the institution—published during the Civil Rights movement of the 1960s—states the following:

> There was no segregation or discrimination against race or religion at Harper. Among the wounded soldiers in the military hospital and the veterans in the Soldiers' Home, there were Indians and Negroes. Later, in the civilian hospital, Negro patients are often listed. ... Harper Hospital served all groups and classes of people and fulfilled all of the requirements of a truly civic institution.[33]

Michigan's official history of the Civil War described the facility thus:

> It was made up of eleven one-story buildings, with a capacity for eight hundred patients, and costing about sixty thousand dollars, the use of the grounds being given gratis by the "Harper Hospital Association." Much care had been observed in regard to ventilation, drainage, and superior water arrangements. Opening with an exceedingly capable management, it had soon the reputation of being one of the most complete, comfortable, and best regulated hospitals in the West.

The hospital served incapacitated soldiers until December 1865, including former prisoners of war such as Joseph Doherty of Detroit,

---

33. *Harper of Detroit*, 133.

a Private in the 7th Michigan Cavalry who was incarcerated at Pemberton, Libby, and Belle Isle prisons in Virginia, Andersonville, Camp Lawton, Georgia, and Salisbury, North Carolina.[34] Before the Federal Government transferred the property back to the trustees, it insisted on a condition that sufficient accommodation should be at all times afforded for a Soldiers' Home to house invalid and destitute Michigan soldiers and sailors. Tripler had served as a consulting surgeon and on the surgical staff via its Board of Consultation. The other surgeon was Dr. Zina Pitcher, president of the US Army Medical Board, American Medical Association president, two-time mayor of Detroit, leader in founding the University of Michigan Medical School, and member of the University's Board of Regents.[35]

Opening the facility enabled transfer of Michigan men from Eastern hospitals, bringing them close to family and friends. The State's Adjutant-General vowed that the people would "never forget the efforts of those gentlemen to secure it, while the soldiers will in all time hold them in most grateful remembrance."[36] In his second Inaugural Address, the President called upon the nation to "care for him who shall have borne the battle." That mission was now Tripler's. Those wounded by Rebel ordnance at Gettysburg, the Wilderness, Spotsylvania, and on Western Theater battlegrounds came to Harper. At its peak, the facility housed 645 patients.[37]

The year did not pass without another familiar duty. Tripler met in Cincinnati on October 18, 1864, with two other surgeons to examine

---

34. William O. Lee, *Personal and Historical Sketches and Facial History of and by Members of the Seventh Regiment Michigan Volunteer Cavalry 1862-1865* (Detroit: 7th Cavalry Association, 1902), 235.
35. *Constitution and Rules of the Harper Hospital, Together with the Report and Statement of the Trustees* (Detroit: William Graham, 1866), 25. *American Medical Biographies*, 917-918. The 1964 centennial history characterized the initial role as a military hospital as a disappointing failure of the founders' vision, inexplicably demeaning its role in providing care to those who fought for Union and liberty. *Harper of Detroit*, 81.
36. John Robertson, *Michigan in the War* (Lansing: W.S. George & Co., 1882), 115-116.
37. *Harper of Detroit*, 84-86.

candidates for addition to the Medical Corps. Surgeon-General Barnes appointed him its President, and the board approved two of the five applicants. A more extended stint was required in September 1865. A board manned by Tripler and two others met in New York City, carefully reviewed qualifications, and approved nineteen for appointment to the Army out of sixty-seven candidates who appeared for examination. The process extended from February 15, 1866.[38]

As Medical Director of the Department, Tripler had duties beyond Michigan. Included were a wide-ranging number of hospitals, reported years later as follows:

Name	Locality	Beds
Officers'	Cincinnati	75
Marine	"	122
Washington Park	"	150
West End	"	120
Seminary	Columbus	150
Dennison	Camp Dennison, Ohio	1,716
US General	Camp Chase, Ohio	200
US General	Cleveland	330
US General	Gallipolis, Ohio	350
US General	Evansville, Ind.	702
US General	Indianapolis	256
US General	New Albany, Ind.	860
Ohio	"	300
Corps d'Afrique	"	146
Madison	Madison, Ind.	2,430
Desmarres	Chicago	150
Marine	"	110
US General	Quincy, Ill.	950
US General	Camp Butler, Ill.	525
US General	Camp Douglas, Ill.	137

---

38. Brown, *Medical Department*, 238, 242; Surgeon-General's Order of Sept. 21, 1864, *Daily Ohio State Journal*, Oct. 20, 1864, 1.

Simons	Mound City, Ill.	788
Harper	Detroit	578
St. Mary's	"	276

Total: 11,421[39]

Until the Civil War, the honor of a "brevet"—a special designation awarded to a candidate without actual promotion, change in status, or increase in pay—had been bestowed on only one medical officer, Surgeon-General Lawson, after the Mexican-American War. This situation changed late in the conflict, with more officers being brevetted for heroism, unspecified contributions to victory, and other lauded deeds. One of those honored was Tripler. He received a brevet promotion to Colonel on November 29, 1864.[40] The US Senate confirmed the honor, recommended by Lincoln and Stanton, a partial vindication and tacit admission of error by those, including Jacob Howard, who had once opposed his advancement.

As an original member of the Aztec Club, no doubt Tripler hoped for a similar social organization to be founded at a successful conclusion to the War of the Rebellion. Indeed—he joined the Military Order of the Loyal Legion at its founding in May 1865.

It did not mean he slacked off in the performance of his duties; a prime example was his management of the US Army General Hospital constructed three miles west of Columbus, Ohio, along the Scioto River adjacent to the Columbus, Dayton & Cincinnati Railroad. It came to be known as "Tripler General Hospital" or simply "Tripler Hospital"—a strange title if convention dictates not naming institutions after failures. The institution's record of care appeared quite successful: an early 1865 report boasted that only two deaths had occurred since its founding the prior December, with five hundred patients currently being treated. (See Illustration 14) The Official

---

39. *Medical and Surgical History*, Pt. III, Vol. I, 961, as of Dec. 17, 1864. This volume was published in 1888.
40. Shrady, Vol. II, 425.

Roster of the Soldiers of the State of Ohio in the War of the Rebellion mentions soldiers who were mustered out while there, apparently as patients.[41]

On June 20, 1865, acting upon a request from the Governor of Ohio, the War Department issued this order:

> Medical Director Tripler has this day been instructed to turn over the hospital to you or your legal representative, so soon as it can be done without detriment to the public service.[42]

The new purpose—"a Home for Ohio Soldiers" who lacked the ability to be on their own—replaced the purely medical reason for its existence.[43] It opened in October and housed veterans regardless of race.

In July 1865, another change was made in the Army structure in the Midwest. The headquarters of the Department of the Ohio was moved to Detroit, enabling Tripler to center his time there again. His "many friends" welcomed his return "with pleasure."[44]

Although based in Detroit, Tripler continued to take part in medical conferences far from home. In October 1865, he attended a session of the New York Academy of Medicine. In response to a report on gunshot fractures of the thigh in which amputation was favored, he gave a rather politic rebuttal, concluding that exsection should be the rule and amputation as the exception. Such learning, he noted, dated from the Schleswig-Holstein War of 1848-1851. He also commented on a paper dealing with pneumonia.[45] At the January 17,

---

41. Thomas H. Smith, *The Mapping of Ohio* (Kent: Kent State University Press, 1977), 112-113, 115; *Daily Ohio State Journal*, Mar. 9, 1865, 3; Mar. 31, 1865, 3; Sept. 9, 1865, 3; Oct. 10, 1865, 3; *Columbus Morning Journal*, Jan. 3, 1866, 2. The site is today in the neighborhood known as Franklinton.
42. *Message and Annual Reports for 1865, Made to the Fifty-Seventh General Assembly of Ohio*, Pt. I (Columbus: Richard Nevins, 1866), 296-297.
43. *Daily Ohio State Journal*, June 28, 1865, 3.
44. *Detroit Free Press*, Jul. 8, 1865, 1.
45. *Bulletin of the New York Academy of Medicine*, Vol. II (New York: Bailliere Bros., 1866), 479, 487, 495-496, 526.

1866, meeting, he spoke on the Surgeon-General's circular describing the project to construct the medical/surgical history of the Civil War.[46]

Charles Tripler had not much time to experience the fruits of his long labors. In the Spring of 1866, as Eunice phrased it, trouble developed in his right ear. Three small glands on that side of the face "became implicated, one after another."[47] At first the condition was not painful. But it must have been, to a doctor of such credentials, apparent that his disease was significant, and that it was progressing.

---

46. Id. 532.
47. *Heart in Tatters*, 80.

The Final Act

The Civil War had come to a close. Union officers emerged triumphant, even those for whom the unpredictable fortunes of war had wreaked havoc. One such figure was Major-General Joseph Hooker. Resignation just before the Battle of Gettysburg shelved him for a space, then a transfer to the Western Theater during late 1863 rescued his military reputation. Incensed not to receive a coveted command, he asked to be relieved and was assigned to the Midwest as leader of the Northern Department, replacing Heintzelman. In June 1865, the War Department merged this command with the Department of the Ohio, and Hooker ended up in charge of the Department of the Lakes.[1] On August 23, 1866, he assumed command, with headquarters at Detroit. He formally appointed the members of his staff; Brevet Colonel Tripler was announced as his Medical Director.[2]

Dr. Tripler was ailing. By the time President Andrew Johnson came to town during his "swinging round the circle" campaign to build public support for his Administration, the Colonel was confined to his bed. Two of the dignitaries accompanying the President were the General-in-Chief of the Army, U.S. Grant, and Surgeon-General Barnes. They arrived at the Tripler house shortly after breakfast and went upstairs to the room where Tripler lay, suffering. The malignancy was apparent. Barnes did most of the talking—he unburdened himself, explaining that he accepted the Surgeon-Generalship in order to steer it in the right direction. "The Sanitary Commission

---

1. John Eicher & David Eicher, *Civil War High Commands* (Stanford: Stanford University Press, 2001), 304, 838.
2. *Detroit Free Press*, Aug. 25, 1866, 5.

was making and unmaking everything," he confirmed; it had secured Hammond's elevation in order to gain a willing ally for its agenda. Hammond, so Barnes represented, had accepted a bargain that Tripler would never have tolerated, and within months been "cashiered" by Secretary Stanton. The message: the blow to Tripler's career had been undeserved. Grant overheard the account. Ironically, his life would be cut short by cancer in 1885. Eunice Tripler recalled that "[t]he attention of this call from the General of the Army and the Surgeon General was very gratifying to Dr. Tripler. He regarded it as a personal testimony that his own character and services were esteemed far above the indication by the rank accorded him."[3]

The Triplers received a visit by another old acquaintance, Bishop McCoskry. The underlying purpose: to provide the dying man with whatever spiritual succor was necessary and appropriate. Eunice came home during the visit and met the Bishop on the stairs. "Mrs. Tripler," he uttered with much emotion, "I called to teach your husband, but I find he has taught me."[4]

In likely his final words to appear in print, Tripler authored an article on the issue of proper rank for medical practitioners in the US Army. The effort had been completed on April 23, in Detroit, time enough for it to be presented at the American Medical Association meeting in Baltimore in May. The signatories to the document were Tripler and Thomas Antisell, surgeon for the "Red Star" Division and the XX Corps under A.S. Williams. But the title page as it appeared in a national journal attributed the item only to Tripler, perhaps in recognition of his ultimate fate that year. The report commended pending legislation in Congress that would grant medical officers the same rank as other officers. The language, as per Tripler's wont, was direct:

---

3. *Heart in Tatters*, 80. Cancer was the diagnosis; lymphoma of some sort appears to fit the description. Barnes served as acting Surgeon-General from September 3, 1863, until August 24, 1864, when he was confirmed to the position. His tenure lasted until 1882. Pilcher, 60, 63.
4. *Heart in Tatters*, 80-81.

Your Committee are gratified to be able to report that the language of these acts is the same precisely as to the rank of the officers of all the Staff Departments, and that if either of these bills should become a law, the rank of the medical officers will be clearly defined, stripped of all ambiguities and untrammelled by any proviso that can render it nugatory, or afford a pretext for any arbitrary construction that would render a medical officer subject to any disabilities that would not equally apply to an Adjutant-General, Quartermaster, or a Subsistence officer. The odious principle that has, up to this epoch, controlled legislation and disfigured military law, by refusing any recognition of medical officers as military men, and has subjected them to the command of Cadets having the brevet of Second Lieutenant, is by the provisions of these acts abandoned, and no subtlety of reasoning can revive it.

Despite this advancement, the bill did not completely remedy discriminatory treatment. Such disrespect brought forth incredulity and indignation, for not only was it an insult to the profession but a diminishment of an appropriate pension once the physician "is worn out in service." To remedy this wrong, the AMA was encouraged to lobby Congress. The final version of the bill should mete out equivalent treatment to Army doctors "for services equally faithful, equally important, and equally indispensable."[5]

The first week in October, the Triplers went to Cincinnati to consult with Dr. George Curtis Blackman, co-author of the *Hand-Book*. Since their collaboration, the war had sent Tripler east while Curtis remained in the west. He had helped save lives at the Battle of Shiloh.

---

5. "Report of the Committee on Rank in the Medical Department of the Army" in *The Transactions of the American Medical Association*, Vol. XVII (Philadelphia: Collins, 1866), 513-518. The Act of July 28, 1866, §17, 39th Congress, 1st Session, *United States Statutes at Large*, Vol. XIV, George P. Sanger ed. (Boston: Little, Brown & Co., 1868), 332-334, was the bill in question, further dealt with by Act of March 2, 1867, id. 422-423.

As a renowned surgeon, perhaps Blackman might have a miracle within his medical bag.[6]

It was not to be. On October 20, 1866, while in Cincinnati, Charles Stuart Tripler died. His wife remembered how "death came finally and released him from his anguish."[7] Those few words hint at the pain the doctor endured. Ironically, his death came ten days shy of the anniversary of his original Army commission.

One of the hometown newspapers published a lengthy obituary:

Death of Dr. Charles S. Tripler

Another of the prominent actors in the late war has passed away, and his numerous friends, both in and out of the army, are called to mourn for one who had few equals and no superior in all those qualities which make men honored among men. Dr. Tripler died of a cancer on the 20th instant, at Cincinnati, where he had gone for the purpose of being under the care of his friend Dr. Blackburn, in whose skill and judgment he had the greatest possible confidence. He was born in the city of New York in August, 1806, and was therefore in the sixty-first year of his age. He studied medicine and graduated at the College of Physicians and Surgeons of New York in 1830, and at once received the appointment of Assistant Surgeon in the army, and was promoted to be Surgeon on the second of July, 1838. He was stationed at different times at Detroit, Fort Gratiot and Mackinaw. During the Mexican war he served with distinction as the medical director of General Twiggs' division, and subsequently as medical director of the Department of California. At the commencement of the rebellion he was at Newport, Kentucky, but was at once assigned to the army under General Patterson for duty. Immediately after

---

6. *Heart in Tatters,* 81; *American Medical Biographies,* 107-108.
7. From "epithelioma" according to *American Medical Biographies,* 1161.

the disastrous defeat at Bull Run, when the President called General McClellan to the command of all the armies of the United States, Surgeon Tripler, who was then second to no one in his profession, was appointed the Medical Director of the Army of the Potomac. It is not too much to say that when he received this appointment the Government had in truth taken no steps towards organizing the Medical Department of the Army. There was literally no order, no system, no plan, no preparation, to take care of the sick of a great army in the field, and no real comprehension of the vast wants of such an army as was then being brought together to crush out the rebellion. Dr. Tripler, who was almost the only surgeon in the army who had been in the field and seen active service, at once bent his whole energies to remedy the defects of the organization. The system which, after it was fully organized and perfected, answered the purpose so admirably, was more owing to the great experience and ability of Dr. Tripler than any other man in the nation. He grasped, as with a master mind, everything which was necessary for the army, and he labored with unwearied zeal until all was accomplished. He should have been placed at Washington as Surgeon-General, but through the influence of interested parties another was preferred before him; and that man, whose name is not worthy to be mentioned on the same page with that of Dr. Tripler, maligned, misrepresented, vilified, and traduced him until he was compelled to ask to be relieved from his position in the army of the Potomac. He lived, however, to see the Surgeon-General who was so false to his profession and his country, cashiered and disgraced.

On his retirement from the position of Medical Director of the Army of the Potomac he was ordered to Detroit, and at once undertook to secure the establishment of large hospitals in all the States where the sick and wounded soldiers could be well cared for near to their homes and friends. The erection of the large hospital here was entirely owing to his unwearied efforts. He married Miss Hunt, in this city, in the year 1843, and he leaves his wife and several children to mourn his death.

As a professional man he had few or no superiors; as a friend he was faultless; as a citizen, above all reproach. He will be followed to his last resting place, Elmwood, by his numerous friends, who will mourn ever the death of one they so much loved and respected.

Dr. Tripler received the rank of Colonel and was brevetted Brigadier-General for his arduous services in behalf of his country.[8]

When his widow died in 1910, this summary appeared of her long-departed husband:

> Dr. Tripler died in 1866, leaving an enviable record for professional attainment and for integrity and uprightness in every relation of life.

The funeral was appropriately elaborate for someone of such rank, reputation, and accomplishment. Present were "a large number of sorrowing friends." Bishop McCoskry officiated. The military escort consisted of a section of Battery G, 4th US Artillery, and two companies of US infantry. Pallbearers included Generals Hooker, Silas Casey, and Orlando Bolivar Willcox. Other notables attended.[9] The Board of Trustees of Harper Hospital adopted a resolution of sorrow. Tripler's remains were carried by hearse from the family residence to the Episcopal Church, thence to Elmwood Cemetery where they were interred in the family plot, Section B, Lot 31, next to the graves of Thomas and Alice Hunt and the Triplers' infants.

By subscription of the medical members of the Army, a marble

---

8. *Detroit Free Press*, Oct. 23, 1866, 4.
9. Id. Oct. 24, 1866, 5.

monument was proposed for the gravesite. Barnes issued a circular inviting participation, limited in amount, encouraging wide subscription. Surgeons were not to give over $10 each and Assistant-surgeons not over $5. A very large proportion donated towards the neoclassical memorial, which consisted of a stone base topped by a tall cross. The Surgeon-General's official history included these observations:

> The death of Surgeon Charles S. Tripler, which occurred at Cincinnati, Ohio, on the twentieth of October, after a long and painful illness, left a vacant place in the ranks of the Medical Staff difficult to be filled. He was one of its most distinguished members, who during upwards of thirty-five years service had ever been foremost in all enterprises for the advancement of the interests of the Corps, and the dignity of the medical profession.

It also republished the text of the notice issued by the War Department:

> Adjutant General's Office,
> Washington, October 27, 1866.
> General Orders, No. 89.
>
> The following notice of the decease of a distinguished officer of the Medical Department of the army, by the chief of his Department, is published to the army:
>
> Surgeon General's Office,
> Washington, October 23, 1866.
>
> To the Adjutant General, U. S. Army:
> Sir: I have the honor to report the death, at Cincinnati, on the 20th instant, of Brevet Brigadier General C.S. Tripler, Surgeon, U.S. Army, Medical Director, Department of the Lakes.

Entering the army as assistant surgeon, October, 1830, General Tripler served continuously for thirty-six years, during which time he held with credit to himself and advantage to the government, positions of high trust and responsibility, taking part in the Seminole war, the war with Mexico, the occupation of California, and being the first Medical Director of the Army of the Potomac.

His skilful [sic] administration and conscientious discharge of duty, has been rewarded by three brevets for 'faithful and meritorious services.' The Medical Corps possesses in his distinguished career a bright example of the union of great professional attainments, with the military zeal and pride of an officer, and those qualities which mark the christian gentleman.

Very respectfully, your obedient servant,

J.K. Barnes,
Surgeon General.

By Order of the Secretary Of War:
E. D. Townsend,
Assistant Adjutant General.[10]

The official history also included "brief lines by the one who knew him best in this world"—suggestive that the author was his widow Eunice. The few lines were:

He made many friends at West Point during the time he lived there, among the Professors as well as among the future officers of the army. He was always a student, though he described himself as a lazy boy, who learned nothing unless it

---

10. *Medical and Surgical Reporter*, Vol. XV (Nov. 10, 1866), 408.

was beaten into him. He certainly was beaten into the habit of study; he went through the mathematical course pursued by the cadets while he was at West Point; he afterwards learned the French language so as to be able to translate with fluency and elegance, the same with Italian and Spanish. He made no attempt to speak any but the Spanish. He was no mean musician. His great desire seemed to be to learn well, what he did learn.

He wrote less than he studied, but his stores of knowledge were always at the service of his professional friends in civil life, who had less time than himself to give to books. As far as I know he printed but the following: 1. Remarks on Delirium Tremens, 1827, being his graduating Thesis, published by request. 2. A Treatise on the duties of physicians in regard to popular delusions. 3. A Treatise on the nature, cause and treatment of scurvy. 4. Manual for the medical officers of the army of the United States. Part I. Recruiting and the inspection of recruits, 1858. 5. Hand-book for the military surgeon, 1861. These last two were incomplete, the latter on account of his going to the field at the beginning of the Rebellion, and the former being only the first part of the work, which he hoped to live to complete to his own satisfaction.

There is little more to say. Any record of Doctor Tripler should tell of prompt obedience of orders, of twenty-three years of service at one time without a leave, of thirty years of devotion to his corps and to every duty to his country, of his services in three wars so ill rewarded.

He was not in the habit of talking about himself. He was one of the most self-denying and charitable of men, but no one would have dreamed it from anything he said. With nothing but his pay, he supported his own mother for twenty years and his wife's mother and sister for half that time, and never to his own wife mentioned the money which was sent each quarter with unfailing regularity. A devout christian, he avoided the subject of religion in general conversation most carefully only to make more telling some private talk which souls now on earth and many in Paradise listened to, to their eternal welfare. His own faith never wavered; he bore his painful sickness, his horrible pangs more than patiently, he bore them thankfully; when he was struck he gave the ring of the true metal, and so died.[11]

Mrs. Tripler never remarried. She fought to keep her husband's memory alive, in part through pressing Congress for a share of the royalties associated with the 1858 *Manual*. After years of narrowly losing out, she finally obtained some recompense when a bill was passed to award her the sum of three thousand dollars—far less than sought, and with a waiver of any further rights. More than the money involved, the signature by President Theodore Roosevelt on the measure proved that Charles Tripler had written a seminal book that had yielded countless benefits to his nation's armed forces.[12] Eunice lived to a ripe old age and died at her daughter's home in Grand Island, Nebraska, in 1910.

One important memorial she pursued for her husband was an honorary promotion to generalship. On December 11, 1866, the War Department submitted to the President, and Johnson forwarded to Congress, the appointment of "Brevet Colonel Charles S. Tripler, surgeon, for faithful and meritorious services during the war, to date from March 13, 1865."[13] On February 23, 1867, her efforts were rewarded by the United States Senate with a posthumous promotion to Brevet Brigadier-General, United States Army, effective March 13, 1865.[14]

---

11. Brown, *Medical Department*, 252-253.
12. Act approved January 25, 1907, 59th Congress, 2nd Session. *The Statutes at Large from December 1905 to March 1907*, Vol. XXXIV, Part 2 (Washington: Government Printing Office, 1907), 2308; *Heart in Tatters*, 85.
13. *Senate Executive Journal*, Dec. 14, 1866, 33.
14. *Senate Executive Journal*, Feb. 23, 1867, 246; *Civil War High Commands*, 536. He is recorded here as Medical Director of the Northern Department from October 28, 1864, until his death.

For the second time, former opponents such as Senator Jacob Howard honored Tripler after previously denigrating his service record.

Doctor—Surgeon—Medical Director—General—unselfish patriot. The legacy of Charles Stuart Tripler, properly grounded in fact and on the record, rises along with greater appreciation for the service of Civil War medical personnel. He lacked the facility of self-promotion,[15] and that attribute contributed to a false narrative that has played out over the past century's historical writing.[16]

---

15. He does not appear to have contributed to the *Medical and Surgical History*. Perhaps he was repelled by Hammond's crassness in promising each contributor's name would appear in the publication, giving "full credit." The Surgeon-General expected full cooperation "since no one will neglect this opportunity of advancing ... his own reputation." Circular No. 5, June 9, 1862.

16. Even a recent fairly favorable treatment of Tripler repeats some of that narrative (e.g., Hammond was sympathetic). Jessica M. Shiepko, *William Alexander Hammond's Transformation of the Army Medical Department During the American Civil War*, Department of History, Sam Houston State University, December 2018, p. 128.

Epitaph

1866

In the same year of Tripler's death, his successor published a 200-page account of his service under McClellan. The preface to *Medical Recollections of the Army of the Potomac* was dated February 1, 1866, from "Near San Buenaventura, Cal.", now known simply as Ventura. Significantly, its first page recounted arriving at White House landing on the Pamunkey on June 28, 1862, and how "I met Mr. Olmstead [sic] and several other members of the Sanitary Commission" before his first meeting with McClellan or Tripler.

1870

Eunice was living in Detroit and "keeping house." The Census recorded her as having a personal estate of $1,000 and real estate valued of $6,000. Ellen, Edward, Eunice, and Henry lived with her, as did 24-year old Charles whose occupation was "Officer U.S.A." She had two boarders and an Irish household worker in the house.[1]

1872

On February 25, an article in the *Detroit Free Press* about Historic Elmwood Cemetery included a description of "The Tomb and Life of Tripler." It called him "the victim of unfounded prejudice as medical chief." It also reported on the inscription on the memorial that

---

1. *US Census*, County of Wayne, City of Detroit, Ward 1, Enumeration pages 57-58.

had been erected over his grave: "Faithful unto death. Erected to the memory of a loved and revered brother officer by the Medical Corps of the Army."[2]

On March 15, Jonathan Letterman died in San Francisco, age 47.

1880

Eunice remained in Detroit at 86 Howard Street, widowed and keeping house. Edward, Eunice, and Henry remained at home. The sons were employed, and an Irish household worker lived in the house.[3]

1882

On January 30, Henry W. Bellows died in New York City. Burial was in the Village Cemetery in Walpole, New Hampshire. In addition to birth and death dates, and his position as Minister at All Souls Church in New York, his gravestone records: "President of the United States Sanitary Commission 1861-1878." A bronze memorial tablet by sculptor Augustus Saint-Gaudens was unveiled in All Souls Church in 1886, containing birth and death dates and his positions as minister and Commission President.

Robert N. Scott, the editor of the *Official Records of the War of the Rebellion*, reported on October 23 that Volume V of Series I had been published in the interval since his last report on October 12, 1881. This volume contained the first part of Dr. Tripler's 1863 report to McClellan.

1884

Scott reported on October 14, 1884, that Parts I and II of Volume XI of Series I had been published in the interval since October 14, 1883.[4] This volume contained the remaining part of Dr. Tripler's report to McClellan.

---

2. See Appendix.
3. *US Census*, County of Wayne, City of Detroit, Ward 1, Enumeration District 270, page 18. The street location in Detroit no longer exists.
4. Dates of publication are drawn from Secretary of War annual reports to Congress.

1885

On October 29, George B. McClellan died at Orange, New Jersey. Burial was at Riverview Cemetery in Trenton. The massive monument above his grave contains these words: "Organizer and Commander of the Army of the Potomac and Commanding General of the Armies of the United States."

1887

McClellan's posthumous memoir was published. He opined that "difficulties to be overcome in organizing and making effective the Medical Department were very great" during the first months after he took command of the Army of the Potomac. He made no distinction between the two physicians who served as Medical Director, instead asserting that "by the successive exertions of Surgeons Tripler and Letterman the medical corps was brought to a very high degree of efficiency."

1900

On January 5, William A. Hammond died in Washington, D.C., and was buried in Arlington National Cemetery. The inscription on his gravestone mentions "Brigadier General and Surgeon General, U.S.A." with birth and death dates, and: "loyal and true."

On June 6, Eunice was recorded in the Federal Census at Grand Island, Nebraska. She, along with her daughter and son-in-law, lived in the Palmer House hotel located on the corner of Third and Sycamore Streets. Eunice was recorded as widowed and that five of nine child she had borne were living.[5]

1903

Frederick Law Olmsted died on August 28 at the McLean Hospital in Belmont, Massachusetts. Burial was in the Old North Cemetery in Hartford, Connecticut. The National Park Service continues today

---

5. *US Census*, County of Hall, Enumeration District 83, page 237.

to operate the Frederick Law Olmsted National Historic Site near Brookline, Massachusetts.

1906

Letterman's remains were relocated to Arlington National Cemetery. The inscription on this gravestone reads: "Medical Director of the Army of the Potomac June 23, 1862, to December 30, 1863. Who brought order and efficiency into the medical service and was the originator of modern methods of medical organization in armies."

1910

Eunice Hunt Tripler died on March 28 in Grand Island, Nebraska, and was buried in Historic Elmwood Cemetery in Detroit on March 31. Her memoir was published posthumously by her son-in-law.

1920

The US Army opened a medical facility on the island of Oahu in the Territory of Hawaii and named it the Tripler Memorial Hospital.

1942

An article in the April issue of the *Army Medical Bulletin* entitled "Charles Stuart Tripler (1806-1866)" constituted the first, though general, biography of the surgeon.[6]

In General

The legacy of these two Medical Directors began on July 4, 1863, in quite contrasting styles. One would have a hospital named for him on the sacred ground at Gettysburg, and "Camp Letterman" would go down in history as a memento to the great work done by a fine physician to alleviate horrible suffering. For the other, a medical facility in the capital of Ohio would have to suffice when "Tripler Hospital" was founded, after the Civil War to be converted into a soldiers' home for

---

6. By James M. Phalen, No. 61, Apr. 1942, 176-181.

the infirm who could not afford their own care, eventually to be torn down and forgotten.

Letterman appears to have almost immediately lost the unalloyed endorsement of the Sanitary Commission. The relationship became "strained at best," with Bellows resenting "what he viewed as Letterman's intent to keep the commission in its place and subservient to the medical department."[7] Similar complaints had been lodged against the predecessor. Letterman persuaded McClellan to issue orders to rectify conditions resulting from the rapid and unplanned maneuver to Harrison's Landing, and in the camps erected in that crowded space. But withdrawal of the Army northward, and the Battle of Second Bull Run, put it again in what Letterman described as "a deplorable condition" reminiscent of July 4, 1862. Any progress he had made was "largely gutted."[8] Over the next sixteen months, Letterman coped with the costly battles of the 1862 Maryland and 1863 Pennsylvania campaigns, between which came the bloody contests at Fredericksburg and Chancellorsville. In December 1863, he asked to be relieved of his post with the Army of the Potomac and for a transfer to Pennsylvania. Newly married and with Hammond under a cloud, his new assignment as a medical inspector of hospitals promised far less trauma. When he faced transfer to Missouri, Letterman made a decision that Tripler had not: he submitted his resignation from the Army on December 22, 1864. He never revealed his reasons, but disenchantment, exhaustion, and "increasingly chronic poor health" must have contributed.[9]

Letterman moved to California to make money in the petroleum business, failed, set up a medical practice, and published his memoir. He was elected coroner in San Francisco "on largely white supremacy sentiment" with an anti-Chinese immigration platform. His wife predeceased him; he became ill and died on March 15, 1872, age 47.[10]

---

7. McGaugh, 77-78.
8. Id. 93-96, 99.
9. Id. 204-205, 209-210, 213, 223-224.
10. Letterman, 185; Phalen, "The Life Of Jonathan Letterman," 159-160;

The memoir was not a magnanimous book. Letterman mentioned his predecessor but once, referring to him as "that experienced officer," damning with faint praise.[11] The gist of the early sections is that a myriad of issues rendered the health of the Army of the Potomac highly problematic when he took over. Such an interpretation helped set the stage for historians to castigate Tripler as nothing more than "a spinner of bureaucratic red tape."[12] The resulting trope enshrined Letterman as the "originator of modern methods" of military medical care and Tripler as one of the feeble old guard who clung to old practices. Ironically, an early biographer of Letterman found it unnecessary to trash Tripler in order to burnish the successor's reputation, writing:

> Perhaps no one in the responsible position of Medical Director of an army had ever before encountered more serious difficulties than did Dr Letterman's predecessor, Surgeon Charles Tripler, of the United States Army. Experienced in the war with Mexico, of military instincts and soldierly training, Dr. Tripler brought to this high duty the most untiring zeal and devotion to the interest of the soldier and the service. Delay and disappointment met him at every turn, as indeed was inevitable, for the whole army were alike inexperienced, and its appointments new and untried, and, above all, but few of the medical officers had any military training or habits.

McGaugh, 252, 261; Jeffry D. Wert, "Dr. Letterman's War" in *Civil War Times*, Vol. 45, No. 7 (Sept. 2006). The McGaugh work contains a quote of McClellan extolling Letterman, id. 73-74, found in Bennett A. Clements, "Memoir of Jonathan Letterman, M.D." as reprint from *Journal of the Military Service Institution*, Vol. IV, No. 15 (1883), 26-27, from a letter of February 26, 1883, not long before McClellan's death. See John T. Greenwood, "Hammond and Letterman: A Tale of Two Men Who Changed Army Medicine" in *Landpower Essay: An Institute of Land Warfare Publication*, No. 03-1, June 2003, 3, available at: https://www.ausa.org/sites/default/files/LPE-03-1-Hammond-and-Letterman-A-Tale-of-Two-Men-Who-Changed-Army-Medicine.pdf
11. Letterman, 6.
12. Sears, *To the Gates of Richmond*, 147.

They shared with all other departments the misfortunes of inexperience.[13]

Not an accurate portrayal of Tripler's tenure, but one not approaching fiction as with other chroniclers. Letterman's star ascended but is now subject to closer examination, and several commentators find it overblown.[14] If Tripler's successor had done such a magnificent job as some historians claim, why did the Sanitary Commission succeed in supplying medical stores to the Antietam battleground more quickly than the Army of the Potomac? How could it be, after that Army's "Mud March" in January 1863, that "disease ran rampant through the dispirited Union ranks, exacerbating by overcrowding, poor nutrition, and poor sanitation"? A new commander would take over a "diseased army" under the vaunted director's regime.[15]

The best writing of history relies on evidence and persuasive argument to make its case; it does not slant; it does not generalize a verdict by regurgitating previous assessments. It does not oversimplify.[16] Unquestioning acceptance of clichés, no matter how recently formed, "can cloud the realities behind the façade."[17] A recent biography of Letterman requires critical review. For example, Tripler is said to have become overwhelmed on the Peninsula and "conceded professional defeat" by asking for transfer to Detroit.[18] The evidence conclusively demonstrates that the transfer transpired because a well-deserved promotion was blocked, that Tripler sought the move while the Army was

---

13. Clements, 6.
14. E.g., Stouffer, Hood.
15. Browning & Silver, 5.
16. Compare: "The Union Army quickly reorganized its Medical Department in 1862 after prodding by a Sanitary Commission created by President Lincoln." M.M. Manring, Alan Hawk, Jason H. Calhoun & Romney C. Andersen, "Treatment of War Wounds: A Historical Review" in *Clinical Orthopaedics and Related Research*, Vol. 467, No. 8, Aug. 2009, 2169.
17. William C. Davis, *The Cause Lost: Myths and Realities of the Confederacy* (Lawrence: University Press of Kansas, 1996), 139.
18. McGaugh, 72-73.

poised on the brink of success, and that Letterman arrived when the Army had just fought the Seven Days Battles and was reeling from the effects of combat, fatigue, and poor generalship, soon to be joined by over-crowding.

Both behavioral and environmental factors have proven critical to human health. The volunteers who enlisted with little awareness of the importance of good "habits of self care"—eating, exercising, washing, sleeping, sheltering—but who followed medical advice such as Tripler's proved to be the soldiers with "the best health and the highest morale."[19] McClellan chose an advance against the Confederate capital over terrain and in conditions "increasing their vulnerability to illness." Sickness continued to plague the Army of the Potomac through the Summer in the face of Letterman's efforts. McClellan had chosen the "worst possible location" for his thrust at Richmond, and environmental complications impacted the combat readiness of his troops.[20] During the later campaigns of the Army of the Potomac, disease became less a factor.

Some critics of Tripler end in mixed judgment, labeling him "energetic" as well as "spasmodic" and "crotchety."[21] At best he was "important," but he "took an exaggerated pride in the prerogatives and privileges of military position."[22] One history paints him as "ascerbic" for being disgusted with how the line officers subverted the well-being of their men by not caring for their food and shelter properly.[23]

---

19. Kathryn S. Meier, "'No Place for the Sick': Nature's War on Civil War Soldier Mental and Physical Health in the 1862 Peninsula and Shenandoah Valley Campaigns" in *Journal of the Civil War Era*, Vol. 1, No. 2 (June 2011), 177. This historian maintains that self-care was a more critical element to a soldier's welfare than locale. Id. 178.
20. Browning & Silver, 397, 401-403, 407, 409.
21. Gillett, 166, a quotation from George Templeton Strong of the US Sanitary Commission. See Appendix.
22. William Q. Maxwell, *Lincoln's Fifth Wheel: The Political History of the United States Sanitary Commission* (New York: Longmans, Green & Co., 1956), 13.
23. Kenneth W. Noe, "I Am Completely Checked by the Weather: George B. McClellan, Weather, and the Peninsula Campaign" in Andrew S. Bledsoe & Andrew F. Lang eds., *Upon the Fields of Battle: Essays on the Military History of*

Another incorporates these assessments: "the feeling was widely held that the Medical Department, and more particularly Medical Director Tripler, had let the Army down," followed by "Tripler was not as inept as was thought" since his suggested system "was good; but he was not the man to head it."[24] A lone observer remarked on the recovery of the ill and their rapid return to the ranks under Tripler's regime, opining that the number of sick at home very likely took on the same dimensions.[25]

In one way, the two Medical Directors had something in common: they both brought order out of chaos. In Tripler's case, the challenge arose from mobilizing the largest army in US history and seeking to instill a professionalism and organization that would help carry it to victory. In Letterman's case, the chaos he met in taking over came about because of the Seven Days Battles, the unplanned and rapid retreat, and the confined encampment of the Army of the Potomac for succeeding weeks until withdrawn.

In the 20th century, two developments revived the possibility of remembering Tripler's service and contributions. In 1920, the Army opened a hospital in Hawaii and named it after the Civil War surgeon (today known as Tripler Army Medical Center). During World War II, it published in a medical bulletin a biographical sketch of Tripler. In part, it read:

> Throughout his army career he took every opportunity to improve his professional knowledge and skill. He was a talented physician and an able surgeon. He was the medical adviser of many individuals high in military and civil activities. He was what is known in the parlance of the Episcopal

---

America's Civil War (Baton Rouge: Louisiana State University Press, 2018), 56-57. Presumably, the term here means "forthright."
24. George W. Adams, *Doctors in Blue: The Medical History of the Union Army in the Civil War* (New York: Henry Schuman, 1952), 72, all unsourced. Similar is Louis C. Duncan, *The Medical Department of the United States Army in the Civil War* (n.p., n.d.).
25. Stewart, 78.

Church as a churchman, joining actively in the affairs of that denomination as church or lay reader wherever he was stationed.

His lasting fame throughout the Medical Corps of the Army has rested upon his *Manual*, which for half a century was the guide for recruit examiners. Though the form in which these instructions are given has been changed, the essence of Tripler's work will remain with them as long as diseases and deformities have to be sought for in the recruit. With the passing of the *Manual*, Tripler's memory is kept green to the army in the naming of the Hawaiian Department general hospital at Honolulu, the Tripler General Hospital.[26]

In 1990, the National Museum of Civil War Medicine came into existence. It began holding an annual national conference on Civil War-era medicine in 1993 and opened a museum to the public in 1996. In 2006, the organization published its first in a line of books and materials on Civil War medicine and began operating the Pry House Field Hospital Museum at the Antietam National Battlefield in association with the National Park Service. Its efforts to educate on the more accurate story of the practitioners and patients of the country's most violent and costly war have proven instrumental in changing traditional viewpoints about this sphere. Among its assessments is this, available on its website:

> As the first Medical Director of the Army of the Potomac, it was Tripler's job to ensure that both the raw recruits and surgeons adhered to the best medical practices of the day. While his successor, Jonathan Letterman, is better remembered for

---

26. *Army Medical Bulletin*, 176-181; a corresponding webpage states the Tripler facility was named for "the legendary American Civil War medic who made significant contributions to military medicine." https://defenseeconomy.hawaii.gov/tripler-army-medical-center/ See also online resources of the US Army Medical Department (AMEDD) found at: https://achh.army.mil

revolutionizing battlefield medicine, Tripler himself faced a gigantic challenge in creating and streamlining the medical organization of the largest army the United States had ever seen.[27]

Hammond's reputation has, in some respects, been subject to a similar complicated history. His tenure also was of short duration. The *Detroit Free Press*, no friend of the Lincoln Administration, would nonetheless praise it when suited to the newspaper's purposes. One such occasion came with the end of Hammond's tenure, captured by an item appearing under a surprising, laudatory headline:

> A Commendible [*Sic*] Act of Secretary Stanton.

> The Surgeon General, before he was ordered away from Washington, undertook to remove every Surgeon of the army who, he thought, dangerous to his plans and schemes. With that object in view, he made out a long list of Surgeons, and sent them to the Secretary of War, with the recommendation that they be placed on the retired list. At the head stood the name of Dr. Tripler. When the list was laid before Secretary Stanton, he at once dashed his pen through it, and wrote opposite it, absurd. This was right, and now his hand is in, we wish he would, if consistent with his other duties, spare time enough to look into the reasons which influenced the Surgeon General to exert his powerful influence to have Dr. Tripler rejected as Inspector General of the army. That it was to subserve the selfish ends and views of the Surgeon General, can be demonstrated ....[28]

By the time these words were printed, the political leverage by which

---

27. https://www.civilwarmed.org/event/facebook-live-tripler/
28. *Detroit Free Press*, Sept. 22, 1863, 2.

Hammond achieved his post had vanished. Engaging in "an essentially personal struggle" with Stanton had been costly.[29] While away, he was "relieved from the charge of the Medical Department in Washington."[30] The situation concerned his supporters, and a public relations campaign ran on Hammond's behalf. It consisted of:

- advertisements hailing his elimination of certain medicines[31]
- op-eds that ruled out any notion that he had fallen out of favor within the War Department[32]
- at least one adulatory biography, with head-and-shoulders illustration[33]

The Sanitary Commission pressed for a court-martial in order that its man could clear himself of Stanton's charges,[34] and a proceeding was ordered. But Hammond was convicted of most charges, and he was removed from service in August 1864. Hammond was "impulsive" and "not always wise or prudent; his ways of doing things were not always judicious."[35] Whether or not his actions deserved cashiering, he had been drummed out before two years in office elapsed.

By then, Letterman had left his position with the Army of the Potomac. Contemporaries seemed not to make a connection: "It was not known to even his intimate friends, and it can hardly concern

---

29. Marvel, 313-318.
30. Hammond, 25.
31. *Harper's Weekly,* July 18, 1863, 462; July 25, 1863, 478; Aug. 8, 1863, 511; Aug. 15, 1863, 527.
32. Id. Sept. 26, 1863, 611; Oct. 31, 1863, 691.
33. Id. Nov. 21, 1863, 748.
34. Hammond, 29.
35. *Personal Memoirs of John H. Brinton, Major and Surgeon U.S.V., 1861-1865* (New York: Neale Pub. Co., 1914), 170-171. Brinton wrote of being "a friend of Hammond's" and "a blood relative of General McClellan." Id. 310. A memoir critical of Tripler by a doctor "convinced" that "the negroes" were happiest and the most cared for "in the cotton and sugar growing States of the South" was dedicated to McClellan. Thomas T. Ellis, *Leaves from the Diary of an Army Surgeon* (New York: John Bradburn, 1863), 11.

those now living, why he took this step."[36] Their friendship did not end with their service in uniform. In 1872, Hammond went all the way to California to visit Letterman before death.[37]

The court-martial may not have been conducted with rigorous fairness, but a different outcome would not mean that Hammond's conduct was unimpeachable. A lamentable case demonstrated his rigidity in some circumstances, which proved fatal to a heroic patient. Surgeon Swinburne had examined a Colonel who was convalescing in the National Hotel in Washington. Wounded in the foot, the officer's injury did not, in the estimation of the field staff, require amputation. Swinburne concurred with that judgment, which conflicted with the hospital physician on duty. Others called to the case lined up against surgery. Hammond upbraided Swinburne, instructing him that the hospital surgeon had charge of the patient and the case was none of his business. Surgery proceeded; the patient died. The Surgeon-General's conduct provided evidence that he was not necessarily the dedicated opponent of red tape. He could demonstrate animus, rather than open-mindedness.[38] Tripler addressed a shortcoming in his final official report since he lacked some records from his office in Washington. Quartermaster-General Meigs had kindly aided his work by sending records to Detroit, but the locked chest in which they were stored, it turned out, had been opened in Surgeon-General Hammond's office. Some documents had been removed.[39] His nephew, Lieutenant Charles T. Bissell, replied to Tripler's request for records:

> I have all your letter books, as well as the one for telegrams. I did not forward them to you before because Dr. Letterman said they did not belong to you but were the property and

---
36. Clements, 20.
37. Id. 24. This work states that Letterman suffered from a chronic intestinal disease, became very ill on March 13, 1872, and died two days later, indicating "the dark shadow" of his wife's death in 1867 contributed to his own.
38. *A Typical American*, 50-57.
39. *OR*, V, 91. Ironically, Hammond would complain of the same obstruction when he sought documents during his court-martial.

records of the Med. Director's Office of the Army. I will forward them immediately by express.[40]

Of special interest is a trade press op-ed on July 30, 1864, at a point when Letterman had stepped away from the Army of the Potomac and Hammond would soon be court-martialed. Entitled "Union of Civil and Military Surgeons," the piece extolled how the War had brought the two branches of the profession together, increasing the technical expertise of Army doctors while elevating the moral tone of the civilians. As to the latter, it related how surgeons working with their military counterparts "feel that they are in the presence of men who hold in proper esteem their official position and profession." Under that influence, civilian doctors stepped up, so that all medical staffers "occupied a most enviable position in the army. The medical officer was everywhere regarded as the soul of honor, and as a model of official integrity." Tripler's name was among the six individuals cited. [41]

By contrast, disrespect of Tripler continued a half-century after the Civil War in a popular image-centric collection:

> Dr. Charles S. Tripler was General McClellan's first medical director. Although he had accomplished an immense amount of work, his machinery was not flexible enough to care for 100,000 men, and during the Peninsula campaign there was much confusion and an immense amount of suffering. But for the Sanitary Commission, which had charge of the hospital-boats near White House Landing and which cared for many thousands wounded and carried away hundreds, the distress might have been much greater. Dr. Jonathan Letterman

---

40. Typescript letter dated Jan. 25, 1863, in possession of Dr. David Cullen, Wichita, Kansas. Bissell then was 1st Lieutenant, 5th Michigan Infantry, detached to the "Office of Chief of Artillery, Army of the Potomac" as an aide to Henry J. Hunt. He received a brevet in April 1865 for his services and was discharged in 1870. Robertson, 776.
41. *American Medical Times*, Jul. 30, 1864, 55.

became medical director of the Army of the Potomac July 1, 1862, succeeding Dr. Tripler. Dr. Letterman was a man of great ability; he organized the ambulance corps, improved the field-hospital service, and instituted a method of furnishing medical supplies by brigades instead of by regiments. Many of his innovations continued throughout the war. After the larger part of the Army of the Potomac had returned with General Pope, Dr. Letterman found much difficulty in again organizing it properly. He was successful, however, and the care of the wounded after Antietam marks a distinct advance on anything before this time.[42]

The *Photographic History* was not a scholarly publication and typically did not specify its documentary sources. This assessment came from the pen of an officer in the Army Medical Department, a veteran post-Civil War.[43] Later on in the work, a cite is provided to laud the work and service of Surgeon-General Hammond, enabling the reader to detect how the writer came to the favorable conclusion. This article also conceded an important point: that the Sanitary Commission "took a hand in affairs" to push for Hammond's appointment.[44]

A 2013 biography of Dr. Letterman makes the point that Tripler's "early success" is succeeded in "less than six months" with "public fire"—in reality, the only public involved were the members of the Commission's governing structure who had begun a campaign to "oust" Tripler before he had fairly gotten started. Soon, according to this study, Tripler's behavior "had produced a paralysis that had cost him the confidence of McClellan, the Sanitary Commission, and others." The source for the last quote does not speak to McClellan's loss of

---

42. Holland Thompson ed., *The Photographic History of The Civil War In Ten Volumes*, Volume 7: Prisons and Hospitals (New York: Review of Reviews Co., 1911), 219.
43. Edward L. Munson (1868-1947) was a graduate of the Yale School of Medicine.
44. *Photographic History*, 347.

confidence. To the contrary, McClellan's letter of July 4, 1862 (p. 127, *supra*), expressed "entire satisfaction" with the conduct of the outgoing Medical Director. A post-war reminiscence about the excellence of his staff (p. 42, *supra*), also contradicts dissatisfaction with Tripler's performance.[45]

An award-winning study of the environmental effects of the Civil War addresses the same theme. Tripler became "unpopular in the War Department" by circumventing Surgeon-General Finley, "contributing to his eventual removal in July."[46] Cited support for this assertion is from a single source, an account of the court-martial proceedings in which Finley's abject apology, and Tripler's forgiveness in the matter, caused dismissal.[47] Elsewhere, Tripler is praised since "his medical advice was sound" but criticized as being "ineffectual."[48] And his contemporary, on-the-ground assessment of straggling is repudiated since it was "far more likely" that those who shirked did so "because of illness or fear of falling sick."[49] The latter is tantamount to an admission of Tripler's sagacity.

The matter of Campaign performance by key staff appears in a magisterial 2017 study by a first-rate historian and wordsmith. Within its eight hundred pages is but one mention of Jonathan Letterman. The setting is July 1862, after President Lincoln has paid a visit to the Army of the Potomac in its Harrison's Landing fortress. General McClellan engaged in a purge of officers who had proved lacking during the Peninsula Campaign, seeking "to be rid of" his chief of artillery ("ineffectual"), head of cavalry reserve ("disastrous"), chief quartermaster (the new appointment being "unequalled"), and others.

---

45. McGaugh, 58-63, 301 n.17.
46. Kathryn Shively Meier, *Nature's Civil War: Common Soldiers and the Environment in 1862 Virginia* (Chapel Hill: University of North Carolina Press, 2013), 85.
47. Lowry & Welsh, 174-175. The actual citation is 176; the gist of this chapter is that Tripler deserved to be honored with the naming of the Hawaii medical facility while Finley earned the removal that he—not Tripler—received.
48. Meier, *Nature's Civil War*, 78.
49. Id. 141. No support is cited; this assessment is that of the work's author.

As to the Army's command structure for health and well-being, "[a]nother major staff improvement was the appointment of Jonathan Letterman as the army's medical director."[50] This conclusion is not explained or sourced.

The identity of Letterman's predecessor, though unstated, is not difficult to determine. Both Hammond and Letterman are mentioned without critique. Tripler's 42,000-word report in the *Official Records* is useful to the experienced historian, for it reveals the challenges faced in launching this Army's medical infrastructure and carrying it into the first major campaign. Tripler was not part of the purge.

Tripler is also missing from a recent investigation of "the medical experiences of American physicians who served in the Union Medical Department." A remarkable omission, this, since Tripler did not fit the profile of the doctors who entered the war "without the underpinnings of a proper education or practical experience." He brought training by college and field, and his published works are evidence of a scientifically inquisitive mind. William A. Hammond looms large in this book, uncritically. Letterman's reputation is not tested but, instead, given as someone who would "revolutionize the ambulance system."[51]

Another recent history of the Army of the Potomac treats the department heads under McClellan during the Peninsula Campaign. Some, the author tells the reader, were "highly capable, if not excellent." Without their services, "[t]he army could not have been sustained." The Medical Department is not mentioned.[52] It is difficult to draw a conclusion from this silence.

In a very worthwhile study of women's influence in the work of the Sanitary Commission, the triumvirate of Tripler, Letterman, and

---

50. Stephen W. Sears, *Lincoln's Lieutenants: The High Command of the Army of the Potomac* (Boston: Houghton Mifflin Harcourt, 2017), 282-283.
51. Devine, *Learning from the Wounded*, 43. A prime emphasis in this work is on the experiences of individual Union physicians.
52. Jeffry D. Wert, *The Sword of Lincoln: The Army of the Potomac* (New York: Simon & Schuster, 2005), 93.

Hammond come in for interesting treatment. Tripler is dismissed in two footnotes, the first quoting his petulant judgment of "strong-minded women" in his official report (a statement that did him no credit and is ironic, given the character of his life partner) and the second taking him to task for opposing one of those individuals. Letterman is mentioned once, merely as Tripler's successor. Hammond's opposition to female nurses—a position not held by Tripler—is highlighted, as is his exercise of "virtually unchecked power."[53]

A 2002 study that sought to more accurately portray the state of medical care in the Civil War contains much of relevance.

Ira M. Rutkow's *Bleeding Blue and Gray: Civil War Surgery and the Evolution of American Medicine* (New York: Random House, 2005), is an excellent survey by a clinical professor of surgery, holding a doctorate of public health, on Union military medical conduct. Its dissection of the political machinations engaged in by the Sanitary Commission and Hammond is perhaps the fullest exposure of that story. Olmsted continued in opposition to Tripler because of a struggle "over who officially controlled the hospital ships." Acting upon Olmsted's urging "to revolutionize" things, Hammond began to replace medical directors who were "aging and ineffectual" with someone like "longtime" friend Letterman. When Tripler was nominated for hospital Inspector-General, "the Sanitary Commission's effort to prevent any other important positions from being offered to Tripler" caused it to fail.[54] The assertions that Tripler was "broken" and that Hammond "removed him" from the Army of the Potomac do not comport with evidence adduced herein.

A fuller record is developed in a study of the Army Medical Corps up until the War's end. First is the fluid situation as the great Army of the Potomac left for the Peninsula: "Tripler believed with some justification" that he had brought order out of chaos; thus, "he was

---

53. Judith Ann Giesberg, *Civil War Sisterhood: The U.S. Sanitary Commission and Women's Politics in Transition* (Boston: Northeastern University Press, 2000), 94-97, 188 n.29, n.32.
54. Rutkow, 119-122.

apparently confident of his own ability to deal with the demands of the upcoming campaign." On the Peninsula, "Tripler was forced to act on his own," "insisted upon checking candidates for evacuation," "was thus forced" to extemporize. These characterizations sound like a Medical Director taking initiative and acting resourcefully. When Tripler "begged Hammond for aid and predicted dire consequences" if not provided, the Surgeon-General "obviously sympathized with Tripler's predicament." But his answer "implied that Tripler was not doing all he could to help himself" and that his office "could not always meet all his [Tripler's] needs." Hammond dispatched two doctors to the Peninsula "presumably concluding that Tripler could no longer cope with the situation alone," and "gave Tripler specific instructions"—always a helpful step when what is sought is action, not words. When "the evacuation south to Harrison's Landing" came on June 28—abruptly, despite battlefield success, without advance planning—the term itself suggesting flight, Tripler "had to order more than 600 wounded abandoned." Why? "[B]ecause he had so few ambulances." Why not enough? One reason might have been that Hammond had "pushed to obtain ambulances" from the Quartermaster's Department unsuccessfully. Somehow, the conclusion is that Tripler was "defeated." It is conceded that "Tripler may *well* have done all he could in the situation" (emphasis added), but such admission is trumped by a contemporary's assessment that "he had been proven totally incompetent." By whom? George Templeton Strong, a leader at the Sanitary Commission, who "held that Tripler and his staff were entirely responsible for the sufferings of Union soldiers in Virginia."[55]

Strong (1820-1875) was an attorney, vestryman, and draft shirker—he paid for a substitute. He lacked medical training.[56] His diary came to light in the 1930s, and its attributes consist of being "quotable, opinionated," and "perhaps" the northern counterpart to

---

55. Gillett, 184-190.
56. Ironically, Surgeon-General Hammond criticized appointment of "civilians" to a board that would examine into the affairs of his department, including one whose profession was the law, not medicine. Hammond, 24.

the famous Mary Chestnut diary.[57] In truth, his slants on Tripler began with praise. In a September 1861 letter, Strong castigated rampant "utter idiocy" and the Commission's obligation to "apply the hot end of the poker" to the Surgeon-General; "[f]ortunately, we have the cooperation of McClellan's Medical Director [Tripler]" who "had taken an important step already." Failing change, Strong advised his correspondent that "I shall ask you to help us with a newspaper war before the people." Revealing that the Commission was seeking to "oust Finley," Strong mused that Tripler "might be made to do as head of the [Army Medical] Bureau"—his qualities being "energetic, spasmodic, crotchety, genial." Strong relayed, however, that McClellan "hinted a doubt of his capacity" for remaining on his horse when a wounded soldier needed succor; "[t]his little omission seems to have settled Tripler in McClellan's estimation." It is surpassing strange that the Army commander would then have kept someone of such incapacity in such a vital role. Also interesting was how "'We, the Commission' think well of McClellan." Into the Fall, Strong was still favorably disposed toward Tripler, perhaps because on some issues he "brought over McClellan" to approve.

All was not well, though, in May 1862. Strong saw soldiers lying on bare hospital floors on the Peninsula and "perishing of typhoid" for lack of blankets, beds, food, and clothing. Tripler was "utterly and disgracefully unprovided for the work before him" in front of Yorktown. If so, at "McClellan's headquarters," why had the Army commander not fired Tripler? Strong then headed back to New York. From that location, he recorded a letter from Olmsted on June 13, "giving a fearful, sickening account of the weakness and inefficiency and imbecility of Dr. Tripler and his subordinates on the Peninsula," with "carloads of wounded" and injured not receiving proper attention, "lying neglected and forgotten." A week later, Strong recorded:

---

57. Paula Baker, "New York during the Civil War and Reconstruction" in Milton M. Klein ed., *The Empire State: A History of New York* (Ithaca: Cornell University Press, 2001), 429; C. Vann Woodward ed., *Mary Chestnut's Civil War* (New Haven: Yale University Press, 1981) is one of several versions.

[p]oor, honest, irascible, feeble old Tripler's nomination as Inspector General unanimously rejected by the Senate. Not surprising, for Senators have been visiting the White House and seeing for themselves what he can accomplish. Letterman and Vollum are to report to McClellan as Medical Director and Inspector. Tripler is relieved, and McClellan's army still more so.

Strong recorded another letter from Olmsted on July 4 on his voyage "to make a report to the Surgeon-General on the sanitary condition of the army." Medical affairs were not the only subject of the visit to Washington: "and to plead for reinforcements for Burnside or somebody, and for 50,000 more men. Where can we find them on demand? Why was recruiting stopped? Letterman, surgeon U.S.A., says our loss is 30,000, residue 60,000. Sanitary aspect of the army very bad. No camp police; no time for it." Another from Olmsted on the 7th exhibited a "still darker mood. Seems to think McClellan's whole army may be cut off from its supplies and destroyed."[58]

Strong is quotable and revelatory. His painting of the Sanitary Commission as highly political, with its members holding opinions based on rumor and "fake news," seems not to have registered with many historians. Olmsted's mission to lobby for more reinforcements after the hasty retreat to Harrison's Landing, in the light of the factual situation on the Peninsula, has him carrying McClellan's water. It clearly exceeded the Commission's jurisdiction. Olmsted's later recanting of the condemnation of Tripler, upon mature reflection, should have trumped Strong's private gossiping had historians reviewed and reflected upon the whole record.

Those regarding the New York lawyer as an excellent source may have overlooked a certain kind of horse-trading that he, and the

---

58. Allan Nevins ed., *The Diary of George Templeton Strong: The Civil War, 1860-1865* (New York: MacMillan Co., 1952, 1962), xxxviii, 181, 184, 187, 222, 231, 240. Nevins adds a laudatory encomium of Letterman's legacy in extensive footnote 26 on 240.

Commission, were not averse to undertaking. When Hammond was in grave trouble after his court-martial conviction, Strong and another Commission leader visited the Secretary of War. The Commission's continuing role and Hammond's fate came up together, "and a deal was made." The Secretary could "get rid of Hammond," and the Commission could continue its work.[59] So much for the untarnished integrity of the Sanitary Commission and the notion that it was an apolitical organization.

Unlike the medical practitioners and other volunteers of the Sanitary Commission, who temporarily withdrew "from positions far more remunerative," Tripler stayed a soldier, foregoing financial reward from the same "motives of the highest benevolence and patriotism."[60] He also appears to have stayed as an associate member of the Sanitary Commission.[61]

Particularly revealing is a speech given by President Bellows in Philadelphia in 1863. In reviewing the history of the Commission's activities, Bellows went back to the beginning of the war when, he said, the Army Medical Bureau consisted of "excellent" physicians

---

59. Rutkow, 293-294. In 1878, Hammond mounted a "crusade" to clear his name; President Rutherford B. Hayes referred the matter to a military board, which recertified the guilty verdicts; Hammond once again played the political game, and his name was added to the retired list with the stipulation that he never receive a government pension. In 1899, he was broke and sought to break the 1879 deal. He died from a heart attack before achieving his goal. Id. 322-323. The fact of passage of a private bill to authorize (i.e., virtually instruct) the President to review his case and, if he shall deem it proper, to restore him to the retired list as Surgeon-General without back pay or pension is established in 20 Stat. 511 (ch. 35). A favorable biography is Bonnie Ellen Blustein, *Preserve Your Love for Science: Life of William A. Hammond, American Neurologist* (Cambridge: Cambridge University Press, 1991). See also Pat Leonard, "William Hammond and the End of the Medical Middle Ages" in the "Disunion" Civil War Sesquicentennial weblog in *New York Times*, Apr. 27, 2012. Hayes may not have become President but for successful surgery after his wounding at the Battle of South Mountain in September 1862.
60. *Succinct Narrative*, 20-21.
61. U.S. Sanitary Commission, *Publication No. 74, Associate Members as of March 15th, 1864*, 20.

and surgeons; "[i]t was an admirable department, strong from the knowledge gained in previous wars;" "the discipline of rigid machinery" was essential to an army's success, and the Commission looked at such conduct "with a kind of jealousy;" and problems in the Medical Department were largely created by the addition of civilian doctors into the ranks.[62] Such platitudes were in direct conflict with the intraboard member chatter that evinced a group intent on dramatic changes in the Department because of—not in spite of—its leadership.

The Commission's allies sought to gild its legacy late in and after the war. In 1864, Strong published a revelatory article about its "struggles." He confessed that no one "fully understood the herculean nature of the business" of constructing the military and medical apparatus necessary to win the war. But the Commission, he argued, had been the prime force in improving the health of the Army.[63] A retrospective published a half-century later, perhaps removed from the immediacy involved in war-time politics, boasted of the improvement in the medical condition of the Eastern army. Large credit lay at the Commission's door, according to this slender pamphlet, but the Army itself had done the hard work. The ragged condition of the Union combatants after First Bull Run equaled that of the medical organization until improvement materialized:

> A reorganization of the army followed, and it went forward with tremendous vigor. Order, discipline, cleanliness, the policing of camps, the training of inexperienced officers and men, soon made a new army out of the old one, and three months later the very measures which the Commission urged, and which it was said could not be enforced, were now

---

62. *Speech of the Rev. Dr. Bellows, President of the United States Sanitary Commission, Made at the Academy of Music, Philadelphia, Tuesday Evening, Feb. 24, 1863* (Philadelphia: C. Sherman, Son & Co., 1863), 9-10.
63. George T. Strong, *Origin, Struggles and Principles of the U.S. Sanitary Commission* (Boston: U.S. Sanitary Commission, 1864), 11.

submitted to and enforced, and the best disciplined regiments were the most contented regiments. …

New vigor was at once infused into every part of the medical service, and adequate provision was made for coming campaigns. The new hospital system which had been previously planned by the Commission was organized on a scale unprecedented in war, and resulted in a lower rate of mortality than had been recorded in history, and all this was accomplished within a year after the firing upon Fort Sumter.[64]

What of the legacy of the last Medical Director of the Army of the Potomac, Thomas A. McParlin? Suffice to say that few histories treat the subject, and hardly any have adopted the view that "[a]s Letterman had built upon the foundation of Tripler, McParlin built on Letterman's achievements."[65] The fourth Medical chief served from January 14, 1864, until beyond the war's conclusion in September 1865. He, too, faced a daunting challenge, dealing with the immense casualties of the Overland Campaign during the Spring and Summer of 1864. His performance was "a credit to the medical director and his organization." McParlin, however, has received "scant credit" in the literature about medical care during the Civil War.[66]

Letterman may have written the best viewpoint on the historiography sought to be rectified in this study. It came in a defense of the conduct of the medical staff at Antietam, but its applicability here is obvious:

> Gross misrepresentations of the conduct of medical officers have been made and scattered broadcast over the country, causing deep and heart-rending anxiety to those who had

---

64. William H. Reed, *The Heroic Story of the United States Sanitary Commission, 1861-1865* (Boston: Geo. H. Ellis Co., 1910), 7, 8.
65. Hood, 155.
66. James M. Phalen, "Surgeon Thomas A. McParlin: Letterman's Successor with the Army of the Potomac" in *The Military Surgeon*, July 1940, 68, 70.

friends or relatives in the army, who might at any moment require the services of a surgeon. It is not to be supposed that there were no incompetent surgeons in the army. It is certainly true that there were; but these sweeping denunciations against a class of men who will favorably compare with the military surgeons of any country, because of the incompetency and short-comings of a few, are wrong, and do injustice to a body of men who have labored faithfully and well. It is easy to magnify an existing evil until it is beyond the bounds of truth. It is equally easy to pass by the good that has been done on the other side.[67]

Historians have been quick to magnify shortcomings in Tripler's performance from August 1861 to July 1862. It has been equally too easy to pass by his achievements, given the task. He had been required "to do what had never been done."[68] That McClellan's force was poised for success just a few miles from the Confederacy's capital—not sapped by poor health, with thoughtful plans made for a structured care of casualties—reflects a major achievement unprecedented in US Army medical history.

Looking back after a quarter-century, a fellow physician who had been taken prisoner at Savage's Station could add another dimension to Tripler's legacy. The reminiscence noted that President Lincoln had nominated the Army Medical Director "to be medical inspector-general of the United States Army"—a promotion, rather than merely a paper elevation. He was deserving of such recognition:

> Dr. Tripler's experience had been wide, and his training of such a nature as well suited him to the responsibilities of the office he had so long and admirably filled; but the difficulties

---

67. *OR*, XIX, pt. I, 113.
68. William J. Miller, "Scarcely Any Parallel in History: Logistics, Friction and McClellan's Strategy for the Peninsula Campaign" in *The Peninsula Campaign*, Vol. Two, 129, 130.

to overcome had been many and various, and while the campaign just ended had taxed his energy and capacity to their uttermost, it had yet left as a heritage other and newer experiences, as well as a trained medical staff, — resources of inestimable value to be drawn upon by his successor.[69]

Letterman had thus built on an earnestly constructed system, making improvements upon the "heritage" bequeathed to him by a worthy predecessor.

The 1862 landscape from Fortress Monroe to Richmond, and the battlegrounds that spread out across the swamps ranging from the York River to the James, were sites of "what is good and bad, noble and mean, wise and foolish, brave and cowardly" in human behavior.[70] Scenes of quietude today, they represent a "sublime awfulness" where 19th century soldiers wounded and killed each other in scores and hundreds and thousands.[71] In the midst of this awful carnage, confronting sickness and disease, Charles Stuart Tripler and other earnest physicians labored, sacrificed, and exposed themselves at great personal risk and cost, working faithfully for as great a cause as earth has ever known. Cut off from the land of the living before his time, Tripler did not have opportunity to burnish his legacy, and history has done his name no favors. He was one of the "men set apart"[72]—men in uniform, in this case wearing a special sash—who sought to do his duty—in this case, a combination of civic, moral, and medical obligations.

The monument above his grave in the old Detroit cemetery signifies respect, admiration, and fondness by the colleagues who knew him best. As such memorials go, it is far from imposing or grand.

---

69. Potter, 8-9.
70. John S. Salmon, *The Official Virginia Civil War Battlefield Guide* (Mechanicsburg: Stackpole Books, 2001), ix.
71. Stephen Berry, *Weirding the War: Stories from the Civil War's Ragged Edges* (Athens: University of Georgia Press, 2011), 191.
72. Bruce Catton, *Waiting for the Morning Train: An American Boyhood* (Garden City: Doubleday & Co., 1972), 189.

Upon a block base sits a square stone inscribed with "M.S."—signifying the "Medical Service" of the Army to which the grave's occupant devoted so much of his life. Above those is an urn-shaped and carved piece upon which his life's span was inscribed. Above it all is a cross, symbol of the faith in a higher power and the faithfulness to medicine exhibited by the man remembered. It is altogether a fitting monument, one that should be visited and tended, the physician remembered and his service to a free nation venerated.

Appendix [1]

I. Tripler's Published Writings

Based on a list provided in Eunice Tripler's memoirs,[2] in *The Medical History*, and elsewhere, the following titles can be attributed to Charles Tripler in what is believed to be chronological order.

1. *Remarks on Delirium Tremens, or the Irritative Fever of Drunkenness: An Inaugural Dissertation, Submitted to the Examination of the Faculty of the College of Physicians and Surgeons of the University of the State of New York* (New York: J. Seymour, [April 3,] 1827), a 22-page pamphlet. It was republished in 1857 by Tripler with an introductory paragraph. *Delirium Tremens: Its Nature and Treatment* (n.p., ca. 1857)

2. "Case of Secondary Hemorrhage after Amputation at the Shoulder-Joint" in S.S. Purple M.D. ed., *New-York Journal of Medicine, and the Collateral Sciences*, Vol. III—New Series (New York: Daniel Fanshaw, 1849) 40-43

3. *The Causes, Nature, and Treatment of Scurvy: A Paper Read Before the Covington and Newport (Ky.) Medical Society* (n.p., ca. 1858) (20 pages)

---

1. This volume follows the appendix format of the classic work by Kenneth P. Williams originally entitled *Lincoln Finds a General*, two volumes of which were republished by the University of Nebraska Press in 1999, the first as *Grant Rises in the West: The First Year, 1861-1862*.
2. *Heart in Tatters*, 85-86.

4. *Manual of the Medical Officer of the Army of the United States, Part I, Recruiting and the Inspection of Recruits*, by Charles S. Tripler, M.D., Surgeon U.S.A.; Fellow of the College of Physicians and Surgeons of the University of the State of New York (Cincinnati: Wrightson & Co., 1858)

5. *The Duties of Physicians in Relation to Popular Medical Delusions: An Address Delivered Before the Covington and Newport Medical Society, June 14, 1859* (Covington: S.G. Cobb, 1859)

6. *Hand-Book of the Military Surgeon* (Cincinnati: Robert Clarke & Co., 1861), co-authored with George Curtis Blackman (1819–1871), professor of surgery at the College

7. *Hospital Gangrene: A Lecture Delivered to Prof. Blackman's Class at the Medical College of Ohio, Session of 1860-61* in The Cincinnati Lancet and Observer, Vol. VI, No. 10 (Cincinnati: n.p., Oct. 1863)

8. *Report of the Committee on Rank in the Medical Department of the Army*, co-authored with Thomas Antisell. *The Transactions of the American Medical Association*, Vol. XVII (Philadelphia: Collins, 1866)

II. Tripler's Mexico Report

Puebla, Mexico,
6th July, 1847.

Sir:

Agreeably to your instructions of the third instant, I called together yesterday the medical officers of the second division for the purpose of consultation, and the interchange of opinion, upon the causes of the diseases now so extensively prevailing among the troops. I have the honor to submit the result.

We consider the origin of the evil, the inferior physical constitution of so many of the men that are enlisted for the service. In peace, when we have good comfortable quarters, good hospitals, abundance of clothing and bedding, and no exposure for our men, the greatest care and caution are exercised in the inspection of recruits, and it is seldom a man gains admission into the ranks who is not qualified to perform the duties of a soldier. But in war, where a still greater degree of physical vigor in the soldier is required, from the necessary privation and exposure to which he must be subjected, a relaxation in the scrutiny the recruit is submitted to, is winked at and even encouraged, with the effects of giving us armies on paper, filling our hospitals and embarrassing the operations of our Generals in the field. It is undeniable that the recruits the regiments of this division have received within the past year, have been of the most inferior description, and it is among them the greatest proportion of disease has occurred.

Another cause of disease is the necessary and rapid transition of climate. It is believed that few individuals in private life make a rapid transit from one climate to another, without experiencing some disturbance of healthy function. This cause would of course operate to a greater extent among soldiers from the peculiarity of their circumstances, and it is one that cannot be obviated.

Deficiency of clothing is another cause. In many and perhaps most instances, this is the fault of the soldier himself. Men will throw away their clothing on a march to relieve their knapsacks, preferring future pain, disease and death to present fatigue. This evil has prevailed extensively on the march from Vera Cruz to Puebla.

The sudden and violent change of habits the recruit must undergo in becoming a soldier produces an unfavorable influence upon the power of his constitution to resist disease. This cause is also irremediable.

The neglect of personal cleanliness is another cause of disease. It is a fact that numbers of our men, particularly those reporting sick, neglect to a shameful extent such ablutions as are necessary to health.

The quarters occupied by our troops are for the most part open to the weather, those which are within doors are small and ill ventilated apartments, the floors upon which the men sleep are of brick, and at least one-half on the ground floor and necessarily damp. This is a palpable cause of disease. It has been mitigated to some degree by the issue of mats to the men.

The use of fresh provisions extensively no doubt occasions disturbance of the digestive organs and swells the number of our cases of diarrhoea. The imprudent use of the fruits of the climate occasions many cases and is a great impediment in the way of convalescence. It is also thought that a proper attention is not given to the cooking of the rations; that the cooks are frequently careless in the performance of their duties and that bad cooking makes a doubtful diet positively injurious.

But an important reason for the increase in the number of the sick report may be found in the climatic influence. Ordinarily men when relieved of disease rapidly recover strength and flesh, and are able to return to duty. Here this is not the case, convalescence is astonishingly slow, and an improvement scarcely perceptible is made from day to day in men who do not want any further medical treatment. Of this class are most of those now on the surgeon's reports.

Very respectfully, your obedient servant,

Chs. S. Tripler,
Medical Director, 2nd Division.[3]

---

3. Brown, *Medical Department*, 188-189.

III. Official Formation of the United States Sanitary Commission

War Department,
Washington, June 9, 1861.

The Secretary of War has learned, with great satisfaction, that at the instance and in pursuance of the suggestion of the Medical Bureau, in a communication to this office, dated May 22, 1861, Henry W. Bellows, D.D., Prof. A.D. Bache, LL.D., Prof. Jeffries Wyman, M.D., Prof. Wolcott Gibbs, M.D., W.H. Van Buren, M.D. Samuel G. Howe, M.D., R.C. Wood, Surgeon U.S.A., G.W. Cullum, U.S.A., Alexander E. Shiras, U.S.A., have mostly consented, in connection with such others as they may choose to associate with them, to act as "A Commission of Inquiry and Advice in respect of the Sanitary Interests of the United States Forces," and without remuneration from the Government. The Secretary has submitted their patriotic proposal to the consideration of the President, who directs the acceptance of the services thus generously offered.

The Commission, in connection with a Surgeon of the U.S.A., to be designated by the Secretary, will direct its inquiries to the principles and practices connected with the inspection of recruits and enlisted men; the sanitary condition of the volunteers; to the means of preserving and restoring the health, and of securing the general comfort and efficiency of troops; to the proper provision of cooks, nurses, and hospitals; and to other subjects of like nature.

The Commission will frame such rules and regulations, in respect of the objects and modes of its inquiry, as may seem best adapted to the purpose of its constitution, which, when approved by the Secretary, will be established as general guides of its investigations and action.

A room with necessary conveniences will be provided in the City of Washington for the use of the Commission, and the members will meet when and at such places as may be convenient to them for consultation, and for the determination of such questions as may come properly before the Commission.

In the progress of its inquiries, the Commission will correspond freely with the Department and with the Medical Bureau, and will communicate to each, from time to time, such observations and results as it may deem expedient and important.

The Commission will exist until the Secretary of War shall otherwise direct, unless sooner dissolved by its own action.

Simon Cameron
Secretary of War.[4]

The original structure of the Commission was comprised of a Board of Commissioners and a Secretary, who acted as the chief executive officer. For that position, Frederick Law Olmsted was selected. Although women had fostered its creation, none was named to the Board. Instead, its membership consisted of men who "came from wealthy, privileged backgrounds and were related by familial and educational ties to the elites of their areas." All but Olmsted possessed a college degree; most had never served in a benevolent organization. A minority were physicians.[5]

Olmsted had significant administrative experience gained from his work on design and construction of Central Park in New York City. He also brought limitations to the job: he was stubborn, proved to be a difficult subordinate, did not manage finances carefully, and did not expect a long tenure as Secretary.[6]

---

4. Stille, 532-533.
5. *Olmsted Papers*, 4-5.
6. Id. 7-8.

IV. Olmsted

The most recent biography of F.L. Olmsted contains a number of interesting insights regarding his Civil War service.

In modern times, the man is best known for his landscape design work, most notably at Central Park in New York. This identification may gloss over the fundamental point that "Olmsted viewed the world as a social reformer, first and foremost."[7] A reformer may let idealism cloud realities that are difficult, or even impossible, to overcome. Thus, he ran into cognitive dissonance in seeking to influence the levers of power inside the District of Columbia: "Olmsted's tenure in the capital would be marked by extreme impatience, particularly at the outset. He'd grown used to making rapid-fire changes in his own life. Washington felt so sluggish by contrast."[8] Instead, he found an intellectual companion in Henry Bellows, head of the Sanitary Commission, whose sermons were "generously laced with progressive social ideas."[9] Both were members of the Century Club[10]— the "Century Association," founded in 1847, located at 7 West 43rd Street near Fifth Avenue in Midtown. It became headquarters for the Sanitary Commission. For his part, Bellows regarded Olmsted as "a severe judge, seldom pleased."[11] He pled a special case for his colleague:

> You also understand his impracticable temper, his irritable brain, his unappreciation of human nature in its undivided form and his very imperfect sympathies to weak, mixed, and inconsequent people.[12]

---

7. Id. 178.
8. Martin, 178.
9. Id. 180.
10. Id. 182.
11. Id. 191.
12. Id. 216. Strong recorded Olmsted traits: "a monomania for system and organization ... and appetite for power." Nevins, *The Diary of George Templeton Strong*, 304-305.

When Olmsted drafted up a report for the Board, his first effort proved unsatisfactory. The Board was concerned about the political fall-out from the approach, and it ended up becoming only a privately printed edition.[13]

Olmsted's kind of impatience extended to intersecting the careers of high individuals. Surgeon-General Finley was the first target. Olmsted met with General McClellan in his private quarters on September 12, 1861, to advocate for Finley to be replaced. He camped out "in the lobbies and anterooms of the Washington power elite" to achieve his ends. He and several commissioners met with the President on October 17 to press for Finley's removal.[14]

Soon after Tripler departed the Peninsula, so did Olmsted. He sailed to New York in mid-July. He was exhausted—and then suffered a breakdown, perhaps a form of post-traumatic stress disorder. His recuperation was lengthy.[15] By the time of Gettysburg, "his relationship with the United States Sanitary Commission was souring fast."[16] He resigned as Secretary as of September 1. His next job had little of the reformer's bent: for a nice annual salary of $10,000, he moved to California to manage the Mariposa Estate, leaving New York City on September 14, 1863—almost a year to the date of Antietam.[17] On November 21, 1865, he was back in New York.[18] The Civil War had been over for several months.

Perhaps the most telling insight by this biography is the assessment that "nothing in Olmsted's background really qualified him to run a medical commission."[19] By contrast, Tripler's background eminently qualified him to be an army medical director. Letterman's performance seems to have avoided much criticism, but at Antietam the

---

13. Martin, 189-190; see *Olmsted Papers*, 153-187.
14. Martin, 191.
15. Id. 205, 209-210. Roper, *F.L.O.*, 231, mentions his "fatigue."
16. Martin, 223.
17. Id. 232-233.
18. Id. 270.
19. Id. 182.

Commission's supplies arrived "a full day before those of the Medical Bureau."[20]

V. Savage's Station Hospital

Publicizing the locations of Civil War field hospitals to increase public awareness is a relatively recent development. The 1993 national report on the condition of Civil War battlefields concurred in the value of such sites as part of preservation programs. However, "[u]nable to study all these thousands of sites" such as "hospitals and prisons," principal effort was devoted to battlegrounds themselves.[21] The same kinds of forces threaten field hospital locations as they do battle ground. That Americans bled and died at both is a truth that needs to be better understood. A military hospital is a sphere in which brave men are succored; alone, that fact deserves memorialization. It is sacred ground, consecrated by bloodshed.

The National Museum of Civil War Medicine was established in 1990; its first site opened in 1996 in Frederick, Maryland. It began operating the Pry House, site of McClellan's headquarters during the Battle of Antietam, as a museum to commemorate its use as a Union hospital in 2005. At Gettysburg, the George Spangler Farm & Field Hospital now serves as a site to learn about the treatment on its grounds of nearly two thousand wounded soldiers, not all of whom survived.

A greater focus on preservation of hospital sites associated with other Civil War battles would increase comprehension of the real human cost of the nation's most costly conflict. The location of the Union field hospital at Savage's Station is one such worthy site.

The National Park Service Richmond National Battlefield Park map of its constituent units puts the hospital/station location northeast of the junction of I-295 and I-64 and Richmond International Airport. Historical signage in a turn-off along Meadow Road east of

---

20. Id. 213.
21. Civil War Sites Advisory Commission, *Report on the Nation's Civil War Battlefields* (1993), 12.

Grapevine Road (both VA-76), and the Park's map route, pinpoint the site. The single line of the old Richmond & York River Rail Road remains across the field to the south, as does the Old Williamsburg Road on the opposite side of the interstate. Texts of signs at the turn-off, and derivation in brackets, recount what happened there:

> In the field beyond this marker was fought June 29, 1862, the battle of Savage Station in which Confederate forces under command of Major-General John B. Magruder attacked indecisively the rearguard of the Federal Army moving toward James River. This was the Third Battle of the Seven Days' Campaign. [Virginia Conservation & Development Commission, 1932]
>
> Here, facing west, stretched the Union line in the afternoon of June 29, 1862. Brook's brigade was south of the road with Gorman's and Burn's brigades to the north. In a furious conflict Burn's line was broken but was restored by Sumner in person. Darkness ended the conflict. The Unionists withdrew southward. [Battlefield Markers Association]
>
> On the night of June 27, 1862, following the Battle of Gaines' Mill, Gen. George McClellan ordered a withdrawal of his Union army to the James River. In the wake of the retreating army, Savage's Station, located one half mile in front of you along the Richmond and York River Railroad, was ordered abandoned. Having served as the army's advance supply base during the previous month, the immense stockpiles of equipment, ordnance, and commissary stores located there were to be destroyed.
>
> Hoping to catch McClellan on the move, Gen. Robert E. Lee ordered an attack at Savage's Station on June 29. Confederate troops under Gen. John B. Magruder encountered the Federal rear guard near the station in the late afternoon. In a twilight battle, Union forces under Gen. Edwin V. "Bull" Sumner held back the Southern assaults while McClellan

proceeded southward. When darkness put an end to the battle, 444 Confederates and 919 Northerners were counted as casualties. That night, Sumner withdrew from the station and followed McClellan south across White Oak Swamp. [Civil War Trails, Inc.]

Of related interest are other nearby sites:

- the Trent house, McClellan's headquarters between June 12 and June 28, 1862, on Grapevine Road south of Old Hanover Road, on the west side of the road
- Allen's Farm, where the Confederate offensive against Sumner's rear guard began on June 29, 1862, and from which Sumner retired east to Savage's Station

The nearby battlefield is largely under the sprawling interstate cloverleaf, but the area around the Station and its field hospital have not been lost to permanent development. Instead, the farm field now hosts a solar array that fills up most of the acreage and, with required screening, will be obscured other than from the historic sign turn-out.

Is it an effort worth pursuing? Only when one considers that the "story of the hospitals is symbolic. It is the end of battle, and the end of war." In that vital sense, a battlefield preservation movement needs to save, and to educate about, all of the ground that has been hallowed by those who offered and were burdened by a full measure of devotion. These hospital sites "exist as the only monuments and memorials to those days of suffering." Saving them for posterity is more than just a grand idea: "the preservation of these sites is a duty of our generation to that generation which found the necessity to use them." Just as human misery necessitated "urgency about the work of the surgeons," looming threats to the memorialization of these places sanctified by blood and gore and lifesaving work require a commitment to preserving, saving, and cherishing.[22]

---

22. Kathleen Georg Harrison, "Foreword" in Coco, *A Vast Sea of Misery*, vii.

The Savage's Station field hospital site, where lives were saved and no doubt lost, could still be preserved and commemorated, if there were the will to do so.[23] War is terrible; war is hell. At the location where "[f]athers parted with sons, and friends with friends"—where "invalids cried out, and some struggled with renewed strength to escape certain capture"[24]—solar arrays now occupy the landscape. A visit to such hallowed ground could make even more real the contemporary image drawn by the poet:

> *. . . to the rows of the hospital tent, or under the roof'd hospital,*
> *To the long rows of cots, up and down, each side, I return;*
> *To each and all, one after another, I draw near—not one do I miss;*
> *An attendant follows, holding a tray—he carries a refuse pail,*
> *Soon to be fill'd with clotted rags and blood, emptied, and fill'd again.*
> *I onward go, I stop,*
> *With hinged knees and steady hand, to dress wounds;*
> *I am firm with each—the pangs are sharp, yet unavoidable;*
> *One turns to me his appealing eyes—(poor boy! I never knew you,*
> *Yet I think I could not refuse this moment to die for you, if that would save you.)*[25]

VI. Data

Students of the Civil War are well aware of the less than perfect accuracy of casualty reports. A long-accepted total of just over 600,000

---

23. Location information is derived in part from: Salmon, 110; Brian K. Burton, *The Peninsula and Seven Days: A Battlefield Guide* (Lincoln: University of Nebraska Press, 2007), 92, which showed the route from the main road to the station could still be seen on the land recently. It also prophetically entitled the chapter "The Mess at Savage Station."
24. Burton, *A Battlefield Guide*, 94.
25. "The Dresser" in *Walt Whitman's Drum-Taps* (New York: Gibson Brothers, 1865), 31-34. For a contemporaneous account of the field hospital in operation, see Marks, 189-193.

recently has been adjusted to some 750,000. The same difficulty adheres in sick reports. Some officers were dutiful in turning in their numbers; others were not as duty-conscious. Discrepancies resulted from differing counts turned in to the Medical Bureau as opposed to the Adjutant-General's office.

An example is found in Tripler's more than 40,000-word final report:

> I am able from the reports in my hands to compare the true sick lists in brigades with those sent in to the Adjutant-General's Office. Among the brigades to which my attention was directed are the following. I arrange them in tabular form, to show how widely the reports of the brigade surgeons differ from those in the table appended to your letter: [omitted]
>
> The above are sufficient for my present purpose, which is to show that numbers of men are reported sick by their captains who are not found upon the reports of the medical officers of their regiments. The true number of the sick is large enough to give me much concern, but I am unwilling it should be represented to be larger than it really is through the careless manner in which company reports are too frequently made out. Considering the season of the year and the unfavorable state of the weather it cannot be disputed that this is the most healthy army the world has ever seen. The general health of the whole force is rather improving than deteriorating; still, certain corps are at a stand-still, while others are sadly falling off.[26]

An extensive analysis by physician Edward Jarvis, a member of numerous learned societies and president of the American Statistical Association from 1852 until 1884, made a similar conclusion as to McClellan's force: "our Union army is one of the healthiest on

---

26. *OR*, V, 107–108.

record."[27] A letter of June 21, 1862, reported two Corps of the Army of the Potomac to be in good health.[28]

Just as with casualty data, analysis needs to be cautiously applied to the numbers of sick contained in documentation from the war. Over a half-century ago, one study provided these war-time data:

Union deaths by "Disease"	224,586
Confederate deaths by "Disease, etc."	164,000[29]

With more than twice as many Union enlistments, the clear inference is that US military medical care was superior.

VII. Ambulances

As mentioned in the text, a Civil War ambulance was a horse-drawn wagon. According to the National Museum of Health and Medicine, Otis Historical Archives, the US Army had no specially designed means of transport for conveyance of its wounded or infirm soldiers from the time of the Revolutionary War until just before the Civil War. In 1858, a board of Army surgeons reviewed and recommended use of an ambulance wagon designed by a New York doctor. No record exists, however, showing that the ambulances were built. In 1859, a Board of Medical Officers, on which Tripler sat, made further recommendations. One involved a design of Tripler's, which transported patients as well as medical supplies. It was heavily used at the beginning of the war but, requiring four horses for its motive power, was succeeded by two-horse wagon designs. Still, the federal government

---

27. Edward Jarvis, "Sanitary Condition of the Army" in *The Atlantic Monthly*, Vol. X (Boston: Ticknor & Fields, 1862), 463, 473; James G. Wilson & John Fiske eds., *Appletons' Cyclopædia of American Biography*, Vol. III (New York: D. Appleton & Co., 1887), 406.
28. Frank R. Freemon, *Microbes and Minie Balls: An Annotated Bibliography of Civil War Medicine* (Rutherford: Fairleigh Dickinson University Press, 1993), 107.
29. Brooks, 126. This volume asserted Tripler "had some good ideas" and the medical situation during the Seven Days was a "fiasco." Id. 14.

"produced the Tripler by the hundreds and used it throughout the Civil War." Platform springs reduced jolting so as to aid the comfort of the patients it transported.[30]

The Fort Scott National Historic Site administered by the National Park Service, located on Old Fort Boulevard in Fort Scott, Kansas, has among its displays such an artifact. The vehicle is a reproduction based on photographic and other evidence, since no original or reproduction model or measured drawings exist to guide construction. This "Tripler Wagon" is shown in Illustration 15.

Circular No. 6 issued by the Army Surgeon General's Office on November 1, 1865, is known as *Reports on the Extent and Nature of the Materials Available for the Preparation of a Medical and Surgical History of the Rebellion.*[31] A section entitled "On Means of Transportation of the Wounded" describes, and portrays in images, the types of conveyances used, including litters (both carried by hand, by horse, and by carriage), stretchers, and cacolets (a seat, like a saddle, attached to the side of a horse or mule). It further stated:

> At the beginning of the war, the one-horse ambulances, designed by Surgeon General Finley and Surgeon Coolidge, and the four-horse ambulances, designed by Surgeon Tripler, were chiefly employed.
>
> The former were intended to transport two wounded men in a recumbent position. The latter accommodated eight men, lying down. The beds in all of these ambulances were movable, and could be used as hand-litters.
>
> The one-horse ambulances were too frail for the rough roads on which they were employed, and soon fell into disrepute. The four-horse ambulance rendered good service, but it was very heavy. What is commonly known as the "Wheeling" ambulance, from having been first constructed at Wheeling,

---

30. Haller, *Farmcarts*, 46-47.
31. Philadelphia: J.B. Lippincott & Co., 1865.

Virginia, from a design of General Rosecrans, soon came into very general use. It is drawn by two horses, and carries ten or twelve persons sitting, or two or three sitting and two lying down. It combines lightness and strength.[32]

A complete survey of ambulance designs resulting from the needs arising from the nation's greatest conflict is beyond the scope of this work. Suffice that others sought to contribute, one example being Clarissa Britain. She obtained a patent for an improved ambulance design to provide better comfort to wounded soldiers in 1863, listing her address as St. Joseph, Michigan.[33]

VIII. Crimean Ovens

Tripler wrote favorably of this innovation, a radiant underground heating structure for hospital tents.

Vestiges were discovered during an excavation in 2005 in Alexandria, Virginia, on Duke Street near the intersection with Arene Court.[34] An historical marker describes the system as found in Enon, Virginia.[35]

IX. Supplemental to Tripler's Report

The *Official Records* contains the two portions of Tripler's final report; it also contains two separated communiques of his that bear attention in order to see a full record of his performance as Medical Director of the Army of the Potomac.

Tripler to Chief of Staff, Nov. 1861
    Headquarters Army of the Potomac,

---

32. Id. 81-84. See also *Medical And Surgical History*, pt.3, v.2, 946-949.
33. Autumn Stanley, *Mothers and Daughters of Invention: Notes for a Revised History of Technology* (New Brunswick: Rutgers University Press, 1995), 106.
34. https://media.alexandriava.gov/docs-archives/historic/info/archaeology/arsummaryquakerridgeax195=1=.pdf
35. https://www.hmdb.org/m.asp?m=109398

Office Medical Director,
Washington, November 25, 1861.

General R.B. Marcy, U.S.A.,
Chief of Staff Army of the Potomac:

General: The necessity for a better protection for the men than the common tent affords, without going into the construction of extensive huts, which would give the appearance of going into permanent winter quarters, has been for some time engaging my attention. The severity of the winters in this climate renders some protection absolutely necessary, or we must expect a vast increase of disease of the respiratory organs, and unless by our system we can secure a tolerable ventilation, as well as protection against the rains, snow, and cold, we have reason to fear a prevalence of typhus and typhoid fevers among the troops.

To guard against these, so far as practicable, I have the honor to suggest that in the first place, in addition to the ordinary trench about the tents, the trace[36] of every regimental camp shall be provided with a ditch not less than 12 inches wide and deep, to secure a more perfect drainage.

Secondly. That an inclosure equal to the base of each tent shall be constructed of small logs or poles about 3 feet in height, over the top of which the tent shall be secured to serve as a roof. Such constructions have already been made in some of the camps; they can readily be put up by the men themselves.

Upon some of the camp grounds the timber that has been felled will furnish the poles or logs. Where these are not to be had, clapboards or any cheap material will answer the purpose.

---

36. Exterior perimeter.

For warming the tents and drying the ground a modification of the Crimean oven, which has been devised and put in operation by Dr. McRuer, the surgeon of General Sedgwick's brigade, appears to me to be the cheapest and most effective.[37] Dr. McRuer has submitted to me a report on this subject. General Heintzelman, who has inspected his arrangement, informs me that it appears to be perfect in all its details; that it is at the same time efficient and economical. Dr. McRuer thus describes his plan:

A trench 1 foot wide and 20 inches deep to be dug through the center and length of each tent, to be continued for 3 or 4 feet farther, terminating at one end in a covered oven fireplace and at the other in a chimney. By this arrangement the fire-place and chimney are both on the outside of the tent; the fire-place is made about 2 feet wide and arching; its area gradually lessening until it terminates in a throat at the commencement of the straight trench. This part is covered with brick or stone, laid in mortar or cement; the long trench to be covered with sheet-iron in the same manner. The opposite end to the fire-place terminates in a chimney 6 or 8 feet high; the front of the fire-place to be fitted with a tight movable sheet-iron cover, in which an opening is to be made, with a sliding cover to act as a blower. By this contrivance a perfect draught may be obtained, and no more cold air admitted within the furnace than just sufficient to consume the wood and generate the amount of heat required, which not only radiates from the exposed surface of the iron plates, but is conducted throughout the ground floor of the tent so as to keep it both warm and dry, making a board floor entirely unnecessary, thereby avoiding the dampness and filth, which unavoidably accumulates in such places. All noise, smoke, and dust, attendant upon building the fires within the tent are avoided; there

---

37. See VIII, *supra*.

are no currents of cold air, and the heat is so equally diffused, that no difference can be perceived between the temperature of each end or side of the tent. Indeed, the advantages of this mode of warming the hospital tents are so obvious, that it needs only to be seen in operation to convince any observer that it fulfills everything required as regards the warming of hospital tents, and I respectfully ask you to appoint a commissioner to examine the hospital tents of the Eighth Brigade, and ascertain by observation the justness of this report.

The whole cost to the Government of constructing the above apparatus for the four hospitals of the Eighth Brigade is the cost of 112 feet, 1 foot wide, of sheet-iron, one barrel of lime, and four sheet-iron doors, the stone and brick were picked up by the men, who likewise did all the labor.

By this plan floors to the tent are rendered unnecessary; the ground within the tent is kept perfectly dry, and the temperature can be regulated by increasing or diminishing the fires; all smoke, dust, and noise within the tent are obviated; the flues may be carried through a range of five or six tents, making one fire all that is necessary for each set. If the description of this furnace cannot be understood, and it is deemed expedient to put them in general operation, Dr. McRuer might be temporarily detached from his brigade to construct a model in each division in the Army.

I have further to recommend that the men should be required to make daily use of desiccated vegetables in their soups. Where fresh vegetables are to be had, this is not necessary, but in the winter season a sufficient supply of fresh vegetables cannot be depended upon. Soup should form a daily part of a soldier's dinner, and a liberal portion of desiccated vegetables should enter into its composition. Soup requires three and one-half hours for its proper preparation; volunteers will not take so much trouble unless it is enjoined upon them by a positive order, and also made the duty of the company officers to see that it is done. Cold weather and the want of vegetable food are almost sure to engender scurvy. If it is possible to supply an additional allowance of blankets, it would contribute essentially to the preservation of the health of the men.

Very respectfully, your obedient servant,
Chas. S. Tripler,
Surgeon and Medical Director, Army of the Potomac.[38]

❊ ❊ ❊

Tripler to Assistant Adjutant-General, February 1862
Headquarters Army of the Potomac,
Medical Director's Office,
February 6, 1862.

General S. Williams,
Assistant Adjutant-General, Army of the Potomac:

General: In obedience to your instructions, I have the honor to inclose a tabulated report of the sick in the several divisions and brigades of the Army of the Potomac as far as the returns in this office will enable me to do so [omitted here].

I have to observe that these tables show the whole number of sick in the regiments, whether in quarters or hospital, as reported by the medical officers. Of the men thus reported, more than one-half are affected with trivial complaints, that could scarcely justify their being left behind in case the army should be put in motion.

In the cavalry regiments the sick report is swollen considerably in consequence of injuries to the men received from the

---

38.   *OR*, V, 664–665.

horses. A very considerable item in many of the regiments is due to the number of men waiting discharges in consequence of disqualification from old physical infirmities.

Among the regular troops the sick report is seriously increased by the number of venereal cases, some of which were received from California; others contracted here.

Measles, which seems to be scourging the whole Army of the United States, still breaks out from time to time in different regiments. Berdan's Sharpshooters have been and are still severely affected with that disease. It is hoped that hospital and field arrangements already made and in progress will soon abate this evil. It will be perceived that among the Vermont troops in Brooks' brigade there is a wide difference in the ratio of sick between the Second and Third Regiments and the other three. I have already endeavored to give some explanation of this in a former report. I have now to state that I have sent a large detachment of convalescents to Philadelphia in order to make room for the sick of this brigade in the general hospitals, in hopes some beneficial effect may result to the well from removing the sick from their sight, thus avoiding the depressing influence of the daily observation of so much sickness among their comrades.

As a general rule it would seem, as is natural, that the ratio of sick is inversely as the military age of the men. When a departure from this rule is perceived, as it will be in certain brigades, one important reason for it will probably be found in the lax and inefficient discipline of the regiment. I called attention to an instance of that sort a few days since, and was told that the regiment was demoralized from the inefficiency of the officers.

I ask attention in this place to a letter I have received from Brigadier-General Peck, a copy of which I inclose [omitted here] to show how much may be done by attention to certain sanitary measures that I have frequently suggested, and which have been more than once directed from your office. If officers could be impressed with the necessity of such measures, and convinced of their certain beneficial results, I feel sure they would all be zealous in enforcing them.

I am gratified to be able to state that typhoid fever, which I feared would seriously increase with the cold weather, has been much decreased in a very great majority of the regiments, and upon the whole I think I am justified in saying that the sanitary condition of this army is very satisfactory.

I take this occasion to say that I have sent an inspector of hospitals to Lander's division, and that as soon as the inspections of Alexander's and Duane's commands are completed, I shall send another to Perryville, Md., where I have just learned that typhoid fever has appeared and is increasing in one of the regular regiments stationed at that point.

Very respectfully, your obedient servant,
Chas. S. Tripler,
Surgeon and Medical Director Army of the Potomac.[39]

X. Harper Hospital Announced

The April 8, 1864, issue of the Detroit Free Press featured a front-page story headlined: "A NEW HOSPITAL" with subheads "Order for Establishing a Military Hospital in this City. The Harper Hospital Grounds Leased for the Purpose. THE HOSPITAL TO ACCOMODATE FIVE HUNDRED PATIENTS. The Work of Erection to be Commenced Immediately." As for the role that Tripler had played, the article stated:

> The necessity for a regular military hospital in this city has been long felt, and Dr. Tripler, United States Surgeon in charge of the post, has from the first been persistent in his

---

39. Id. 713-714.

efforts to secure such an institution. While from his position he has seen the need of such a hospital and labored zealously for the interests of the people of the State, the members in Congress from this State have worked equally hard to thwart this plan. Of their objects we will say nothing, but it is an undeniable fact that they have left nothing undone to prevent the establishment of a hospital here. The entire credit is therefore due to Dr. Tripler, and the greater credit is due him from the fact that he has brought it about in spite of determined opposition.

Before Dr. Tripler left this city to assume the duties of Medical Director of the Northern Department, he obtained from the Trustees of the Harper Hospital Association an offer to lease their grounds in this city to the government for the purposes of a hospital. This offer, enclosed with the following note, was forwarded to the department in Washington:

Headquarters Northern Department,
Medical Director's Office,
Columbus, O., March 23, 1861[4].

Sir—I have the honor to enclose an offer of the Harper Hospital Association, of Detroit, to convey to the United States a lease of their property for a site upon which to erect a military hospital for such term of years as may suit the government—this to be rent free, subject only to such taxes as may be imposed.

This ground is most eligibly and conveniently situated, with as good facilities for water and drainage as the city of Detroit affords. I have submitted two projects heretofore for providing a general hospital in the city of Detroit. One, so far as I know, has never been acted upon, the other—the conversion of the Detroit Barracks into a hospital—was directed to be carried into effect, but the order was subsequently countermanded.

Thus the patriotic State of Michigan remains to this day without a single establishment of the kind.

I know personally the deep interest the people of Michigan feel in this matter and the intense desire and anxiety they entertain that their interest and desire should be gratified. The State has, I believe, always met promptly the calls of the nation for troops, and is at this moment credited with an excess of men up to completion of the last call. Her people know that general hospitals have been established in all the neighboring States, and they cannot understand how any military consideration can be opposed to their wishes.

For a general hospital in Michigan, the city of Detroit offers manifest advantages over any part of the State. During the season of lake navigation, the most comfortable way of conveying patients to Detroit from the western armies is by rail through Ohio and thence by steamers to Detroit. The only land transportation they would be subjected to being thus reduced to eight or nine hours over some of the best railways in the country and without a change of cars.

The majority of the sick and wounded likely to require a Michigan hospital in the approaching campaign will come from the Western armies, as will be seen from the distribution of the Michigan regiments as reported in the letter of the Adjutant General of Michigan, forwarded with this letter.

I ask leave to recommend most earnestly the offer of a site now made may be accepted and a hospital of five hundred beds may be erected at once. I urge this from my intimate knowledge of the feelings of the people of Michigan, with which I heartily sympathise, and also because I have reason to hope that these feelings may be gratified at a trifling ultimate outlay of the public money. The Association being willing, as fast as their means will allow, to take and pay for the building at a fair valuation, when the United States shall no longer need it.

I am, Colonel, very respectfully,
Your ob't serv't,

Chas. S. Tripler,
Surgeon U.S.A. Mid. Dis'ct.

Col. Jos. K. Barnes,
Act. Surg. Gen. U.S.A. Washington City.

The article reported that the offer had been accepted and that an architect was at work on the plans. Twelve buildings, "each 120 feet long by 25 feet wide, one story high," would occupy the five acre site on Woodward "near the old Fair grounds" with streetcar access. The facility would be under the direction of Army Surgeon John Henry Rauch, Medical Director of the post.[40]

It was a presidential election year. Tripler mentioned the "people of Michigan"—many of whom were voters—and played on the fact that other Midwest States had been granted such an institution by the Federal Government.

XI. *Detroit Free Press* Retrospective

On page 3 of its February 25, 1872, edition, the newspaper printed an extensive recollection of Tripler as part of an article on Historic Elmwood Cemetery, the site of his grave. In pertinent part, it stated:

> Upon the easterly side of the bank, rising above the valley which now indicates the channel-bed of the ancient Parent's Creek, just south of Elmwood Chapel, a stone has recently been placed, which arrests attention from its perfect

---

40. Rauch "served as assistant medical director of the Army of Virginia, and then in Louisiana till 1864." James G. Wilson & John Fiske eds., *Appletons' Cyclopædia of American Biography*, Vol. V (New York: D. Appleton & Co., 1900), 186. He was succeeded at Harper by Eugene F. Sanger.

proportions, the faultless purity of its marble and exquisite work of the master chisel which molded it into shape.

Upon closer examination the insignia of the United States Medical Corps would seem to indicate that the grave thus marked was of one who in life had been attached to this distinguished branch of army service, and the touching fact was soon revealed that the living members, scattered about in different sections of the country where duty called them, had united to delegate one or more of their number to seek out the spot where reposed the ashes of their dead comrade, to drop the tear of memory and friendship in their behalf, and to rear this tribute to departed worth, beautiful in its design, but still more exquisitely beautiful in the idea of fraternal and professional union thus remarkably illustrated. The monument is of fine Italian marble, polished. From the base the well-modeled shaft rises urn-shaped, capped with a collar of stars, from which ascends a semi-rural cross twined with ivy. The inscription, in raised letters, reads: Charles Stuart Tripler. Born January 19, 1806, Died October 20, 1866. [Wreath—M.S.] Faithful unto death. Erected to the memory of a loved and revered brother officer by the Medical Corps of the Army.

What the modest inscription leaves untold let me briefly relate, that its record may survive, and the characteristic and noble of the living become known and linked to the memory of their honored brother.

Surgeon Tripler was a native of New York City, and an alumni of Columbia College, graduating in his twenty-first year, in the class of 1827. He entered the army October 30, 1830, serving in the Black Hawk, Florida and Mexican war and the war of Southern Rebellion.

Thirty years have passed away since Surgeon Tripler, at that time serving as surgeon of the post, first became known to the citizens of Detroit.

Young, gay, brilliant in his profession, he became a favorite in society, with which he soon identified himself by wedding one of its most beautiful members, distinguished as well for her accomplishments as for her high family position among the old indigenous aristocracy of Detroit.

Three decades form but a short career of life, yet during this brief season Surgeon Tripler's professional honors had been gathered—the highest step had been reached fame and rank won without stain or reproach ere his life had prematurely closed.

In time of peace the honors and rank of an army surgeon are reached by slow and toilsome degrees, years of active duty, home service and border service, near and distant, wherever duty called, painful through the separation which time and distance may create from family and home. In war the responsibilities and labors are tenfold greater. Accumulated duties are laid upon the limited staff before the requisite number and skill are supplied. The reward to the true lover of his art is greater, however, and compensates for the toil in the enlarged field of professional scientific experience.

Surgeon Tripler was breveted Colonel in November, 1864, and Brigadier-General in October, 1866. His career may be said to have culminated when, as Medical Director of the Potomac army, the care of an entire army in the ordinary routine of campaigning, as well as the more capital requirements of the field of battle, was confided to his charge. He was professionally proud of his position, and richly deserved the important post in which he unremittingly and successfully labored to care for the sick and wounded of that ever memorable campaign.

The same political mine which destroyed the foothold of power in the command of that army made Surgeon Tripler the victim of unfounded prejudice as medical chief, and here his active career was brought, in the midst of its well won and highest honors, to an unjust and untimely close.

The professional life of Surgeon Tripler, aside from his professional duties, deserves particular notice. Not alone in the tented hospital or field were his talents called into play. He loved his profession, and was distinguished in times of peace in practice wherever located, and more particularly in the college amphitheatre and highest circles of the most celebrated in the scientific advancement of the medical profession.

....

R.R.E.

XII. The United States Christian Commission

In contrast to the other main voluntary organization, the US Christian Commission emphasized its subordinate position in relation to the Army's medical organization. Its second war-time report made this plain in a section headed "Principles":

> VIII. Respect For Authorities.

Before entering upon its work, the names, organization, purposes, and plans of the Commission, were laid before the President, the Secretaries of War and of the Navy, the General-in-Chief, and the Surgeon-General, and their approbation received.

In each military department, general hospital, permanent camp and separate post or station, the consent and counsel of those in command have been sought and obtained at the threshold.

Delegates are strictly enjoined, in the prosecution of their religious duties, to offer every possible assistance to chaplains, but never to intrude uninvited upon their proper domain. And in their work of ministering to the health and comfort of those under medical treatment and care, to do nothing without instructions from the surgeons in charge, and in all great emergencies on the battle-ground, or in the field hospital, or at points where the wounded are to be fed and cared for, during their removal from the front, always to report themselves to the medical director or surgeon in charge, and place themselves under his instructions for just that service which will most effectually aid him in the work of relieving and saving our wounded heroes.[41]

The document contained a testimonial letter from a Medical Director. "The willingness of your agents to receive instructions and to co-operate with the medical officers in the performance of laborious and responsible duties," it stated, "must render them at all times most welcome assistants to army surgeons."[42]

It is documented that African-American women and men did participate in this Commission's work.[43] Walt Whitman held an association. It should also be noted that this organization's work at the front may not be as well-known as its peer commission. In a vivid and detailed account of his experience after being wounded, one officer recorded the Christian Commission's work at the front to succor wounded Union soldiers, as well as its employment of hospital ships.[44] And the Sanitary Commission sought not to partner with but to "offset" the Christian Commission's prestige.[45]

---

41. United States Christian Commission, for the Army and Navy, *Second Annual Report* (Philadelphia: 1864), 21.
42. Id. 59.
43. According to the US National Library of Medicine, thirteen African-American surgeons served on behalf of the Union during the Civil War. Two received a commission in the Army. William P. Powell Jr. was hired as a contract assistant surgeon at Contraband Hospital in Washington, D.C., a medical facility that cared for emancipated enslaved persons. Powell became surgeon-in-charge and hired several nurses of African-American heritage.
44. J. Gregory Acken, *Inside the Army of the Potomac: The Civil War Experience of Captain Francis Adams Donaldson* (Lanham: Stackpole Books, 1998).
45. Maxwell, 303.

XIII. Medical History of George Brinton McClellan

This topic is well beyond the scope of such a work, except insofar as personal care that Tripler afforded his commanding officer would be of interest. There seems to be no record of that ministration happening. During their tenure together, McClellan first became seriously ill, from the effects of typhoid, just before Christmas in December 1861. He confided his condition to few, apparently, since his wife was by his side and acted as principal caregiver.[46] In late May 1862, he wrote her from the Peninsula that he was "troubled by the old Mexican complaint"—evidently, a recurrence of malaria contracted in the 1840s war.[47] On neither occasion does it appear he consulted the Medical Director of the Army of the Potomac. Whether he would have benefited from Tripler's expertise is uncertain, but the Winter recuperation had wider impact than solely as to the General's health. Having taken to his bed for a period of three weeks, and using his illness as a reason not to see the President but once, McClellan did himself no favor. Suspicions about the commander's plans and strategies grew, and Lincoln and Congress pressed for information and details. When he was less than forthcoming, his stature suffered more than his health had.[48]

During this first period came the well-publicized conversation where the President lamented to a confidant, "What shall I do? The people are impatient, Chase has no money. The General of the Army has typhoid fever. The bottom is out of the tub. What shall I do?"[49] One noted historian opined that nothing "had such long-reaching consequences for the relationship" between the Commander-in-Chief and his lieutenant than this medically induced episode.[50] In

---

46. Sears, *McClellan Papers*, 148 n.4, 152-153.
47. Id. 277-278, 287.
48. Carl Sandburg, *Abraham Lincoln: The War Years*, Vol. One (New York: Harcourt, Brace & World, 1939), 417-421.
49. Geoffrey Perret, *Lincoln's War: The Untold Story of America's Greatest President as Commander in Chief* (New York: Random House, 2004), 112-115.
50. Ethan S. Rafuse, "Typhoid and Tumult: Lincoln's Response to General McClellan's Bout with Typhoid Fever during the Winter of 1861-62" in *Journal*

light of the experience of human transmission of disease during the recent COVID-19 pandemic, McClellan's contracting of the disease was most unfortunate during a time when virtually all of the Army escaped it.[51]

In the second episode, McClellan's poor health may have hampered greater Union success in the Battle of Fair Oaks. His illness began on May 22. He was sick in his tent and summoned a doctor on the 29th. Still feeling unwell, he rose and made it to the battlefield after fighting had commenced—in the afternoon, according to his memoir. His actual whereabouts remain disputed. His counterpart, Joseph Johnston, would be wounded in the affair and forced to relinquish command, potentially offering an opportunity for greater Union success.[52]

Might a healthy McClellan have done more on May 31-June 1? Might Tripler have prevented the recurrence or sped his recovery—and done so back in December? If, indeed, he were suffering from a "state of utter exhaustion,"[53] was it because he did not obtain proper care? One theory is the General "did not take care to remain fit, nor was it in his character to do so."[54] When the Seven Days ended a month later, McClellan still complained of "extreme exhaustion."[55]

The General had "finally called for his surgeon" after his illness worsened on May 29.[56] Instead of consulting with Tripler, however,

---

of the Abraham Lincoln Association, Vol. 18, No. 2 (Summer 1997), 1, 2.
51. Id. 5 n.10.
52. John C. Waugh, *Lincoln and McClellan: The Troubled Partnership Between a President and His General* (New York: Palgrave MacMillan, 2010), 99-100; *McClellan's Own Story*, 365, 395, 397; G.S. Hillard, *Life and Campaigns of George B. McClellan, Major-General U.S. Army* (Philadelphia: J.B. Lippincott & Co., 1865), 227-228 (footnote).
53. Sears, *Young Napoleon*, 196, confined to his tent for a period of ten days.
54. John T. Hubbell, "The Seven Days of George Brinton McClellan" in Gallagher, *The Richmond Campaign*, 41 n.13
55. *OR*, LI, pt. I, 713. He also wrote on September 20, 1862, of being "very sick the last few days"—immediately after Antietam. *OR*, XIX, pt. I, 219.
56. Jack D. Welsh, *Medical Histories of Union Generals* (Kent: Kent State University Press, 1996), 209-210; *McClellan's Own Story*, 397.

it appears that McClellan relied on "homeopathic" practitioners. One was his wife's uncle, Dr. Erastus Edgerton Marcy. Taking this course of treatment ran counter to Army practice and undermined the confidence of leading subordinates in McClellan's judgment. Although he appeared to improve within a week of the onset of the illness, he soon relapsed.[57]

An extensive analysis of the patient published in 1968 makes certain findings: he suffered from "an anxiety state with a paranoid trend in June-July 1862" and, generally, from "neuropsychiatric difficulties" that involved "a deep-seated disorder." This medical historian concluded that McClellan "was mentally not well-balanced" from late 1861 until removed from command and exhibited "pathological" behavior. The well-known condition of W.T. Sherman in Fall 1862 was less severe than McClellan's. His brain affected by physical illness and exhaustion, McClellan's mind failed "to break through to solid reality."[58]

Could matters have proceeded in a more positive manner by seeking the counsel of the Army Medical Director? Precedent supported it: Tripler had provided such services to General Scott, who only requested retirement when McClellan forced him to it.

When McClellan died on October 29, 1885, of, according to newspaper reports, "neuralgia" of the heart, i.e., a heart attack, he had been bedridden for the previous two weeks and in a failing condition

---

57. Rafuse, 6 & n.13, 9, 11. A noted critic of homeopathy was Oliver Wendell Holmes Sr., as evidenced in his *Homœopathy and Its Kindred Delusions* (Boston: William D. Ticknor, 1842). Marcy was a founder and editor of the *North American Homoeopathic Journal* and a practitioner since 1848. An associated New York City physician came with Marcy to attend McClellan; Dr. Alexis M. León had practiced since 1844. William H. King, *History of Homœopathy and Its Institutions In America*, Vol. I (New York: Lewis Pub. Co., 1905), 190; *The Medical Directory of the City of New York* (Medical Society of the County of New York: De Leeuw, Oppenheimer & Myers, 1887), 82; Williams, *Lincoln Finds a General*, 136 & n.46.

58. Paul E. Steiner, *Medical-Military Portraits of Union and Confederate Generals* (Philadelphia: Whitmore Publishing Co., 1968), 10-11, 34-36. Steiner also concluded that his wartime attacks of dysentery were new infections rather than Mexico-related. Id. 12.

for some time prior. In July 1878, he looked much older than his chronological age.[59] He was 58 years old at death. Wife Mary Ellen (Marcy) McClellan died in 1915, age 79.

XIV. Tripler's Opposite

When Robert E. Lee acceded to command of Confederate forces defending Richmond, he appointed LaFayette Guild as chief surgeon and medical director of the Army of Northern Virginia. Guild, then 36 years of age, had graduated from Jefferson Medical College in Philadelphia in 1848 and served in the Army Medical Corps until after Fort Sumter when he allied with the Confederacy.

On August 16, 1862, Guild submitted a consolidated report of sick and wounded in Lee's army, covering the preceding two calendar months. His data were incomplete because no information had been provided by Jackson's and Longstreet's divisions. For history's sake, however, the key is the footnote found in the *Official Records*: "No inclosures found with this report."[60] Many of Guild's other reports contained in the *Official Records* are battle casualties only. General recordkeeping issues during the war preclude accuracy in ascertaining Confederate casualty, disease, and death rates.[61] Thus, anecdotes and estimates must be summoned to provide a picture of the condition of the Rebel army during the Peninsula Campaign.

One insight derives from a letter sent by D.H. Hill to Secretary of War George Randolph in mid-April. He complained of how his force "is diminishing most fearfully by sickness from fatigue, exposure, and stampedes."[62] Six days later, Hill repeated the dire news that "our sick list is fearfully increasing."[63] As another example, on June 16, Brigadier-General Henry A. Wise reported his force on the Varina

---

59. Id. 38.
60. *OR,* XI, pt. II, 501.
61. Faust, xii, 273-274 n.2. This book owes its title to Olmsted. Id. xiii.
62. *OR,* XI, pt. III, 441.
63. Id. 454.

Road at 1,660, of which 364 were on the sick list—an attrition rate of over 20 percent.[64]

It is instructive that some studies address single medical cases rather than overall condition of the Army of Northern Virginia. Thus, Stonewall Jackson is said to have suffered from "stress-exhaustion" during the Seven Days, while he himself blamed "the 'malarial region' of Tidewater for his state" of poor health and mental judgment.[65] The commanding officer of a Georgia regiment reported the necessity of leaving the field at Malvern Hill due to "physical weakness, having been in very feeble health for several weeks," as did the Major who succeeded him for the same reason, finally leaving command to a Captain.[66]

Perhaps documentary issues have prohibited a thorough analysis of the impact of disease on the Confederate military, especially during March-July 1862. A recent statistically valid study of the Army of Northern Virginia concludes that death by disease "accelerated" in 1862 from the prior year, killing one in seven soldiers.[67] Although even Union commanders (like McClellan) believed Southerners would withstand the disease-friendly Peninsula far better than "Yankees," such a notion—as with those regarding the superiority of overall numbers and individual fighting ability—proved to be a Rebel-friendly myth.

Guild served until the surrender at Appomattox and was listed among the parolees.[68] He died on the 4th of July, 1870.[69] An online

---

64. Id. 603-604.
65. Clifford Dowdey, *The Seven Days: The Emergence of Lee* (New York: Fairfax Press, 1978), 197-198. The chapter is entitled "A Study of Stress." The same work cites Letterman on the condition of the Union Army after the Seven Days and does not mention Guild or his army's status. Id. 348.
66. *OR,* XI, pt. II, 702.
67. Joseph T. Glatthaar, *Soldiering in the Army of Northern Virginia: A Statistical Portrait of the Troops Who Served under Robert E. Lee* (Chapel Hill: University of North Carolina Press, 2011), 111-113. This analytic work concluded the Army that fought Tripler's reflected slave ownership in a much greater proportion than the South as a whole. Id. 9.
68. https://www.nps.gov/apco/learn/historyculture/upload/parolelist-g1.pdf
69. Francis B. Heitman, *Historical Register of the United States Army, from its*

resource provides extensive information about his life and career.[70] His name is indexed two times in Freeman's classic four-volume study of Lee and not in the three-volume follow-up.[71]

The Confederacy's Surgeon-General of its armed forces was Samuel P. Moore (1813-1889). He, too, had been a US Army doctor before siding with the Rebel cause.[72] The two leading Confederate medical officers were, then, not home-grown.

XV. *The Horse Soldiers* and More[73]

In this 1959 John Ford-directed motion picture starring John Wayne and William Holden, the enmity between line officers and the medical staff is a central story line. Wayne is Colonel John Marlowe, a hard-bitten cavalry officer who lost his wife to medical malpractice. Holden is Major Henry Kendall, physician. Marlowe is to command a raiding party that will go deep into Confederate Mississippi, and he is ordered to take along Kendall (and his assistant Hoppy). The following portion of dialogue epitomizes the antagonism that Tripler referenced between a Medical head and the commanding officer he is charged with supporting.[74]

> Kendall: Colonel, I gather you're not too happy about my going along.
> Marlowe: I hadn't counted on you, that's all.

Organization, September 29, 1789, to September 29, 1889 (Washington: National Tribune, 1890), 309.
70. https://www.findagrave.com/memorial/18868/lafayette-guild
71. Douglas S. Freeman, *R.E. Lee: A Biography*, Vol. I, 642, Vol. II, 502 (New York: Charles Scribner's Sons, 1934).
72. See Guy R. Hasegawa, *Matchless Organization*; Freemon, *Gangrene and Glory*, 28-34.
73. This item is particularly appropriate given the vocations and experiences of several MCWA board members.
74. The film is also notable for the appearance of tennis legend Althea Gibson.

Kendall: I can understand your reasons for trying to avoid a fight, tactically speaking. But you're going very deep into enemy territory. Tell me, what did you intend to do about your wounded?

Marlowe: I intend to move, and move fast. Those too badly shot up to carry on will be left to the clemency of the enemy. Civilian or military.

Kendall: Including yourself.

Marlowe: Naturally.

Kendall: That's a pretty primitive attitude. Medically speaking.

Marlowe: Well, Doctor, war isn't exactly a civilized business. Of course, I realize that it gives you fellas a wider field of opportunity ...

Kendall: For experimenting, Colonel?

Marlowe: I didn't say that. Mitch.

Mitchell: Yes, sir?

Marlowe: Give the doctor a full roster.

Mitchell: Yes, sir.

Marlowe: Examine every man. Throw out any man who, in your unchallenged opinion, of course, is unfit. Even those who might get sick a week from today.

Kendall: Look, Colonel, I didn't ask to be assigned to this mission. I'm a military doctor. I've been ordered to go and I'm going to do my job. So get off my back.

A 1938 movie, *Of Human Hearts*, starring James Stewart, Beulah Bondi, and Walter Huston, does include a battle scene where Stewart, as Doctor Jason Wilkins, is treating the wounded at a field hospital. He is called away to the White House for a meeting with the President—"maybe it's for a decoration," offers a colleague. Despite not wanting to leave the newly arriving wounded, Wilkins does obey orders but is told not to "dawdle." He and Lincoln (John Carradine) meet:

President: I want to congratulate you, Wilkins. You've been doing great things in the field.
Wilkins: Thank you, Sir. Only my share.
President: More than your share, if what I hear is true. You've saved many lives.
Wilkins: Well, Sir, we're nearer to the lines than most field hospitals, so that when a man is wounded we're able to take care of him before complications set in.
President: Hmm. I've received many letters praising your work. I have here a request from General Grant that you be transferred to his Medical Corps.
Wilkins: Oh, I'd like that, Sir.
President: Well, we'll see. We'll see. You interest me in one particular, Wilkins. I understand you don't amputate except as a last resort.
Wilkins: Well, there's no use crippling a man, Mr. President, unless it's absolutely necessary.
President: Quite right. Quite right. What school did you go to, what medical college?
Wilkins: The Baltimore Free College of Surgery, Sir.
President: Must be a very good school. Sit down; tell me about it.
Wilkins: Thank you, Sir. Well, Sir, it's not much to look at from the outside, but they have very good doctors there. They are very thorough and all that.
President: You have a scholarship?
Wilkins: No, Sir, it's a free school.

The dialogue turns to how Wilkins afforded other expenses: odd jobs, and aid from home—and the motion picture turns to its main message, how the doctor has ignored his faithful, devoted mother at their home in a small town in Ohio and, with the President's encouragement, how he will rectify that failing and embody gratitude. Back at the front, Wilkins saves the arm of his commanding officer, who authorizes the doctor a leave to visit his mother at home.

A Warner Brothers/Vitaphone "short" feature released in 1940, entitled *The Flag of Humanity*, dealt with the story of Clara Barton (played by the versatile Nana Irene Bryant) particularly as to her role in the birth of the American Red Cross. In a vivid, brutal, and brief segment on the Civil War, the film claimed that field hospitals could not cope with the casualties produced in battle, and the Red Cross would have instituted much better conditions. Two actors make the flick more memorable to a later generation. James A. Garfield has an important role in the story on two occasions, played by John Hamilton, who portrayed Perry White in the *Superman* teleplay. In an uncredited appearance, William Hopper—Paul Drake in *Perry Mason*—plays a Union guard.

In the epic *How the West Was Won* (MGM, 1962), a scene involving U.S. Grant and W.T. Sherman (played by Harry Morgan and John Wayne) briefly includes a surgical event that follows traditional lines.

XVI. A Note about the Women

Although this work necessarily is focused on a particular male member of the US military and other males involved in the war, ignoring the vital role that women played in this story would be inappropriate and historically inaccurate. According to one of the most learned employee-volunteers of the Sanitary Commission:

> In the Crimean war, England was eloquent over the good deeds and the philanthropic labors of one woman, but the great Rebellion brought forth hundreds, whose fame is not one whit less brilliant than that of Charlotte [Florence] Nightingale ....[75]

---

75. Steiner, *A Sketch*, 9. A novel-like history asserts there were one hundred thousand "Florence Nightingales." Marjorie B. Greenbie, *Lincoln's Daughters of Mercy* (New York: G.P. Putnam's Sons, 1944).

Women had been instigators of the movement and series of events that gave birth to the Sanitary Commission. Although males comprised the formal leadership of the Commission, the work in the field was managed and performed by women, employing the efforts of 7,000 ladies' aid societies.[76]

Women obtained positions as nurses and provided essential care to numerous soldiers and civilians wounded by the war's hostilities. Several resources tell this story, including Philip A. Kalisch & Beatrice J. Kalisch, "Untrained But Undaunted: The Women Nurses Of The Blue And The Gray" in *Nursing Forum*, Vol. 15, No. 1, Jan. 1976, 4, and, recently, Ronald S. Coddington, *Faces of Civil War Nurses* (Baltimore: Johns Hopkins University Press, 2020).

Women staffed the Soldiers Aid Societies around the North. The first was launched on April 15, 1861, in Bridgeport, Connecticut, reacting to President Lincoln's call for seventy-five thousand volunteers in the wake of the attack on Fort Sumter.[77]

Women—Clara Barton, Dorothea Lynde Dix, Louisa May Alcott—provided critical care to ill and wounded soldiers. Dix acted as leader of an organization of female nurses. Alcott wrote perhaps the first vivid account of nursing, relatively short but exquisitely poignant and contrary to conventional understanding of Civil War medicine.

At least one woman, Mary Edwards Walker, served as a Surgeon.[78]

A marker over the grave of Arabella Wharton Griffith, wife of Brevet Major-General Francis C. Barlow, records that she "served as

---

76. Patricia M. Shields, "Mary Livermore: A Legacy of Caring and Cooperative Womanhood in Service to the State" in Claire L. Felbinger & Wendy A. Haynes eds., *Outstanding Women in Public Administration: Leaders, Mentors & Pioneers* (Armonk: M.E. Sharpe, 2004), 49, 52-55, 61; Tise, i.

77. Robert E. Denney, *Civil War Medicine: Care & Comfort of the Wounded* (New York: Sterling Pub. Co., 1995), 15. This fine, though unfootnoted book, unfortunately switched the captions and identification of two photos, that of Tripler and Letterman. Id. C (following p. 64).

78. See Theresa Kaminski, *Dr. Mary Walker's Civil War: One Woman's Journey to the Medal of Honor and the Fight for Women's Rights* (Guilford: Lyons Press, 2020).

a nurse during the Peninsula, Antietam, and Gettysburg Campaigns" and, specifically, in the hospitals at City Point, Fredericksburg, Port Royal, and White House, and that "she twice nursed back to life from grievous wounds" her husband. She died of typhus fever, contracted in the service of her country, on July 27, 1864, at the age of forty.

One woman—Eunice Tripler—provided support to her physician husband without which he could not have served with the high degree of expertise he offered to his nation. For more information about her unique and powerful story, see *Heart in Tatters*.

All deserve much attention, respect, and study. Without the contributions of this half of the Northern population, it would not have been possible for the Union to be saved, American democracy to be preserved, and for the great cause of human liberty to have triumphed.[79] Many lives were lost in the Civil War, and women experienced those losses as well.[80]

XVII. A Personal Vignette

A half-century after the War, a surgeon recorded recollections of Army medical officers he had known while in service. One was Charles S. Tripler:

> In the fall of 1862 I served as Assistant Surgeon in the Cameron Dragoons, 5th Pennsylvania Cavalry. I was to reach my majority in November. As I had been notified from

---

79. For a "gendered approach" to Civil War medical care, see Margaret Humphreys, *Marrow of Tragedy: The Health Crisis of the American Civil War* (Baltimore: Johns Hopkins University Press, 2013; emphasis in original), 2, which also adopts a different approach for why the Sanitary Commission drew criticism.

80. This work does not delve into the wellness of African-American soldiers, who were not allowed to serve on the front lines until after Tripler left the Army of the Potomac—other than in his connection with Harper Hospital. For information on that topic, see Margaret Humphreys, *Intensely Human: The Health of the Black Soldier in the American Civil War* (Baltimore: Johns Hopkins University Press, 2008).

Philadelphia, my home, that my presence was necessary in assisting to settle my father's estate, it was necessary to procure leave of absence for that purpose. Doctor Tripler was then the Medical Director of the Army of the Potomac, and I called on him at his office on Pennsylvania Avenue near 20th Street in one of the old ramshackle buildings which are still standing. I was received in the anteroom of Doctor Tripler's office by a very amiable and pleasant gentleman who introduced himself as Doctor Greenleaf, Assistant to Doctor Tripler. I told him what I required and after a few minutes he took me in and introduced me to the Medical Director who received me in a very affable and pleasant manner, asking me, however, as it was supposed that the Army might be in a general engagement at any time and my services would be urgently required, why I wanted a seven days' leave at this time. I told him that it was necessary for me to go to Philadelphia for the purpose already mentioned, and he said, "My young friend, our duty to our country is over and above any settlement of estates or any matter requiring legal assistance in such settlement." While he was saying this he smiled very pleasantly and I knew perfectly well that he intended to grant me the leave which he ordered Doctor Greenleaf to prepare at once. He was particularly kind and pleasant and told me that at any time I happened to be in the city he would be glad to see me at his office, and he said, "Do not forget, my young friend that I have a most friendly feeling for the medical institution where you graduated." I never saw Doctor Tripler again, but his pleasant manner made a great impression upon me.[81]

Although the author turned 21 in November 1861, the other details

---

81. Henry Crécy Yarrow (November 19, 1840-July 2, 1929) was author of "Personal Recollections of Some Old Medical Officers" in *The Military Surgeon*, Vol. 59 (Washington: Association of Military Surgeons of the United States, 1926), 344, 345-346.

of this memoir track with the historical record. The 5th Pennsylvania Cavalry was stationed in the Department of Washington until May 8, 1862, when it moved to the James Peninsula with the Army of the Potomac. The medical institution referred to: the University of Pennsylvania in Philadelphia.

XVIII. Tripler, Presidents, and Doctor Willard Bliss

On July 2, 1881, President James A. Garfield, Civil War veteran, was the target of an assassin at the depot in Washington, D.C. of the Baltimore and Potomac Railroad. Secretary of War Robert Lincoln, son of the 16th President, immediately sent for Dr. D. Willard Bliss, one of the physicians who had attended his father in April 1865. Garfield was familiar to Bliss and had supported him when the physician was expelled from the local medical society for opposing a policy of excluding African-American doctors from membership and for embracing homeopathic medicine.[82]

Bliss had practiced medicine for thirty years, part as an Army doctor. Leaving "a thriving practice in Michigan" (Grand Rapids) at the age of 35, he had joined the 3rd Michigan Volunteer Infantry in May 1861 as surgeon.[83] The regiment became part of Brigadier-General Israel B. Richardson's command, who, on September 24, 1861, wrote to McClellan seeking Bliss's appointment to his brigade as its surgeon. The matter was referred by Seth Williams, Assistant Adjutant-General for the Army of the Potomac, to "the Medical Director" on September 29, 1861. An undated notation in the correspondence relates:

> Brigade Surgeon Bliss is now on leave of absence. He will be assigned to Richardson's Brigade when he joins.
> Chs S Tripler
> Surg. & Med Dir'or
> Army of Potomac[84]

---

82. Candice Millard, *Destiny of the Republic: A Tale of Madness, Medicine and the Murder of a President* (New York: Doubleday, 2011), 140.
83. Id. 141; Robertson, 206, 777.
84. Compiled Military Service Record of Surgeon and Major Doctor W.

In 1862, Bliss had been "called" by Lincoln "to organize a system of general hospitals in and about Washington." It was also the President's desire "to have one as complete and comfortable as could be devised" in proximity to the Anacostia River landing. Bliss became superintendent of the Armory Square Hospital, located at 6th Street SW and B Street SW between the Smithsonian Institution building and the Capitol, which Lincoln frequently visited.[85] He served until February 2, 1866, having received a brevet promotion to Lieutenant-Colonel.[86]

Bliss took charge of Garfield's care. After the President died on September 19, Bliss came in for extensive criticism for mismanaging the case. He never recovered "his practice, or his reputation," and died in 1889.[87] His grave is in Rock Creek Cemetery, just north of the summer cottage where President Lincoln took refuge (140 Rock Creek Church Road N.W.).

The connection between the Army's Medical Director, two Commanders-in-Chief, and a physician whose first name was "Doctor"[88] is one more aspect of the Tripler story that has never been related.

XIX. Tripler and Meade

In the action at Glendale (or Frayser's Farm) on June 30, 1862, Brigadier-General George G. Meade suffered two severe wounds, one in the right forearm and the more serious in the right side of his trunk, the ball exiting the back. "[B]ecoming weak from pain and loss of blood," he rode toward the field hospitals in the rear of V Corps. Pennsylvania Reserves Division surgeon Anthony E. Stocker,

---

Bliss, 3rd Michigan Infantry Regiment, National Archives, Record Group 94: Records of the Adjutant General's Office, 1762–1984, available at https://catalog.archives.gov/id/83861337

85. Amanda Akin Stearns, *The Lady Nurse of Ward E* (New York: Baker & Taylor Co., 1909), 7-8.
86. Robertson, 777, 975.
87. Millard, 253-254.
88. Named for the physician who presided at his birth, Dr. Sylvester Willard, of Auburn, N.Y. *New York Times*, July 9, 1881, 3. Willard's house is today the home of the Cayuga Museum of History and Art.

also wounded, was riding toward its hospital and accompanied the General. Finding it crowded, and with the Army withdrawing, the two officers decided to continue on. When Meade's "two-wheeled mess wagon" appeared fortuitously, equipment was tossed out and the General placed inside. They finally arrived at Haxall's Landing after midnight. Stocker regarded the wounds as "not dangerous, though they require immediate and constant medical attendance," especially given potential damage to internal organs. Accordingly, Meade was carried by a hospital transport to Fortress Monroe, then "transferred to one of the regular line of steamers to Baltimore." He could have remained at the hospital there, but his family arranged for transport overnight to Philadelphia. His family physician began to provide care upon his arrival at home on July 4. Meade made such improvement that he left for the Army on August 11.[89]

Surgeon Stocker had received an appointment as Major and Surgeon on August 3, 1861.[90] He passed muster during Tripler's examination of all Army of the Potomac physicians during the Fall of 1861. He was positively mentioned several times in Tripler's extensive report.

Meade suffered from "repeated episodes of jaundice" and incurred pneumonia in January 1863 and 1864, April 1865 (likely), May 1866, and April 1869. He died on November 6, 1872, age 56, prematurely gray:

> Autopsy findings demonstrated he had pneumonia accompanied by enlargement of the liver from congestion. On the surface of the liver was a well-defined scar corresponding to the external skin scar and marking the course of a bullet.[91]

---

89. George Meade, *The Life and Letters of George Gordon Meade*, Vol. I (New York: Charles Scribner's Sons, 1913), 297-298-301; Welsh, *Medical Histories*, 224-225.
90. Samuel P. Bates, *History of Pennsylvania Volunteers, 1861-5*, Vol. V (Harrisburg: B. Singerly, 1871), 1141.
91. Welsh, *Medical Histories*, 225-226.

It seems likely that the bullet had also impacted one of his lungs; the post-mortem examination for General George L. Hartsuff led the attending physician to attribute a bullet wound to the left breast as the origin of the pneumonia that took his life.[92]

Meade survived the Seven Days because, in large part, of (1) immediate medical care by a Division surgeon (2) who had passed the "Tripler test" of professionalism, (3) and a waterborne transport system that carried patients to pre-existing, capable recovery centers. Without that infrastructure, it is questionable whether Meade would have been physically able (even alive) to ascend to command of the Army of the Potomac on June 28, 1863, and to lead during its momentous victory on July 1-3 of that year.

XX. Coffee

Although Charles Tripler ought not be credited as solely responsible for official Army policy to offer coffee as a staple of the soldier's provisions, his report substantiates the medical judgment behind what became critical to Union military success. Several sources undergird this point.

In an excerpt from Chapter II, "The Organization and Make-Up of the Fighting Machine Called 'The Army'" in his memoir, Frederick L. Hitchcock spoke of the beverage's salutary effects:

> Whatever may be said about other portions of the rations, the coffee was always good. I never saw any poor coffee, and it was a blessing it was so, for it became the soldiers' solace and stay, in camp, on picket and on the march. Tired, footsore, and dusty from the march, or wet and cold on picket, or homesick and shivering in camp, there were rest and comfort and new life in a cup of hot coffee. We could not always have it on picket nor on the march. To make a cup of coffee two things were necessary besides the coffee, namely, water and

---

92. Id. 155-157.

fire, both frequently very difficult to obtain. On picket water was generally plentiful, but in the immediate presence of the enemy, fire was forbidden, for obvious reasons. On the march both were usually scarce, as I shall show later on. How was our coffee made? Each man was provided with a pint tin cup. As much coffee as could comfortably be lifted from the haversack by the thumb and two fingers — depending somewhat on the supply — was placed in the cup, which was filled about three-fourths full of water, to leave room for boiling. It was then placed upon some live coals and brought to a boil, being well stirred in the meantime to get the strength of the coffee. A little cold water was then added to settle it. Eggs, gelatin, or other notions of civilization, for settling, were studiously (?) omitted. Sometimes sugar was added, but most of the men, especially the old vets, took it straight. It was astonishing how many of the "wrinkles of grim visaged war" were temporarily smoothed out by a cup of coffee. This was the mainstay of our meals on the march, a cup of coffee and a thin slice of raw pork between two hardtacks frequently constituting a meal.[93]

Hitchcock was Major, 132nd Pennsylvania Volunteer Infantry, and Lieutenant Colonel of the 25th United States Colored Troops.

The classic cited for the salubrious effects of this dietary necessity is, of course, John D. Billings, *Hardtack and Coffee, or The Unwritten Story of Army Life* (Boston: George M. Smith & Co., 1887), 108-142. Andrew Jackson is credited with issuing an executive order in 1832 ordaining the use of coffee in daily Army rations.

XXI. Greenleaf

A key member of Tripler's team of medical experts during his tenure with the Army of the Potomac was a young doctor who went on

---

93. *War from the Inside* (Philadelphia: J.B. Lippincott Co., 1904), 24-25.

to construct his own distinguished military career, witnessed by this obituary:

> Charles Ravenscroft Greenleaf, M. D., Brigadier General, U. S. Army, Retired, died at San Jose, Cal., Sept. 2, 1911, of pulmonary tuberculosis, at the age of 73 years. He was born January 1st, 1838, at Carlisle, Pennsylvania, being the son of Patrick Henry and Margaret Johnson Greenleaf, and descended from the old New England family of that name. Professor Simon Greenleaf of the faculty of Harvard University was his grandfather. His education was received in Boston and Cincinnati and he graduated in medicine at the Ohio State Medical College in 1860. Upon the outbreak of the Civil War he joined the 5th Ohio Infantry as Assistant Surgeon, being the first medical officer commissioned from that State. On August 5th, 1861, he was commissioned Assistant Surgeon in the Medical Corps, U.S. Army, and was not long in receiving recognition of his abilities in the shape of important duties and large responsibilities. He was selected as Assistant by the distinguished Medical Director of the Army of the Potomac, Charles S. Tripler, and served under him through the Peninsular campaign, organizing and taking charge at Yorktown in May, 1862, of a hospital for 2,000 sick collected at that base. During the next summer he prepared the plans for the great Mower Hospital at Philadelphia, of which he later became executive officer. The last two years of the Civil War he spent in the office of the Medical Director at Harrisburg and Baltimore actively engaged in arranging for the care of the vast army of sick and wounded which flowed back in a steady stream from the battlefields of Virginia.
>
> After the close of war he served in various parts of the South and West for more than twenty years, including five years at Fort Lapwai, Idaho, and four at Fort Shaw, Montana. In 1887 Major Greenleaf was brought to Washington as assistant to

the Surgeon General. He devised the system of personal identification, which was in use in the Army for many years up to the time of the Spanish War, and bore an important part in the legislative and administrative changes by which the Medical Department began its advance from its primitive and inchoate condition after the Civil War towards the wider fields of efficiency and usefulness, to which it has since attained. The Spanish War found Colonel Greenleaf nearing the end of his military career, but in the fullest possession of physical and mental vigor, full of energy and alertness, and with the lessons fresh and undimmed by time of that mighty conflict which Virchow declared to have "begun a new era in military medicine." On May 3d, 1898, he was made Chief Surgeon of all the troops in the field on the staff of the General Commanding the Army and at once proceeded to inspect the sites for the camps of mobilization. He then organized the Medical Service of the Porto [sic] Rican Expedition, which he accompanied. Upon his return he proceeded at once to Montauk Point, where he assumed charge of the medical administration of that great hospital camp. Here his administrative ability was soon evident in every direction, and the multitude of sick were cared for and disposed of with the minimum of friction and confusion. On December 2d, 1898, he was detailed Medical Inspector of the Army, but with this most important duty was conferred no increased volunteer rank, although such increased rank was given to a number of officers in staff departments other than the medical, and although he was recommended for commission as brigadier general of volunteers by the Surgeon General of the Army. As Medical Inspector he visited the camps of discharge of volunteers in all parts of the country and contributed much by wise advice and trained criticism to preserve them from the sanitary sins of the camps of mobilization of the year before. To him was due in large part the admirable record of the camp of concentration at San Francisco for the troops sent to the Philippines in 1899.

In December of that year he arrived at Manila and assumed the heavy responsibilities of Chief Surgeon of the Army in the Philippines, which was then about to begin the campaign which crushed the insurrection. The medical administration there had not gone smoothly, having been much hampered by unsympathetic interference from higher authority. This Colonel Greenleaf was able to remove by the tact and suavity which were distinguishing characteristics of his manners, and he met successfully the ever increasing demand for medical personnel and supplies caused by the progressive occupation of the country and the establishment of some 650 military posts in more or less hostile territory. This was undoubtedly the largest and most difficult problem of medical administration which the Spanish War and the Philippine Insurrection presented. He returned to the United States in July, 1901, and on January 1st, 1902, was retired from active service with the rank of Colonel at the age of 64, after more than forty years' active service. He later was advanced to the rank of brigadier general on account of service in the Civil War by virtue of an Act of Congress passed in 1904. The Chief of Staff, General Chaffee, in a letter written to him dated January 13th, 1904, with reference to the findings of a Court of Inquiry, which had investigated certain questions of supplies at Manila, said:

"In transmitting a copy of the findings of the court, with which the Secretary directs that you be furnished, he desires me to say that it gives him great satisfaction to concur in the view entertained by the court as to the character and value of the services rendered by you as Chief Medical Officer of the Division of the Philippines. He is entirely familiar with your long and highly creditable record as a medical officer of the Army, and it is a source of especial gratification to him that the services rendered by you in a distant and difficult field of duty were in keeping with those which have contributed so powerfully to advance the standards of administration in the Medical Department, and to secure the welfare and efficiency of the military establishment."

General Greenleaf's military career began and terminated with the strenuous activities and pressing responsibilities of war. In the long intervening period he saw the rise of aseptic surgery and the swift and wonderful triumphs of bacteriology and preventive medicine. His retentive and logical memory preserved with vivid freshness the great administrative lessons of the Civil War, while his broad and avid intelligence kept pace with the scientific progress of these epoch-making decades. He was by these gifts, together with his industry, studious activity and personal charm of manner well fitted for the conspicuous part which he bore in overcoming the inertia within the medical corps, and the narrow views and antiquated prejudices without it which impeded the progress of military medicine along the new and broader channels, which medical progress and a better conception of its relation to military efficiency have opened up to it.[94]

The "rise of aseptic surgery and the swift and wonderful triumphs of bacteriology" could have alleviated much suffering had such knowledge existed during 1861-1865. Even the Sanitary Commission—for all its self-proclaimed expertise—offered a "confession of ignorance" regarding the cause of malaria.[95]

Greenleaf's grave is in Arlington National Cemetery.

Serving as Assistant to "the distinguished Medical Director of the

---

94. Charles Lynch ed., *The Military Surgeon: Journal of the Association of Military Surgeons of the United States*, Vol. XXIX (Washington: Association of Military Surgeons, 1912), 589-592.
95. *Report of a Committee of the Associate Members of the Sanitary Commission, on the Subject of the Nature and Treatment of Miasmatic Fevers* (New York: Bailliere Brothers, 1862), 5.

Army of the Potomac, Charles S. Tripler," had a profound impact on Greenleaf's career. His work on *Tripler's Epitome* has been earlier noted. Greenleaf published his own military manual in 1864; the relationship between the two physicians is made plain by its dedication:

> To
> Surgeon C.S. Tripler, U. S. A.,
> this little work is inscribed,
> as a token of
> respect and esteem,
> by his friend,
> the compiler.[96]

XXII. Breaking the Color Barrier in US Medicine

Like Charles Tripler, James McCune Smith was born in New York City. His birthdate: April 18, 1813, making him Tripler's contemporary. Unlike his fellow Manhattanite, Smith was born into slavery as a person of color. He was freed, like Michigander Sojourner Truth, under the Emancipation Act of the State of New York in 1827. Educated in Scotland, he returned to New York City where he became a prominent medical person, writer, abolitionist, and community leader. He died on November 17, 1865, a life cut short (similar in that respect to Tripler's).[97]

Rebecca Davis of Delaware is said to be the first woman of color to enter medical school, in 1860.[98]

---

96. *A Manual for the Medical Officers of the United States Army* (Philadelphia: J.B. Lippincott & Co., 1864).
97. Thomas M. Morgan, "The Education and Medical Practice of Dr. James McCune Smith (1813-1865), First Black American to Hold a Medical Degree" in *Journal of the National Medical Association*, Vol. 95, No. 7 (July 2003), 603-614; Anna Mae Duane, *Educated for Freedom: The Incredible Story of Two Fugitive Schoolboys Who Grew Up to Change a Nation* (New York: New York University Press, 2020).
98. Jasmine Brown, *Twice as Hard: The Stories of Black Women Who Fought to Become Physicians, from the Civil War to the 21st Century* (Boston: Beacon Press, 2023).

Alexander Thomas Augusta was born on March 8, 1825, in Norfolk, Virginia, as a free person of color. In the 1840s, he studied medicine with private tutors in Baltimore. Having been denied admittance to a US college, he moved to Canada and obtained his medical degree from Trinity College, University of Toronto, in 1856. Returning to the US in 1862, he obtained an appointment on April 14, 1863, as Surgeon in the US military with the rank of Major. On October 2, he was commissioned regimental Surgeon of the 7th US Colored Troops, becoming the highest-ranking African-American officer in the US military. He also was the first African-American to head an Army hospital. After the war, having received brevet promotion to Lieutenant-Colonel, he served with the Freedman's Bureau, then joined the faculty at Howard University. He died on December 21, 1890, age 65. He was the first burial of an African-American soldier at Arlington National Cemetery, Section 1, Grave 124A. His tombstone reads:

> Commissioned Surgeon of Colored Volunteers April 4, 1863 with rank of Major.
> Commissioned Regimental Surgeon of 7, Regiment U.S. Colored Troops October 2, 1863
> Brevetted Lieutenant Colonel U.S. Volunteers March 13, 1865. "For faithful and meritorious services"[99]

XXIII. Underage Soldiers

A recent groundbreaking study on Civil War underage soldiers estimates that "at least 10 percent of Union enlistees" failed to meet age requirements. Many lied about their age; in some cases, what would appear to be an obvious ineligibility (e.g., an 11-year-old permitted

---

99. Heather M. Butts, "Alexander Thomas Augusta Physician, Teacher and Human Rights Activist" in *Journal of the National Medical Association*, Vol. 97, No. 1, Jan. 2005, 106-109; Gerald S. Henig, "The Indomitable Dr. Augusta: The First Black Physician in the U.S. Army" in *Army History*, No. 87, Spring 2013, 22-31.

to enlist) was not enforced.[100] Such data demonstrate either incompetence or malfeasance by the recruiting officer.

The Tripler *Manual* could not have been more clear about the standards for enlistment in the US Regulars. A male "under twenty-one years of age can not enlist without the consent of his parent, guardian or master, if he have either." Even if written consent were offered, the physician needed to ensure the requisite physical ("able bodied") competency. Tripler referred to the medical consensus of the day, that a male did not typically attain full physical maturity until 21. The medical officer could not categorically reject an underage candidate, but he could reject the applicant if not physically capable:

> We can not but assent entirely to the physiological objections so forcibly urged against the enlistment of minors; and, considering the annoyances and losses to which the service is so constantly exposed from this class of recruits, the perjuries, falsehoods and forgeries they induce in the young and dissolute, the inconsiderable accession of force they bring to the ranks, we think they might profitably be forbidden altogether. But so long as these enlistments are authorized by the Regulations of the Army, the Medical officer can not summarily refuse to recognize them. He must confine himself to the investigation of the physical qualifications of the individual recruit.
>
> Let him then institute a closer scrutiny into the condition ….[101]

---

100. Frances M. Clarke & Rebecca Jo Plant, *Of Age: Boy Soldiers and Military Power in the Civil War Era* (New York: Oxford University Press, 2023), 5.
101. *Manual*, 8-10.

Bibliography[1]

Abbott, John S.C. *The History of the Civil War in America*, Vol. I (New York: Henry Bill, 1863)

Acken, J. Gregory. *Inside the Army of the Potomac: The Civil War Experience of Captain Francis Adams Donaldson* (Lanham: Stackpole Books, 1998)

Act of April 14, 1818, 3 Stat. 426.

Adams, F. Colburn. *The Story of a Trooper, With Much of Interest Concerning the Campaign on the Peninsula, Not Before Written* (New York: Dick & Fitzgerald, 1865)

Adams, George W. "Caring for the Men" in William C. Davis ed., *The Image of War: 1861-1865*, Vol. IV: Fighting for Time (Garden City: Doubleday & Co., 1983)

———. *Doctors in Blue: The Medical History of the Union Army in the Civil War* (New York: Henry Schuman, 1952)

Adams, Michael C.C. *Living Hell: The Dark Side of the Civil War* (Baltimore: Johns Hopkins University Press, 2014)

Adjutant General's Department. *Subject Index of the General Orders of the War Department, from January 1, 1809, to December 31, 1860* (Washington: Government Printing Office, 1886)

Adjutant General's Office. *General Orders Affecting the Volunteer Force, 1861* (Washington: Government Printing Office, 1862)

Adrienne, Carole. *Healing a Divided Nation: How the American Civil War Revolutionized Western Medicine* (New York: Pegasus Books, 2022)

---

1. All works listed were consulted in research for this volume.

Alcott, Louisa May. *Hospital Sketches* (Boston: James Redpath, 1863)

The American Heritage Picture History of the Civil War, narrative by Bruce Catton (New York: American Heritage Pub. Co., 1960)

American Journal of the Medical Sciences (Philadelphia: Lea & Blanchard, 1827)

American Medical Association. *Caring for the Country: A History and Celebration of the First 150 Years of the American Medical Association* (Chicago: n.p., 1997)

The Army Medical Bulletin, No. 61 (Apr. 1942) (James M. Phalen)

Atkinson, Matthew. "'War is a hellish way of settling a dispute'—Dr. Jonathan Letterman and the Tortuous Path of Medical Care from Manassas to Camp Letterman," Gettysburg National Military Park

Atlas to Accompany the Official Records of the Union and Confederate Armies, 1861-1865 (Washington: Government Printing Office, 1891-1895)

Austin, Anne L. *The Woolsey Sisters of New York: A Family's Involvement in the Civil War and a New Profession (1860-1900)* (Philadelphia: American Philosophical Society, 1971)

Bacon, Georgeanna Woolsey & Eliza Woolsey Howland. *Letters of a Family During the War for the Union 1861-1865*, Vols. I & II (n.p., 1899)

Bair, Kevin. "First Battle of Manassas: Unwarranted Deaths of Savable Men" in *Surgeon's Call*, Vol. 25, No. 1, a publication of the National Museum of Civil War Medicine

Baker, Paula. "New York during the Civil War and Reconstruction" in Milton M. Klein ed., *The Empire State: A History of New York* (Ithaca: Cornell University Press, 2001)

Barnard, John G. *The Peninsular Campaign and Its Antecedents* (New York: D. Van Nostrand, 1864)

Barton, William E. *The Life of Clara Barton, Founder of the American Red Cross*, Vols. I-II (Boston: Houghton Mifflin Co., 1922)

Bates, Samuel P. *History of Pennsylvania Volunteers, 1861-5*, Vol. V (Harrisburg: B. Singerly, 1871)

Bauer, K. Jack. *The Mexican War: 1846-1848* (Lincoln: University of Nebraska Press, 1992)

Bearrs, Edwin C. '… Into the very jaws of the enemy…': Jeb Stuart's Ride Around McClellan" in William J. Miller ed., *The Peninsula Campaign Of 1862: Yorktown to the Seven Days*, Vol. One (Campbell: Savas Woodbury, 1997)

Beatie, Russel H. *Army of the Potomac: Birth of Command, November 1860-September 1861* (Cambridge: Da Capo Press, 2002)

———. *Army of the Potomac: McClellan Takes Command, September 1861-February 1862* (Cambridge: Da Capo Press, 2004)

———. *Army of the Potomac: McClellan's First Campaign, March-May 1862* (New York: Savas Beatie, 2007)

Bell, Andrew M. *Mosquito Soldiers: Malaria, Yellow Fever, and the Course of the American Civil War* (Baton Rouge: Louisiana State University Press, 2010)

Berry, Stephen. *Weirding the War: Stories from the Civil War's Ragged Edges* (Athens: University of Georgia Press, 2011)

Bever, Megan Leigh. *War Is A Terrible Enemy to Temperance: Drinking, Self-Control, and the Meaning of Loyalty in The Civil War Era*, Ph.D. Dissertation, University of Alabama (2014), published as *At War with King Alcohol: Debating Drinking and Masculinity in the Civil War* (Chapel Hill: University of North Carolina Press, 2022)

Billings, John S. *Medical Reminiscences of the Civil War* (n.p., n.d.)

Blanton, DeAnne & Lauren M. Cook. *They Fought Like Demons: Women Soldiers in the American Civil War* (Baton Rouge: Louisiana State University Press, 2002)

Blustein, Bonnie Ellen. *Preserve Your Love for Science: Life of William A. Hammond, American Neurologist* (Cambridge: Cambridge University Press, 1991)

Bollet, Alfred J. *Civil War Medicine: Challenges and Triumphs* (Tucson: Galen Press, 2002)

Braun, Lundy. "Spirometry, Measurement, and Race in the Nineteenth Century" in *Journal of the History of Medicine and Allied Sciences*, Vol. 60, No. 2 (Oxford University Press, Apr. 2005)

Brooks, Stewart. *Civil War Medicine* (Springfield: Charles C Thomas, 1966)

Brown, Harvey E. *The Medical Department of the United States Army from 1775 to 1873* (Washington: Surgeon General's Office, 1873)

Brown, Jasmine. *Twice as Hard: The Stories of Black Women Who Fought to Become Physicians, from the Civil War to the 21st Century* (Boston: Beacon Press, 2023)

Brown, T. Allston. *A History of the New York Stage: From the First Performance in 1732 to 1901*, Vol. I (New York: Dodd, Mead & Co., 1903)

Browning, Judkin. *The Seven Days' Battles: The War Begins Anew* (Santa Barbara: Praeger, 2012)

——— & Timothy Silver. "Nature and Human Nature: Environmental Influences on the Union's Failed Peninsula Campaign, 1862" in *Journal of the Civil War Era*, Vol. 8, No. 3 (Sept. 2018)

———. *An Environmental History of the Civil War* (Chapel Hill: University of North Carolina Press, 2020)

Bucklin, Sophronia E. *In Hospital and Camp: A Woman's Record of Thrilling Incidents Among the Wounded in the Late War* (Philadelphia: John E. Potter & Co., 1869)

Bulletin of the New York Academy of Medicine, Vol. II (New York: Bailliere Bros., 1866)

Burr, C.B. ed. *Medical History of Michigan*, Vol. II (Minneapolis: Bruce Pub. Co., 1930)

Burton, Brian K. *Extraordinary Circumstances: The Seven Days Battles* (Bloomington: Indiana University Press, 2011)

———. *The Peninsula and Seven Days: A Battlefield Guide* (Lincoln: University of Nebraska Press, 2007)

Butts, Heather M. "Alexander Thomas Augusta Physician, Teacher and Human Rights Activist" in *Journal of the National Medical Association*, Vol. 97, No. 1, Jan. 2005

Carlisle, Robert J. ed. *An Account of Bellevue Hospital, with a Catalogue of the Medical and Surgical Staff from 1736 to 1894* (New York: Society of the Alumni of Bellevue Hospital, 1893)

Carroll, Dillon. *Invisible Wounds: Mental Illness and Civil War Soldiers* (Baton Rouge: Louisiana State University Press, 2021)

Cashin, Joan E. ed. *The War Was You and Me: Civilians in the American Civil War* (Princeton: Princeton University Press, 2002)

Castleman, Alfred L. *The Army of the Potomac: Behind the Scenes; A Diary of Unwritten History* (Milwaukee: Strickland & Co., 1863)

Catton, Bruce. *The Army of the Potomac Trilogy*, Gary W. Gallagher ed. (New York: Library of America, 2022)

———. *Glory Road: The Bloody Route from Fredericksburg to Gettysburg* (Garden City: Doubleday & Co., 1952)

———. *Mr. Lincoln's Army* (Garden City: Doubleday & Co., 1951)

———. *Waiting for the Morning Train: An American Boyhood* (Garden City: Doubleday & Co., 1972)

Censer, Jane T. ed. *The Papers of Frederick Law Olmsted: Defending the Union*, Vol. IV (Baltimore: Johns Hopkins University Press, 1986)

Chernow, Ron. *Grant* (New York: Penguin Press, 2017)

Chisolm, J. Julian. *A Manual of Military Surgery, for the Use of Surgeons in the Confederate States Army* (Richmond: West & Johnston, 1862)

The Citizens' Association. *A Typical American; or, Incidents in the Life of Dr. John Swinburne* (Albany: n.p., 1888)

Civil War Sites Advisory Commission. *Report on the Nation's Civil War Battlefields* (1993)

Clarke, Frances M. & Rebecca Jo Plant. *Of Age: Boy Soldiers and Military Power in the Civil War Era* (New York: Oxford University Press, 2023)

Clements, Bennett A. "Memoir of Jonathan Letterman, M.D." as reprint from *Journal of the Military Service Institution*, Vol. IV, No. 15 (1883)

Coco, Gregory A. *A Strange and Blighted Land: Gettysburg, the Aftermath of a Battle* (Gettysburg: Thomas Publications, 1995)

———. *A Vast Sea of Misery: A History and Guide to the Union and Confederate Field Hospitals at Gettysburg, July 1-November 20, 1863* (El Dorado: Savas Beatie, 2017)

Coddington, Ronald S. *Faces of Civil War Nurses* (Baltimore: Johns Hopkins University Press, 2020)

Code of Ethics of the American Medical Association, Adopted May, 1847 (Philadelphia: Turner Hamilton, 1871)

Coffman, Edward M. *The Old Army: A Portrait of the American Army in Peacetime, 1784-1898* (New York: Oxford University Press, 1986)

Columbus Morning Journal

Congressional Globe

Connor, Leartus. *The Michigan Medical Society; Its First Eighty-three Years; Present Wants and Suggestions for Their Supply* (Detroit: John Bornman & Son, 1902)

Constitution and Rules of the Harper Hospital, Together with the Report and Statement of the Trustees (Detroit: William Graham, 1866)

Coski, John M. *The Army of the Potomac at Berkeley Plantation: The Harrison's Landing Occupation of 1862* (n.p. 1989)

Croffut, W.A. ed. *Fifty Years in Camp and Field: Diary of Major-General Ethan Allen Hitchcock* (New York: G.P. Putnam's Sons, 1909)

Cullum, George W. *Biographical Register of the Officers and Graduates of the U.S. Military Academy*, Vols. I & II (Boston: Houghton, Mifflin & Co., 1891)

Cunningham, H.H. *Doctors in Gray: The Confederate Medical Service* (Baton Rouge: Louisiana State University Press, 1986)

Daily Ohio State Journal

Damman, Gordon & Alfred J. Bollet eds. *Images of Civil War Medicine: A Photographic History* (New York: Demos Medical Publishing, 2008)

Davis, Jefferson F. *The Rise and Fall of the Confederate Government*, Vol. II (New York: D. Appleton & Co., 1881)

Davis, William C. *The Cause Lost: Myths and Realities of the Confederacy* (Lawrence: University Press of Kansas, 1996)

Dean Jr., Eric T. *Shook over Hell: Post-Traumatic Stress, Vietnam, and the Civil War* (Cambridge: Harvard University Press, 1997)

Democratic Free Press

Denney, Robert E. *Civil War Medicine: Care & Comfort of the Wounded* (New York: Sterling Pub. Co., 1994)

Detroit Free Press

Devine, Shauna. *Learning from the Wounded: The Civil War and the Rise of American Medical Science* (Chapel Hill: University of North Carolina Press, 2014)

———. "'To Make Something Out of the Dying in This War': The Civil War and the Rise of American Medical Science" in *Journal of the Civil War Era*, Vol. 6, No. 2 (June 2016)

Dorwart, Bonnie Brice. *Death is in the Breeze: Disease during the American Civil War* (Frederick: NMCWM, 2009)

Dougherty, Kevin & J. Michael Moore. *The Peninsula Campaign of 1862: A Military Analysis* (Jackson: University Press of Mississippi, 2005)

Dowdey, Clifford. *The Seven Days: The Emergence of Robert E. Lee* (New York: Fairfax Press, 1978)

Downs, Jim. *Maladies of Empire: How Colonialism, Slavery, and War Transformed Medicine* (Cambridge: Belknap Press, 2021)

Duane, Anna Mae. *Educated for Freedom: The Incredible Story of Two Fugitive Schoolboys Who Grew Up to Change a Nation* (New York: New York University Press, 2020)

Duncan, Louis C. *The Medical Department of the United States Army in the Civil War* (n.p., n.d.)

Dyer, J. Franklin. *The Journal of a Civil War Surgeon* (Lincoln: University of Nebraska Press, 2003), Michael B. Chesson ed.

Eggleston, Larry G. *Women in the Civil War: Extraordinary Stories of Soldiers, Spies, Nurses, Doctors, Crusaders, and Others* (Jefferson: McFarland & Co., 2003)

Eicher, John & David Eicher. *Civil War High Commands* (Stanford: Stanford University Press, 2001)

Eisenschiml, Otto. "Medicine in the War" in *Civil War Times Illustrated*, Vol. 1, No. May 1962

Ellis, Thomas T. *Leaves from the Diary of an Army Surgeon* (New York: John Bradburn, 1863)

Erving, Annie Priscilla. *Reminiscences of the Life of a Nurse in Field, Hospital and Camp During the Civil War* (Newburgh: Daily News, 1904)

Faust, Drew Gilpin. *This Republic of Suffering: Death and the American Civil War* (New York: Vintage Books, 2008)

Flannery, Michael A. *Civil War Pharmacy: A History* (Carbondale: Southern Illinois University Press, 2017)

——— & Katherine H. Oomens eds. *The Civil War Journal of Spencer Bonsall* (Carbondale: Southern Illinois University Press, 2007)

Flower, Frank A. *Edwin McMasters Stanton, The Autocrat of Rebellion, Emancipation and Reconstruction* (Boston: Geo. M. Smith & Co., 1905)

Foote, Lorien & Earl J. Hess eds. *The Oxford Handbook of the American Civil War* (New York: Oxford University Press, 2021)

Freeman, Douglas S. *R.E. Lee: A Biography* (New York: Charles Scribner's Sons, 1934)

Freemon, Frank R. *Gangrene and Glory: Medical Care during the American Civil War* (Madison: Fairleigh Dickinson University Press, 1998)

———. "Lincoln Finds a Surgeon General: William A. Hammond and the Transformation of the Union Army Medical Bureau" in *Civil War History*, Vol. 33, No. 1 (March 1987)

———. *Microbes and Minie Balls: An Annotated Bibliography of Civil War Medicine* (Rutherford: Fairleigh Dickinson University Press, 1993)

French, Samuel L. *The Army of the Potomac from 1861 to 1863* (New York: Publishing Society of New York, 1906)

Gallagher, Gary W. "A Civil War Watershed: The 1862 Richmond Campaign in Perspective" in Gary W. Gallagher ed., *The Richmond Campaign of 1862: The Peninsula and the Seven Days* (Chapel Hill: University of North Carolina Press, 2000)

Giesberg, Judith Ann. *Civil War Sisterhood: The U.S. Sanitary Commission and Women's Politics in Transition* (Boston: Northeastern University Press, 2000)

Gillett, Mary C. *The Army Medical Department, 1818–1865* (Washington: Center of Military History, 1987)

Glatthaar, Joseph T. *Soldiering in the Army of Northern Virginia: A Statistical Portrait of the Troops Who Served under Robert E. Lee* (Chapel Hill: University of North Carolina Press, 2011)

Goldsmith, Middleton. *A Report on Hospital Gangrene, Erysipelas and Pyaemia, as Observed in the Departments of the Ohio and the Cumberland* (Louisville: Bradley & Gilbert, 1863)

Goss, Warren L. *Recollections of a Private: A Story of the Army of the Potomac* (New York: Thomas Y. Crowell & Co., 1890)

Gould, Benjamin A. *Investigations in the Military and Anthropological Statistics of American Soldiers* (New York: Hurd & Houghton, 1869)

Grace, William. *The Army Surgeon's Manual, for the Use of Medical Officers, Cadets, Chaplains, and Hospital Stewards* (New York: Bailliere Brothers, 1864)

Graves, Clifford L. *Front Line Surgeons: A History of the Third Auxiliary Surgical Group* (San Diego: Frye & Smith Ltd., 1950)

Greenbie, Marjorie B. *Lincoln's Daughters of Mercy* (New York: G.P. Putnam's Sons, 1944)

Greenleaf, Charles R. *A Manual for the Medical Officers of the United States Army* (Philadelphia: J.B. Lippincott & Co., 1864)

——— ed. *An Epitome of Tripler's Manual and Other Publications on the Examination of Recruits* (Washington: William Ballantyne & Sons, 1890)

Greenwood, John T. "Hammond and Letterman: A Tale of Two Men Who Changed Army Medicine" in *Landpower Essay: An Institute of Land Warfare Publication*, No. 03-1, June 2003

Gross, Samuel D. *A Manual of Military Surgery; or, Hints on the Emergencies of Field, Camp, and Hospital Practice* (Philadelphia: J.B. Lippincott & Co., 1862)

Haller, John S. Jr. *American Medicine in Transition, 1840-1910* (Urbana: University of Illinois Press, 1981)

———. *Farmcarts to Fords: A History of the Military Ambulance, 1790-1925* (Carbondale: Southern Illinois University Press, 1992)

Hammond, William A. *A Statement of The Causes Which Led to the Dismissal of Surgeon-General William A. Hammond from the Army; with a Review of the Evidence Adduced Before the Court* (New York: n.p., 1864)

———. *A Treatise on Hygiene, with Special Reference to the Military Service* (Philadelphia: J.B. Lippincott, 1863)

Handley-Cousins, Sarah. *Bodies in Blue: Disability in the Civil War North* (Athens: University of Georgia Press, 2019)

Harper Hospital (Detroit: Winn & Hammond, 1884)

Harper's Weekly

Hart, Albert G. *The Surgeon and the Hospital in the Civil War* [reprint from Papers of Military Society of Massachusetts] (n.p.: 1902)

Hasegawa, Guy R. *Matchless Organization: The Confederate Army Medical Department* (Carbondale: Southern Illinois University Press, 2021)

———. *Mending Broken Soldiers: The Union and Confederate Programs to Supply Artificial Limbs* (Carbondale: Southern Illinois University Press, 2012)

Hays, Isaac ed. *The American Journal of the Medical Sciences*, New Series, Vol. XLI (Philadelphia: Blanchard & Lea, 1861)

Heitman, Francis B. *Historical Register of the United States Army, from its Organization, September 29, 1789, to September 29, 1889* (Washington: National Tribune, 1890)

Henig, Gerald S. "The Indomitable Dr. Augusta: The First Black Physician in the U.S. Army" in *Army History*, No. 87, Spring 2013

Hennessy, John J. *The First Battle of Manassas: An End to Innocence, July 18-21, 1861* (Mechanicsburg: Stackpole Books, 2015)

Hess, Earl J. *The Union Soldier in Battle: Enduring the Ordeal of Combat* (Lawrence: University Press of Kansas, 1997)

Hicks, Robert D. ed. *Civil War Medicine: A Surgeon's Diary* (Bloomington: Indiana University Press, 2019)

Hill, Daniel H. "Lee's Attacks North of the Chickahominy" in *Battles and Leaders of the Civil War*, Vol. II (New York: Century Co., 1887)

Hillard, G.S. *Life and Campaigns of George B. McClellan, Major-General U.S. Army* (Philadelphia: J.B. Lippincott & Co., 1865)

Records of Historic Elmwood Cemetery, Detroit

Hitchcock, Frederick L. *War from the Inside* (Philadelphia: J.B. Lippincott Co., 1904)

Holmes, Oliver Wendell Sr. *Homœopathy and Its Kindred Delusions* (Boston: William D. Ticknor, 1842)

Holt, Daniel M. *A Surgeon's Civil War: The Letters and Diary of Daniel M. Holt, M.D.* (Kent: Kent State University Press, 1994), James M. Greiner, Janet L. Coryell, & James R. Smither eds.

Hood, Jonathan D. *Jonathan Letterman and the Development of a Battlefield Evacuation System*, Ph.D. Dissertation, Texas Tech University, Dec. 2004

https://history.army.mil/html/faq/oaths.html

Hubbell, John T. "The Seven Days of George Brinton McClellan" in Gary W. Gallagher ed., *The Richmond Campaign of 1862: The Peninsula and the Seven Days* (Chapel Hill: University of North Carolina Press, 2000)

Humphreys, Margaret. *Intensely Human: The Health of the Black Soldier in the American Civil War* (Baltimore: Johns Hopkins University Press, 2008)

———. *Marrow of Tragedy: The Health Crisis of the American Civil War* (Baltimore: Johns Hopkins University Press, 2013)

Irwin, Bernard J.D. "Notes on the Introduction of Tent Field Hospitals in War" from *Proceedings of the Association of Military Surgeons of the United States* (n.p., ca. 1894)

Irwin, Richard B. "The Administration in the Peninsular Campaign" in *Battles & Leaders*, Vol. II

Jackson, Kenneth T. ed. *The Encyclopedia of New York City* (New Haven: Yale University Press, 2010)

Jarrow, Gail. *Blood and Germs: The Civil War Battle Against Wounds and Disease* (New York: Calkins Creek, 2020)

Jarvis, Edward. "Sanitary Condition of the Army" in *The Atlantic Monthly*, Vol. X (Boston: Ticknor & Fields, 1862)

Johnson, Robert U. & Buel, Clarence C. eds. *Battles and Leaders of the Civil War*, Vol. II (New York: Century Co., 1887)

Jones, Gordon W. "Sanitation in the Civil War" in *Civil War Times Illustrated*, Vol. V, No. 7, November 1963

———. "Wartime Surgery" in *Civil War Times Illustrated*, Vol. II, No. 5, May 1963

Jones, Terry L. "Down the Peninsula with Richard Ewell: Captain Campbell Brown's Memoirs in the Seven Days Battles" in William J. Miller ed., *The Peninsula Campaign of 1862: Yorktown to the Seven Days*, Vol. Two (Campbell: Savas Woodbury, 1997)

Josyph, Peter ed. *The Wounded River: The Civil War Letters of John Vance Lauderdale, M.D.* (East Lansing: Michigan State University Press, 1993)

Journal of Civil War Medicine

Journal of the Executive Proceedings of the Senate of the United States of America from December 2, 1861, to July 17, 1862, Inclusive, Vol. XII (Washington: Government Printing Office, 1887)

Kalisch Philip A. & Beatrice J. Kalisch. "Untrained But Undaunted: The Women Nurses Of The Blue And The Gray" in *Nursing Forum*, Vol. 15, No. 1, Jan. 1976

Kaminski, Theresa. *Dr. Mary Walker's Civil War: One Woman's Journey to the Medal of Honor and the Fight for Women's Rights* (Guilford: Lyons Press, 2020)

Katcher, Philip. *American Civil War Armies (3): Staff, Specialist and Maritime Services* (London: Osprey Publishing, 1986)

Keen, William W. *Surgical Reminiscences of the Civil War* (Philadelphia: Transactions of the College of Physicians of Philadelphia, 1905)

Kelly, Howard A. & Walter L. Barrage. *American Medical Biographies* (Baltimore: Norman, Remington Co., 1920)

Killblane, Richard E. *White House Landing: Sustaining the Army of the Potomac during the Peninsula Campaign* [https://transportation.army.mil/historian/documents/White%20House%20Landing%20paper.pdf]

Kilmer, George L. "The Army of the Potomac at Harrison's Landing" in *Battles and Leaders of the Civil War*, Vol. II (New York: Century Co., 1887)

King, William H. *History of Homœopathy and Its Institutions In America*, Vol. I (New York: Lewis Pub. Co., 1905)

Landis, H.R.M. *The History of the Development of Medical Science in America as Recorded in The American Journal of the Medical Sciences* (Philadelphia: Lea Brothers & Co., 1901)

Lee, William O. *Personal and Historical Sketches and Facial History of and by Members of the Seventh Regiment Michigan Volunteer Cavalry 1862-1865* (Detroit: 7th Cavalry Association, 1902)

Legislative History of the General Staff of the Army of the United States (Its Organization, Duties, Pay, and Allowances), from 1775 to 1901, 56th Congress, 2d Session, Doc. No. 229 (Washington: Government Printing Office, 1901)

Leonard, Pat. "William Hammond and the End of the Medical Middle Ages" in the "Disunion" Civil War Sesquicentennial weblog in *New York Times*, Apr. 27, 2012

Letterman, Jonathan. *Medical Recollections of the Army of the Potomac* (New York: D. Appleton & Co., 1866)

Lewis, Lloyd. *Captain Sam Grant* (Boston: Little, Brown & Co., 1950)

Library of Congress

Linderman, Gerald E. *Embattled Courage: The Experience of Combat in the American Civil War* (New York: The Free Press, 1987)

Livermore, Mary A. *My Story of the War* (Hartford: A.D. Worthington & Co., 1889)

Locke, E.W. *Three Years in Camp and Hospital* (Boston: Geo. D. Russell & Co., 1870)

Long, Lisa A. *Rehabilitating Bodies: Health, History, and the American Civil War* (Philadelphia: University of Pennsylvania Press, 2004)

Longacre, Edward G. *The Man Behind the Guns: A Military Biography of General Henry J. Hunt, Commander Of Artillery, Army Of The Potomac* (Cambridge: Da Capo Press, 2003)

Loperfido, Christopher E. ed. *Death, Disease, and Life at War: The Civil War Letters of Surgeon James D. Benton, 111th and 98th New York Infantry Regiments, 1862-1865* (El Dorado Hills: Savas Beatie, 2018)

Lowry, Thomas P. & Jack D. Welsh. *Tarnished Scalpels: The Court-Martials of Fifty Union Surgeons* (Mechanicsburg: Stackpole Books, 2000)

Lustrea, John. "How Civil War Cooks Kept Soldiers Healthy with History's Worst Vegetables," Aug. 11, 2022, at https://www.historynet.com/civil-war-desiccated-vegetables/

Manring, M.M., Alan Hawk, Jason H. Calhoun & Romney C. Andersen. "Treatment of War Wounds: A Historical Review" in *Clinical Orthopaedics and Related Research*, Vol. 467, No. 8, Aug. 2009

Marks, James J. *The Peninsular Campaign in Virginia* (Philadelphia: J.B. Lippincott & Co., 1864)

Martin, Justin. *Genius of Place: The Life of Frederick Law Olmsted* (Boston: Da Capo Press, 2011)

Marvel, William. *Lincoln's Autocrat: The Life of Edwin Stanton* (Chapel Hill: University of North Carolina Press, 2015)

Maxwell, William Q. *Lincoln's Fifth Wheel: The Political History of the United States Sanitary Commission* (New York: Longmans, Green & Co., 1956)

May, George S. *Michigan and the Civil War Years, 1860-1866: A Wartime Chronicle* (Lansing: Michigan Civil War Centennial Observance Commission, 1964)

———. ed. *Michigan Civil War History: An Annotated Bibliography* (Detroit: Wayne State University Press, 1961)

McClellan, George B. "From the Peninsula to Antietam" in *Battles and Leaders of the Civil War*, Vol. II (New York: Century Co., 1887)

———. *McClellan's Own Story: The War for the Union, the Soldiers Who Fought It, the Civilians Who Directed It and His Relations to It and to Them* (New York: Charles L. Webster & Co., 1887)

———. "The Peninsular Campaign" in *Battles and Leaders of the Civil War*, Vol. II (New York: Century Co., 1887)

McGaugh, Scott. *Surgeon in Blue: Jonathan Letterman, the Civil War Doctor Who Pioneered Battlefield Care* (New York: Arcade Publishing, 2013)

McKay, Charlotte E. *Stories of Hospital and Camp* (Philadelphia: Claxton, Remsen & Haffelfinger, 1876)

McPherson, James M. *Battle Cry of Freedom* (New York: Oxford University Press, 1988)

McRae, Norman. *Negroes in Michigan During the Civil War* (Lansing: Michigan Civil War Centennial Observance Commission, 1966)

Meade, George. *The Life and Letters of George Gordon Meade*, Vol. I (New York: Charles Scribner's Sons, 1913)

The Medical and Surgical Reporter

The Medical Directory of the City of New York (Medical Society of the County of New York: De Leeuw, Oppenheimer & Myers, 1887)

Meier, Kathryn Shively. *Nature's Civil War: Common Soldiers and the Environment in 1862 Virginia* (Chapel Hill: University of North Carolina Press, 2013)

———, "'No Place for the Sick': Nature's War on Civil War Soldier Mental and Physical Health in the 1862 Peninsula and Shenandoah Valley Campaigns" in *Journal of the Civil War Era*, Vol. 1, No. 2 (June 2011)

Message and Annual Reports for 1865, Made to the Fifty-Seventh General Assembly of Ohio (Columbus: Richard Nevins, 1866)

Message of the President of the United States to the Two Houses of Congress, 37th Congress, Vol. II, Report of the Secretary of War, Senate Ex. Doc. No. 1 (Washington: Government Printing Office, 1861)

Michigan Civil War Association. *Heart in Tatters: Eunice Hunt Tripler and the Civil War* (Traverse City: Mission Point Press, 2022)

Miers, Earl S. ed. *Lincoln Day By Day: A Chronology, 1809-1865*, Vol. III (Washington: Lincoln Sesquicentennial Commission, 1960)

The Military Surgeon: Journal of the Association of Military Surgeons of the United States, Vol. XXIX (Washington: Association of Military Surgeons, 1912), Charles Lynch ed.

Millard, Candice. *Destiny of the Republic: A Tale of Madness, Medicine and the Murder of a President* (New York: Doubleday, 2011)

Miller, William J. "Scarcely Any Parallel in History: Logistics, Friction and McClellan's Strategy for the Peninsula Campaign" in William J. Miller ed., *The Peninsula Campaign of 1862: Yorktown to the Seven Days*, Vol. Two (Campbell: Savas Woodbury, 1997)

——— ed. *The Peninsula Campaign of 1862: Yorktown to the Seven Days*, Vol. One (Campbell: Savas Woodbury, 1997)

———. *The Peninsula Campaign Of 1862: Yorktown to the Seven Days*, Vol. Three (Campbell: Savas Pub. Co., 1997)

Mitchell, S. Weir. "The Medical Department in the Civil War" in *Journal of the American Medical Association*, Vol. LXII, No. 19 (May 9, 1914)

Mitchill, Samuel L., Edward Miller & Elihu H. Smith. *The Medical Repository* (New York: T & J. Swords, 1797)

Moore, Frank. *Women of the War: Their Heroism and Self-Sacrifice* (Hartford: S.S. Scranton & Co., 1868)

Morgan, Thomas M. "The Education and Medical Practice of Dr. James McCune Smith (1813-1865), First Black American to Hold a Medical Degree" in *Journal of the National Medical Association*, Vol. 95, No. 7 (July 2003)

Munroe, James Phinney ed. *Adventures of an Army Nurse in Two Wars: Edited from the Diary and Correspondence of Mary Phinney, Baroness von Olnhausen* (Boston: Little, Brown & Co., 1904)

Murison, Justine S. "Quacks, Nostrums, and Miraculous Cures: Narratives of Medical Modernity in the Nineteenth-Century United States" in *Literature and Medicine*, Vol. 32, No. 2, Fall 2014, Johns Hopkins University Press

The National Cyclopaedia of American Biography, Vol. VII (New York: James T. White & Co., 1897)

Nevins, Allan. "The United States Sanitary Commission and Secretary Stanton" in *Proceedings of the Massachusetts Historical Society*, Third Series, Vol. 67 (Oct. 1941-May 1944)

———. *The War for the Union: The Improvised War, 1861-1862*, Vol. I (New York: Charles Scribner's Sons, 1959)

——— ed. *The Diary of George Templeton Strong: The Civil War, 1860-1865* (New York: MacMillan Co., 1952, 1962)

New York Times

Newmark, Jill L. *Without Concealment, Without Compromise: The Courageous Lives of Black Civil War Surgeons* (Carbondale: Southern Illinois University Press, 2023)

Noe, Kenneth W. "I Am Completely Checked by the Weather: George B. McClellan, Weather, and the Peninsula Campaign" in Andrew S. Bledsoe & Andrew F. Lang eds., *Upon the Fields of Battle: Essays on the Military History of America's Civil War* (Baton Rouge: Louisiana State University Press, 2018)

Oates, Stephen B. *A Woman of Valor: Clara Barton and the Civil War* (New York: The Free Press, 1994)

Official Register of the Officers and Cadets of the U.S. Military Academy, West Point, New-York, June 1841 (New York: J.P. Wright, 1841)

Olmsted, Frederick L. *Hospital Transports: A Memoir of the Embarkation of the Sick and Wounded from the Peninsula of Virginia in the Summer of 1862* (Boston: Ticknor & Fields, 1863)

Ordronaux, John. *Hints on the Preservation of Health in Armies: For the Use of Volunteer Officers and Soldiers* (New York: D. Appleton & Co., 1861)

Palmer, Friend. *Early Days in Detroit* (Detroit: Hunt & June, 1906)

Papers of Abraham Lincoln

Patterson, Robert. *A Narrative of the Campaign in the Valley of the Shenandoah, in 1861* (Philadelphia: John Campbell, 1865)

Perret, Geoffrey. *Lincoln's War: The Untold Story of America's Greatest President as Commander in Chief* (New York: Random House, 2004)

Perry, Martha Derby ed. *Letters from a Surgeon of the Civil War* (Boston: Little, Brown & Co., 1906)

Personal Memoirs of John H. Brinton, Major and Surgeon U.S.V., 1861-1865 (New York: Neale Pub. Co., 1914)

Personal Memoirs of U.S. Grant, Vol. II (New York: Charles L. Webster & Co., 1886)

Pfanz, Donald C. *Clara Barton's Civil War: Between Bullet and Hospital* (Yardley: Westholme Publishing, 2018)

Phalen, James M. "The Life Of Jonathan Letterman" in *Records of the American Catholic Historical Society of Philadelphia*, Vol. 58, No. 2 (June 1947)

———. "Surgeon Thomas A. McParlin: Letterman's Successor with the Army of the Potomac" in *The Military Surgeon*, July 1940

Philippe, Comte de Paris. "McClellan Organizing the Grand Army" in *Battles and Leaders of the Civil War*, Vol. II (New York: Century Co., 1887)

Pilcher, James E. *The Surgeon Generals of the Army of the United States of America* (Carlisle: Association of Military Surgeons, 1905)

Porter, Fitz John. "Hanover Court House and Gaines's Mill" in Robert U. Johnson & Clarence C. Buel eds., *Battles and Leaders of the Civil War*, Vol. II (New York: Century Co., 1887)

Potter, William W. *Reminiscences of Field-Hospital Service with the Army of the Potomac* (Buffalo: *Buffalo Medical and Surgical Journal*, Oct.-Nov. 1889) [reprint]

Powers, Elvira J. *Hospital Pencillings: Being a Diary while in Jefferson General Hospital, Jeffersonville, Ind., and Others at Nashville, Tennessee, as Matron and Visitor* (Boston: Edward L. Mitchell, 1866)

Priest, John Michael ed. *One Surgeon's Private War: Doctor William W. Potter of the 57th New York* (Shippensburg: White Mane Pub. Co., 1996)

Puzzilla, Anthony G. *Hospital Trains and Vessels during the Civil War: The Evolution in the Handling and Transportation of the Wounded* (Manchester: Canoe Tree Press, 2020)

Rafuse, Ethan S. "Typhoid and Tumult: Lincoln's Response to General McClellan's Bout with Typhoid Fever during the Winter of 1861-62" in *Journal of the Abraham Lincoln Association*, Vol. 18, No. 2 (Summer 1997)

Reception of the American Medical Association at Independence Hall, Philadelphia, May 2, 1855 (Philadelphia: T.K. & P.G. Collins, 1855)

Records of the Quartermaster General, National Archives and Records Administration, Washington

Reed, William H. *The Heroic Story of the United States Sanitary Commission, 1861-1865* (Boston: Geo. H. Ellis Co., 1910)

Regulations for the Medical Department of the Army (Washington: George W. Bowman, 1860)

Report of a Committee of the Associate Members of the Sanitary Commission, on the Subject of the Nature and Treatment of Miasmatic Fevers (New York: Bailliere Brothers, 1862)

Report of the Secretary of War, Communicating the Report of Captain George B. McClellan, Senate Ex. Doc. No. 1 (Washington: A.O.P. Nicholson, 1857)

Reports on the Extent and Nature of the Materials Available for the Preparation of a Medical and Surgical History of the Rebellion (Philadelphia: J.B. Lippincott & Co., 1865)

Rhode, Michael G. "The Rise and Fall of the Army Medical Museum and Library" in *Washington History*, Vol. 18, No. 1/2 (2006)

Rhodes, James F. "The First Six Weeks of McClellan's Peninsular Campaign" in *The American Historical Review*, Vol. I, No. III (New York: Macmillan Co., 1896)

Rhodes, Robert H. ed. *All For the Union; The Civil War Diary and Letters of Elisha Hunt Rhodes* (New York: Vintage Books, 1992)

Robarts, William H. *Mexican War Veterans: A Complete Roster of the Regular and Volunteer Regiments in the War Between the United States and Mexico, from 1846 to 1848* (Washington: Brentano's, 1887)

Roberts, William C. *An Address Delivered Before the Alumni Association of the College of Physicians and Surgeons, Medical Department of Columbia College, New-York, at the Spring Commencement, March 12, 1863* (New York: John A. Gray & Green, 1864)

Robertson, John. *Michigan in the War* (Lansing: W.S. George & Co., 1882)

Roger Hepburn, Sharon A. ed. *Private No More: The Civil War Letters of John Lovejoy Murray, 102nd United States Colored Infantry* (Athens: University of Georgia Press, 2023)

Roper, Laura Wood. *F.L.O.: A Biography of Frederick Law Olmsted* (Baltimore: Johns Hopkins University Press, 1973)

Rutkow, Ira M. *Bleeding Blue and Gray: Civil War Surgery and the Evolution of American Medicine* (New York: Random House, 2005)

Salmon, John S. *The Official Virginia Civil War Battlefield Guide* (Mechanicsburg: Stackpole Books, 2001)

Sandburg, Carl. *Abraham Lincoln: The War Years*, Vol. One (New York: Harcourt, Brace & World, 1939)

Sanger, George P. ed. *The Statutes at Large*, Vol. XII (Boston: Little, Brown & Co., 1863) (37th Congress, 1st Session)

———. *United States Statutes at Large*, Vol. XIV (Boston: Little, Brown & Co., 1868) (39th Congress, 1st Session)

The Sanitary Commission of the United States Army: A Succinct Narrative of Its Work and Purposes (New York: n.p., 1864)

Sartin, Jeffrey S. "Infectious Diseases during the Civil War: The Triumph of the 'Third Army'" in *Clinical Infectious Diseases*, Vol. 16, No. 4 (Apr. 1993)

Schaadt, Mark J. *Civil War Medicine: An Illustrated History* (Quincy: Cedarwood Publishing, 1998)

Schmidt, James M. & Guy R. Hasegawa eds. *Years of Change and Suffering: Modern Perspectives on Civil War Medicine* (Roseville: Edinborough Press, 2009)

Schroeder-Lein, Glenna R. *The Encyclopedia of Civil War Medicine* (Armonk: M.E. Sharpe, Inc., 2008)

———. *Lincoln and Medicine* (Carbondale: Southern Illinois University Press, 2012)

Schultz, Jane E. *Women at the Front: Hospital Workers in Civil War America* (Chapel Hill: University of North Carolina Press, 2004)

Schwalm, Leslie A. "A Body of 'Truly Scientific Work': The U.S. Sanitary Commission and the Elaboration of Race in the Civil War Era" in *Journal of the Civil War Era*, Vol. 8, No. 4 (University of North Carolina Press, Dec. 2018)

Scientific American

Sears, Stephen W. *George B. McClellan: The Young Napoleon* (New York: Ticknor & Fields, 1988)

———. *Lincoln's Lieutenants: The High Command of the Army of the Potomac* (Boston: Houghton Mifflin Harcourt, 2017)

———. *To the Gates of Richmond: The Peninsula Campaign* (Boston: Houghton Mifflin Co., 2001)

——— ed. *The Civil War Papers of George B. McClellan: Selected Correspondence, 1860-1865* (New York: Ticknor & Fields, 1989)

Seed, David, Stephen C. Kenny & Chris Williams eds. *Life and Limb: Perspectives on the American Civil War* (Liverpool: Liverpool University Press, 2015)

Seiple, Samantha. *Louisa on the Front Lines: Louisa May Alcott in the Civil War* (New York: Seal Press, 2019)

Shields, Patricia M. "Mary Livermore: A Legacy of Caring and Cooperative Womanhood in Service to the State" in Claire L.

Felbinger & Wendy A. Haynes eds., *Outstanding Women in Public Administration: Leaders, Mentors & Pioneers* (Armonk: M.E. Sharpe, 2004)

Shiepko, Jessica M. *William Alexander Hammond's Transformation of the Army Medical Department During the American Civil War*, Department of History, Sam Houston State University, December 2018 [dissertation]

Shrady, John ed. *The College of Physicians and Surgeons, New York, and Its Founders, Officers, Instructors, Benefactors and Alumni: A History*, Vols. I & II (New York: Lewis Pub. Co., 1903)

Simon, John Y. ed. *The Personal Memoirs of Julia Dent Grant* (New York: G.G. Putnam's Sons, 1975)

Slawson, Robert G. "Medical Training in the United States Prior to the Civil War" in *Journal of Evidence-Based Complementary & Alternative Medicine* 17(1) 11-27 (2012) [https://journals.sagepub.com/doi/pdf/10.1177/2156587211427404]

────── & Carl W. Mansfield. *Prologue to Change: African Americans in Medicine in the Civil War Era* (NMCWM Press, 2006)

Smith, Adelaide W. *Reminiscences of an Army Nurse During the Civil War* (New York: Greaves Pub. Co., 1911)

Smith, Michael O. "Raising a Black Regiment in Michigan: Adversity and Triumph" in Darlene Clark Hine & Earnestine Jenkins eds., *A Question of Manhood: A Reader in Black Men's History and Masculinity*, Vol. I (Bloomington: Indiana University Press, 1999)

Smith, Stephen ed. *The American Medical Times: Being a Weekly Series of the New York Journal of Medicine*, Volume III, July to December, 1861 (New York: Bailliere Brothers, 1861)

Smith, Thomas H. *The Mapping of Ohio* (Kent: Kent State University Press, 1977)

Speech of the Rev. Dr. Bellows, President of the United States Sanitary Commission, Made at the Academy of Music, Philadelphia, Tuesday Evening, Feb. 24, 1863 (Philadelphia: C. Sherman, Son & Co., 1863)

Spruill, Matt. *Decisions of the Seven Days: The Sixteen Critical Decisions That Defined the Operation* (Knoxville: University of Tennessee Press, 2021)

Stanley, Autumn. *Mothers and Daughters of Invention: Notes for a Revised History of Technology* (New Brunswick: Rutgers University Press, 1995)

The Statutes at Large from December 1905 to March 1907, Vol. XXXIV, Part 2 (Washington: Government Printing Office, 1907)

Stearns, Amanda Akin. *The Lady Nurse of Ward E* (New York: Baker & Taylor Co., 1909)

Steiner, Lewis H. *A Sketch of the History, Plan of Organization, and Operations of the U.S. Sanitary Commission* (Philadelphia: Jas. B. Rodgers, 1866)

Steiner, Paul E. *Disease in the Civil War: Natural Biological Warfare in 1861-1865* (Springfield: Charles C Thomas, 1968)

———. *Medical-Military Portraits of Union and Confederate Generals* (Philadelphia: Whitmore Publishing Co., 1968)

———. *Physician-Generals in the Civil War: A Study in Nineteenth Mid-Century American Medicine* (Springfield: Charles C Thomas, 1966)

Stephenson, Michael. *The Last Full Measure: How Soldiers Die in Battle* (New York: Crown Publishers, 2012)

Stevens, George T. *Three Years in the Sixth Corps* (Albany: S.R. Gray, 1866)

Stevenson, Elizabeth. "Olmsted on F Street: The Beginnings of the United States Sanitary Commission" in *Records of the Columbia Historical Society, Washington, D.C.*, Vol. 49 (1973/1974)

Stewart, Alexander M. *Camp, March and Battle-field; or, Three Years and a Half with the Army of the Potomac* (Philadelphia: Jas. B. Rodgers,1865)

Stille, Charles J. *History of the United States Sanitary Commission, Being the General Report of Its Work During the War of the Rebellion* (Philadelphia: J.B. Lippincott & Co., 1866)

Stouffer, Dan. "Officer Autopsy: Dissecting the Legacy of Jonathan Letterman" in *Surgeon's Call: Journal of the Museum of Civil War Medicine* (Special Edition 2015)

Straubing, Harold E. *In Hospital and Camp: The Civil War Through the Eyes of its Doctors and Nurses* (Harrisburg: Stackpole Books, 1993)

Strong, George T. *Origin, Struggles and Principles of the U.S. Sanitary Commission* (Boston: U.S. Sanitary Commission, 1864)

Swinburne, John. *Reports on the Peninsular Campaign, Surgical Experience, &c.* (Albany: C. Van Benthuysen, 1863)

Swinton, William. *Campaigns of the Army of the Potomac* (New York: Charles B. Richardson, 1866)

Tap, Bruce. *Over Lincoln's Shoulder: The Committee on the Conduct of the War* (Lawrence: University Press of Kansas, 1998)

Thomas, Emory M. "The Peninsular Campaign" in William C. Davis ed., *The Image of War: 1861-1865*, Vol. II: The Guns of '62 (Garden City: Doubleday & Co., 1982)

Thompson, Holland ed. *The Photographic History of the Civil War in Ten Volumes*, Volume 7: Prisons and Hospitals (New York: Review of Reviews Co., 1911)

Tiffany, Francis. *Life of Dorothea Lynde Dix* (Boston: Houghton, Mifflin & Co., 1890)

Tise, Pam. *A Fragile Legacy: The Contributions of Women in the United States Sanitary Commission to the United States Administrative State*, Masters Thesis, Texas State University-San Marcos, 2013

Tripler, Charles S. "Case of Gun Shot Wound to the Stomach" in *The Peninsular Journal of Medicine and the Collateral Sciences*, Vol. IV, No. 1, July 1856 (Detroit: John A. Kerr & Co.)

———. *The Duties of Physicians in Relation to Popular Medical Delusions: An Address Delivered Before the Covington and Newport Medical Society, June 14, 1859* (Covington: S.G. Cobb, 1859)

———. *Hand-Book for the Military Surgeon* (Cincinnati: Robert Clarke & Co., 1861)

———. *Manual of the Medical Officer of the Army of the United States, Part I, Recruiting and the Inspection of Recruits, by Charles*

S. Tripler, M.D., Surgeon U.S.A.; Fellow of the College of Physicians and Surgeons of the University of the State of New York (Cincinnati: Wrightson & Co., 1858)

————— & Thomas Antisell. "Report of the Committee on Rank in the Medical Department of the Army" in *The Transactions of the American Medical Association*, Vol. XVII (Philadelphia: Collins, 1866)

Tripler, Eunice. *Some Notes of her Personal Recollections* (New York: The Grafton Press, 1910)

United States Christian Commission, for the Army and Navy. *First Annual Report* (Philadelphia: 1863)

—————. *Second Annual Report* (Philadelphia: 1864)

United States Sanitary Commission. *Publication No. 74, Associate Members as of March 15th, 1864*

—————. *Statement of the Object and Methods of the Sanitary Commission* (New York: Wm. C. Bryant Co., 1863)

—————. *Surgical Memoirs of the War of the Rebellion* (New York: Hurd & Houghton, 1870-1871), by John A. Lidell, Frank H. Hamilton ed. (2 vols.)

U.S. Census

U.S. Navy Department, *Dictionary of American Naval Fighting Ships*, Vol. IV (Washington: Government Printing Office, 1969)

U.S. War Department. *The Medical and Surgical History of the War of the Rebellion* (Washington: Government Printing Office, 1870-1888)

—————. *Revised Regulations for the Army of the United States, 1861* (Philadelphia: J.B. Lippincott & Co., 1861)

Wagner, Margaret E., Gary W. Gallagher & Paul Finkelman eds. *The Library of Congress Civil War Desk Reference* (New York: Simon & Schuster, 2002)

Walt Whitman's Drum-Taps (New York: Gibson Brothers, 1865)

The War of the Rebellion: A Compilation of the Official Records of the Union and Confederate Armies (Washington: Government Printing Office, 1880-1901)

Waugh, John C. *Lincoln and McClellan: The Troubled Partnership Between a President and His General* (New York: Palgrave MacMillan, 2010)

Webb, Alexander S. *The Peninsula: McClellan's Campaign of 1862* (New York: Charles Scribner's Sons, 1882)

Welsh, Jack D. *Medical Histories of Union Generals* (Kent: Kent State University Press, 1996)

Wert, Jeffry D. "Dr. Letterman's War" in *Civil War Times*, Vol. 45, No. 7 (Sept. 2006)

———. *The Sword of Lincoln: The Army of the Potomac* (New York: Simon & Schuster, 2005)

The Western Sanitary Commission: A Sketch (St. Louis: R.P. Studley & Co., 1864)

Wheelock, Julia S. *The Boys in White; The Experience of a Hospital Agent in and Around Washington* (New York: Lange & Hillman, 1870)

White, Ronald C. *American Ulysses: A Life of Ulysses S. Grant* (New York: Random House, 2016)

Wilcox, Cadmus M. *History of the Mexican War* (Washington: Church News Pub. Co., 1892)

Willard, Sylvester D. *Conservative Surgery, with a List of the Medical and Surgical Force of New York in the War of the Rebellion, 1861-2* (Albany: Charles Van Benthuysen, 1862)

Williams, Kenneth P. *Lincoln Finds a General*, Vol. I (Bloomington: Indiana University Press, 1949)

Williams, T. Harry. *Lincoln and the Radicals* (Madison: University of Wisconsin Press, 1941)

Wills, Brian S. *Inglorious Passages: Noncombat Deaths in the American Civil War* (Lawrence: University Press of Kansas, 2017)

Wilson James G. & John Fiske eds., *Appletons' Cyclopædia of American Biography*, Vol. III (New York: D. Appleton & Co., 1887)

———. *Appletons' Cyclopædia of American Biography*, Vol. V (New York: D. Appleton & Co., 1900)

Winkle, Kenneth J. *Lincoln's Citadel: The Civil War in Washington, DC* (New York: W.W. Norton & Co., 2013)

Wittenmyer, Annie. *Under the Guns: A Woman's Reminiscences of the Civil War* (Boston: E.B. Stillings & Co., 1895)

Woodford, Frank B. & Mason, Philip P. *Harper of Detroit: The Origin and Growth of a Great Metropolitan Hospital* (Detroit: Wayne State University Press, 1964)

Woodward, C. Vann ed. *Mary Chestnut's Civil War* (New Haven: Yale University Press, 1981)

Woolsey, Jane Stuart. *Hospital Days: Reminiscence of a Civil War Nurse* (Roseville: Edinborough Press, 1996)

Wormeley, Katherine Prescott. *The Other Side of War with the Army of the Potomac* (Boston: Ticknor & Co., 1889)

Yarrow, Henry Crécy. "Personal Recollections of Some Old Medical Officers" in *The Military Surgeon*, Vol. 59 (Washington: Association of Military Surgeons of the United States, 1926)

Index

abolition, xiii, 86, 124, 251
Adjutant-General, 20 n.33, 63, 125, 213
African-Americans ("negro"), xix, 23, 86-87, 150, 252
Albany, N.Y., 96, 102
alcohol, 18-19, 65 n.73
Alcott, Louisa May, 13 n.10, 109 n.88, 239
Alexandria, Va., 35, 47, 92, 96, 216
ambulance, xvii, xx, 24, 50-51, 53, 69, 134, 191, 214
ambulance corps, 57, 66, 67, 187
American Journal of the Medical Sciences, 16, 39
American Medical Association, 14-15, 24, 162
American Revolutionary War, xix, 214
amputation, 11, 13, 23, 52, 158, 185
An Act for the Release of certain Persons held to Service or Labor, 85
An Epitome of Tripler's Manual and Other Publications on the Examination of Recruits, 21 n.39, 251
Anderson, Robert, xx
Annapolis, Md., 70, 94, 96
Antisell, Thomas, 162
Arlington, Va., 37, 62,
Army Medical Board, 9, 24, 48, 49, 66, 152, 156, 214

Army Medical Museum, xix, 86 n.49
Army of Northern Virginia, xxi, 110, 233-234
Army of the Potomac, xiii, xx, 41, 61, 75, 90, 121, 149
Army of Virginia, 110 n.92
artificial limb, 151
assistant-surgeons, 38, 167
Association of Military Surgeons, 85
Augusta, Alexander T., 252
Aztec Club, 12, 157

Baltimore, Md., 96, 162, 244
Banks, Nathaniel P., 38
Barnard, John G., 42, 117 n.125, 128
Barnes, Joseph, 44, 151, 156, 161, 167
Bartholow, Roberts, 92
Barton, Clara, 238, 239
Battle of Antietam, 118, 140, 179, 182
Battle of Ball's Bluff, 69
Battle of Chancellorsville, 140, 177
Battle of First Bull Run, 34, 37, 96, 101, 125
Battle of Fredericksburg, 109 n.88, 177, 240
Battle of Gaines Mill, 110, 111, 114
Battle of Gettysburg, 118, 155, 209
Battle of Hanover Court House, 100, 102
Battle of Malvern Hill, 110, 117, 126
Battle of Seven Pines, 101, 109, 124

Battle of Shiloh, 113, 118
Battle of Williamsburg, 96, 121, 137
Bellevue Hospital, 5
Bellows, Henry W., 77, 81, 86
Berkeley Plantation, Va., 114
Billings, John Shaw, 42, 43
Bissell, Charles T., 8 n.17, 185
Blackman, George Curtis, 163
Blair, Austin, 153
Bliss, D. Willard, 242
Boston, Ma., 76, 96, 103
Bowery, 3
Bragg, Braxton, 73 n.101
brevet promotion, 157
brigade surgeons, 50, 64, 68, 149, 213
Brinton, John H., 184 n.35
Britain, Clarissa, 216
Budd's Ferry, Md., 63
Buffalo Barracks, 7
Bunker Hill, Va., 33
Bureau of Sanitary Inspection, 122
bureaucracy, 16, 73, 76, 91, 105
Burnside, Ambrose E., 151

cacolets, 66, 215
cadets, 38, 78
Camp Ward, 150
Camp Winfield Scott, 93
Campbell, C.F.H., 32 n.5
camps, policing of, 62, 195
cancer, 162, 164
Capitol Hill, 83, 119, 123
Capitol Prison, 62
carbolic acid, 61
Casey, Silas, 166
Castleman, Alfred L., 71 n.94
casualties, 34, 38, 69, 96, 103, 108, 109, 118
Chandler, Zachariah, 119
Charlestown, (West) Va., 33
Chase, Salmon P., 119
Cheeseman's Landing, Va., 94

Chesapeake Bay, 89
Chickahominy River, 101, 110, 113, 117, 142
Civil Rights movement, xiii, 154
chlorine, 61
Chopart's operation, 52
climate, 139, 142, 150, 203, 217
coffee, 53, 116, 245
Cold Harbor, Va., 100
College of Physicians and Surgeons, Columbia College, 4, 148, 164
Commodore, 91, 94, 99
Confederate States of America, 25
Congress, 6, 9, 37, 79, 105, 125, 151, 170
Cooper, George E., 33 n.7, 123
court-martial, 54, 72, 184, 194
COVID-19, 54 n.44, 231
Crimean ovens, 216
Crimean War, xxi, 22, 23, 43, 238
Cumberland Landing, Va., 98, 99
Cumberland, Md., 63
Cuyler, John M., 44, 92

Dances with Wolves, xvii n.7
Daniel Webster No. 1, 94, 103
Daniel Webster No. 2, 101
Davis, Jefferson F., 111
Davis, Rebecca, 251
delirium tremens, 5
Department of the Lakes, 161, 167
Department of the Ohio, 151 n.19, 158, 161
Department of the Pacific, 19
Department of Pennsylvania, 32
Departments of Washington and of Northeastern Virginia, 32, 41
Detroit, Mich., 7, 8, 10, 14, 17, 20, 125, 145, 150, 152, 158, 161
Detroit Advertiser & Tribune, 131
Detroit Barracks, 7, 11, 14, 145, 233
diarrhea, 100 n.48

disability, 50, 63
disease, 13, 15, 22, 44 n.18, 48, 50, 60, 95, 138, 146, 203
disorder of the heart, 76, 232
Dispatch Station, 100
Division of the Potomac, 41, 47
Dix, Dorothea, 85, 100
Doherty, Joseph, 154
Dr. Trent's house, 103, 116, 211
Dr. William Gaines's house, 101, 103 n.63
Dranesville, Va., 69
Drewry's Bluff, Va., 99
Du Bois, W.E.B., 87
dysentery, 22, 60

East India Company, 5
Ellis, Thomas T., 184
Elm City, 101, 133
Emancipation Proclamation, xii, 150
epidemic, 15, 64
eruptive-fever, 64
Etheridge, Annie, 101 n.53
examining board, 9, 152
exsection, 51, 158

Fair Oaks Station, 101, 102
Fairfax Court House, 67
Farrand, David O., 153
Finley, Clement A., 26, 56, 69, 72, 76, 91, 188, 208
First Michigan Colored Infantry, 150
The Flag of Humanity, 238
Forsyth, Robert Allen, 8
Fort Donelson, 89
Fort Gratiot, 4, 14, 16, 164
Fort Henry, 89
Fort Mackinac, 33, 77, 164
Fort Monroe, 44, 90, 109 n.89, 198, 244
Fort Pulaski, 89
Fort Scott National Historic Site, 215
Fort Sullivan, 6, 7

Fort Sumter, 26, 196
Fort Towson, 6
Fort Vancouver, 44

gangrene, 71
Gardiner, William, 54
Garfield, James A., 238, 242
General Orders No. 9, 52, 54, 66
General Orders No. 17, 152 n.25
General Orders No. 20, 51 n.39, 66
General Orders No. 25, 48 n.32
General Orders No. 35, 49
General Orders No. 89, 167
General Regulations for the Army, 22
Georgetown, 33, 47, 96
germ theory of disease, 61, 146
Gone With The Wind, xvi
Gould, Benjamin A., 86 n.49
Grant, Julia Dent, 19
Grant, Ulysses S., 17, 161
Great Lakes, 42
Greene, George S., xx
Greenleaf, Charles R., 21 n.39, 241, 246
Guild, LaFayette, 233

Hagerstown, Md., 32, 33
Hall, Norman J., xiii, 128
Hammond, William A., 43, 70 n.92, 76, 81, 104, 121, 125, 129, 183
Hampton Roads, Va., 89, 113, 137
Hancock Barracks, 6
Hand-Book of the Military Surgeon, 21, 38, 163
hand-stretchers, 50, 51
Harper Hospital, 148, 152, 166, 222
Harpers Ferry, (West) Va., 33, 125
Harper's Weekly, 76, 97
Harrison's Landing, Va., 110, 112, 117, 118 n.129, 126, 142, 177, 188
Hartsuff, George L., 245
Harvard University, 77
Haxall's Landing, Va., 114, 244
Hayes, Rutherford B., 194 n.59

Heintzelman, Samuel P., 152, 161, 218
Hill, Bennett H., 150
Historic Elmwood Cemetery, 166, 176, 225
Holmes, Oliver Wendell Sr., 232 n.57
homeopathy, 232
Hooker, Joseph, 19, 161, 166
The Horse Soldiers, xvi, 235
hospital attendants, 17, 50, 71, 114
hospital transports, 95, 96
hospitals, 12, 26, 32, 33, 43, 47, 55, 65, 70, 93, 96
How the West Was Won, 238
Howard, Jacob M., 124, 131, 157, 171
Humphreys, Andrew A., 128
Hunt, Henry J., 8, 128,
Hunt, Thomas V., 7
hygiene, 48, 62, 79, 146

Ingalls, Rufus, 132
Inspector-General, 78, 121, 131, 190
inspectors, 43, 63, 75, 78, 91

Jackson, Andrew, 6, 246
Jackson, Thomas J., 32, 234
James Peninsula, 61, 90, 141
James River, 90, 112, 118, 142, 198
Jarvis, Edward, 213
Jefferson Medical College, 42, 233
Jim Crow, 87
John Quincy Adams house, 83
Johnson, Andrew, 161
Johnston, Albert Sidney, xx
Johnston, Joseph E., 32

Kane, Elisha Kent, 17
Keene, Laura, 4 n.4
King, William S., 34
Knickerbocker, 101
Koch, H.H.R., 61

Lawson, Thomas, 14, 26, 157
Lee, George W., 153

Lee, Mary Custis, 62 n.68, 98, 105
Lee, Robert E., 62 n.68, 110, 210, 233
Lemaire, Jules, 61
León, Alexis M., 232 n.57
Letterman, Jonathan, 43, 70 n.92, 119, 125, 129, 177, 208
Lincoln, Abraham, xi, 20 n.34, 31, 46, 59, 79, 123, 157, 197
Lind, Jennie, 3
Lister, Joseph, 61
litters, 50, 66, 215
logistics, xii, 98 n.305, 118 n.129
Lovell, Joseph, 6

Mackinaw, Mich., 77
Magruder, David L., 34
Magruder, John B., 210
malaria, 53, 61, 65, 93, 132, 230, 250
Manassas Junction, Va., 34
Manual of the Medical Officer of the Army of the United States, 21, 63
Marcy, Erastus E., 232
Marks, James J., 141
Martinsburg, Va., 32
Massachusetts, 94
McClellan, Dr. Ely, 106 n.79
McClellan, Dr. George, 42, 106 n.79
McClellan, Dr. Samuel, 106 n.79
McClellan, George B., xxi, 37, 41, 56, 90, 127, 142
McCoskry, Samuel A., 8, 162, 166
McDowell, Irvin, 34-37
McParlin, Thomas A., 196
Meade, George G., 42, 243
measles, 63, 221
Medical and Surgical History, 24 n.50, 85, 171, 215
Medical and Surgical Reporter, 70, 107
Medical College of Ohio, 21 n.40, 43
Medical Department of the Army, 6, 9, 14, 26, 36, 58, 72, 78, 86, 122-123, 140, 147, 167
Medical Reform Bill, 68, 77-78, 85, 121

The Medical Repository, 16
Meigs, Montgomery C., 25 n.56, 146 n.5, 185
Mercy Street, xxiv
Metcalfe, John T., 44
Mexican–American War, 11, 23, 164
Mexico City, 11, 14, 23
Michigan State Medical Society, 14, 15 n.16
Midwest, 31, 145, 161, 225
Military Order of the Loyal Legion of the United States, 157
Minié ball, xx
Mississippi River, 11, 89
Moore, Samuel P., 235
Munson, Edward L., 187 n.43

Nashville, Tn., 89
Natchitoches, La., 6
National Museum of Civil War Medicine, xviii, 182, 209
National Museum of Health and Medicine, xix, 214
Navy Department, 23, 25, 228
"negro," 23, 25, 86, 154, 184 n.35
New Bridge, Va., 103 n.63
New Kent Court House, Va., 98
New Orleans, La., 11, 89
New York Academy of Medicine, 158
New York City, 3, 4, 5, 19, 44, 70, 78, 96, 152, 156
New York Times, 35
New York University, 76
Newport Barracks, 11, 21
Norfolk, Va., 26, 137, 252
Northern Department, 152, 161, 170 n.14, 223
Northwest Ordinance of 1787, 85
nurses, 38, 55, 57, 85 n.47, 101 n.53, 116, 137, 146, 190, 229 n.43

Ocean Queen, 94
Of Human Hearts, 236

Olmsted, Frederick Law, 78, 80, 103-104, 106, 132, 136, 175, 207
Ontario, Canada, 68
Ord, E.O.C., 69
Overland Campaign, 196

Pamunkey River, 98, 100, 105, 113
Panama, Isthmus of, 16
pandemic, 231
Pasteur, Louis, 61
Patterson, Robert, 32
Peninsula Campaign, 61, 67, 89, 138, 142, 188
The Peninsular Journal of Medicine and the Collateral Sciences, 20
Perry, John G., 109 n.89
Petersburg, Va., 90
Philadelphia, Pa., 42, 58, 69, 76, 96
Picolata, Fl., 7
Pirigoff's operation, 52
Pitcher, Zina, 153 n.32, 155
pneumonia, 158, 244, 245
Point Lookout, Md., 89
Pope, John, 110 n.92, 187
Poquosin River, 93 n.14
Port Royal Sound, 89, 136
Porter, Fitz John, 100 n.52
Potomac River, 32, 89
Potter, John F., 105 n.77
Powell, William P. Jr., 229 n.43
prisoners of war, 35, 96, 113, 115, 154, 197
protocol, 76
psycho-traumatic effects of war, 13
Puebla, Mex., 14, 202
purveyors, 78

Quartermaster Department, 23, 53, 56, 93, 95, 132
Quartermaster-General, 26, 66, 146 n.5, 185
quinine, 65, 75, 118

racial stereotypes, 86-87
railroads (see specific), 77
Rappahannock River, 89, 90
Rauch, John Henry, 225
Reconstruction, 87
reforms, 72, 78, 121, 149, 207
religious faith, 12, 168, 169, 170
Republican Party, 124
Richardson, Israel B., 242
Richmond, Va., 31, 89, 180
Richmond & York River Rail Road, 98, 100, 115, 210
Roosevelt, Theodore, 170
Rosecrans, William, 43-44, 216

San Francisco, Ca., 19, 23, 174
Sanger, Eugene F., 225
sanitary conditions, 22, 79, 177, 193, 221
Satterlee, Richard S., 12, 25
Savage's Station, 98, 102, 112, 115, 209
Scott, Thomas A., 77
Scott, Winfield, 10, 31, 46, 123
scurvy, 99, 169, 220
Second Seminole War, 7
segregation, 87, 154
self-care, 146, 180 n.19
Semmelweis, Ignaz P., 61
Senate Committee on Military Affairs and Militia, 124
"Seven Buildings," 46
Seven Days Battles, 110, 113, 114, 126, 180
shelters, 75
Shenandoah Valley, 32, 90-91
Sherman, William T., 20, 232
Ship Point, Va., 94 n.19
Sisters of Charity, 94, 147
slavery, 85, 86, 98, 124
smallpox, 5, 63, 64 n.70, 75
Smith, Charles F., xx
Smith, Henry H., 94
Smith, James McCune, 251
Smith, William F., 93 n.17

Soldiers Aid Societies, 239
Special Orders No. 142, 125
St. Mary's Hospital, 147, 157
Standard Supply Table, 24
Stanton, Edwin M., 75, 78, 83, 105, 121, 162, 183
State of the Union address, 78
Steele, John B., 125
Stephens, Alexander H., 25 n.57
Stevens, George T., 141 n.47
Stocker, Anthony E., 243
Strong, George Templeton, 81 n.22, 191, 207 n.12
Stuart, J.E.B., 69, 110 n.92
Subsistence Department, 53, 95
Sumner, Edwin M., xx, 210, 211
Surgeon-General of the Army, 6, 9, 26, 38, 43, 46
surgeons, 9, 16, 35, 43, 50, 55, 65, 78, 108, 115, 129
Swinburne, John, 102, 115, 138, 185

Taylor, Zachary, 26, 59 n.53
telegraph, 33, 92, 104 n.72, 111, 112
tents, 24, 50, 63, 75, 133, 147, 216
torpedos, 96
Townsend, Edward D., 19-20, 168
training, 41, 60, 68, 189, 191, 195
Treasury Building, 83
Tripler, Alice Hunt, 10
Tripler, Charles Stuart (#1), 10
Tripler, Charles Stuart (#2), 14, 173
Tripler, Edgar Macklin, 21
Tripler, Edward Townsend, 21
Tripler, Ellen Cass, 16
Tripler, Ellen Mackintosh, 14
Tripler, Eunice (Hunt), 7, 12, 16, 45, 68, 121, 162, 170
Tripler, Eunice Montgomery Meigs, 25
Tripler, Henry Hunt, 122
Tripler Ambulance, 214
Tripler General Hospital, 176, 181-182
Tripler Hall, 3
Tripler Hospital, 157

Tunstall's Station, 98, 100
Twiggs, David E., 11, 164
typhoid fever, 5, 20 n.34, 137, 217, 222, 230

uniform, 33
Union Hotel hospital, 33
University of Maryland, 76
University of Michigan, 21, 155
University of Pennsylvania, 44, 242
Urbanna, Va., 89, 90
U.S. Capitol, 70, 122, 243
U.S. Christian Commission, 228
U.S. Military Academy, 5, 44, 128 n.20
U.S. Sanitary Commission, 44-45, 58-59, 64, 75, 97, 121, 146, 205
USS *Galena,* 114
USS *Monitor,* 89

vaccination, 62, 64
Van Buren, Martin, 7
Van Vliet, Stewart, 42, 67, 128
Vera Cruz, Mex., 11, 203
Virginia, 89
Virginia Central Railroad, 100
voyage to the Pacific, 16, 26

Waltham, Ma., 7
War Department, 9, 16, 25, 41, 45, 71, 75, 150
Washington, D.C., 7, 8, 20, 32, 41, 47, 53, 68, 70, 85, 90, 121
Washington, George, 98

weather, 16, 93, 142, 204, 213
Webb, Alexander S., 128
Wellington, Eunice, 7
West Point, Va., 89, 98, 137
Western Theater, 121, 155, 161
Westover Plantation, Va., 112 n.107
Wheaton, Walter V., 5
whisky, 65
Whitaker House, 93 n.17
White House, 46, 83, 119
White House, Va., 90, 98, 100, 113, 126
Whitman, Walt, 212 n.25, 229
Willard, Sylvester D., 243 n.88
Willcox, Orlando B., 166
Williams, Alpheus S., xiii
Williams, Seth, 128, 242
Williams College, 125 n.11
Wilson, Henry, 124
Wilson Small, 113, 114
Winchester, Va., 33
Wm. Whildin, 94, 96
women, 55, 58, 81, 146, 189, 229, 238
Wood, Robert C., 59, 84, 148
Wool, John E., 20
Wormeley, Katherine P., 137
wounds suffered from weapons, 23

Yarrow, Henry Crécy, 241 n.81
yellow fever, 13
York River, 89, 93, 98, 110, 132, 137, 198
Yorktown, Va., 93, 100, 102, 104, 131, 192

Acknowledgments

Grateful appreciation is expressed by the editor to the following, among others: fellow Board members of the Michigan Civil War Association for their dedication to the cause and support for this publication series; Margaret O'Brien and Matt VanAcker for thematic guidance, research assistance, and manuscript reviews; Dr. Brooks D. Simpson for a rigorous review and salient criticism; Jacqueline Tinney for close review of the manuscript; Dr. Dennis Rasbach for a review focusing on medical matters; Dr. Marty Hershock for participation, guidance, and commentary, all volunteered; Brian James Egen for leadership and support for the series; Nadine L. Siak, Public Affairs Specialist, Tripler Army Medical Center, for assistance as to its collections; and Dr. Charles David Cullen, Tripler descendant, for tremendous value added, including the title.

Gratitude preeminently is owed to that Great Physician who heals and whose faithful and meritorious service never wavers or flags.

www.ingramcontent.com/pod-product-compliance
Lightning Source LLC
Chambersburg PA
CBHW070325010526
44107CB00004B/410